Material Requirement Planning System

Heuristics for Improved Performance

Material Requirement Planning System

Heuristics for Improved Performance

R R K Sharma
Professor and Head
Industrial and Management Engineering Department
Indian Institute of Technology, Kanpur, India

Vitasta

Vitasta Publishing Pvt. Ltd.
New Delhi

Published by
Vitasta Publishing Pvt. Ltd.
2/15, First Floor, Ansari Road, Daryaganj,
New Delhi-110 002

ISBN 81-89766-20-1

Typeset by Vitasta Publishing Pvt. Ltd.
Printed at Saurabh Printers, New Delhi
Cover design by Vitasta Publishing Pvt. Ltd.

Contents

Preface

Material Requirement Planning (MRP) systems are over 50 years old. Today, they are a part of Enterprise Resources Planning (ERP) systems. Technical literature on MRP is mostly 'heuristic' based as the problem encountered in real life is too big to be solved optimally in a reasonable time. MRP system in practice focuses more on data integrity, timeliness of input and other practical matters of organisational implementation, and the issue of improving a solution or obtaining a better solution gets relegated to secondary place. This book primarily addresses the need to obtain improved solution in the MRP context.

Research in the past has indicated that decisions in MRP systems, namely lot sizing, scheduling, determination of lead times and capacity planning interact with each other. Due to simplicity the single-pass heuristics are preferred by decision makers. Here, all decision problems are solved separately by a suitable heuristic and the procedure terminates. Such a procedure ignores the interaction between decisions and is obviously far away from even a good solution.

In this book, we present several multi-pass heuristics for MRP systems that seek to improve performance after considering the interactions between decision problems of MRP. This is completely new area of research in MRP systems and the work holds promise for the future.

The commercially available packages have been found to be lacking in the current state-of-the-art procedures that give good solutions. We give in this book an MRP simulator in PASCAL that can be easily understood (as most appropriate variable names are used) and translated in other languages (such as C or C++ etc.) if needed and used in practice to see how a better quality solution can be obtained.

This book offers exciting ideas for researchers as well as practising production managers. We hope our work is applicable in future research works and that it may get incorporated in commercially available MRP/ERP software as well.

Dr R R K Sharma

Acknowledgement

This book is dedicated to my parents, to my father who taught me the value of discipline and hard work and to my mother who taught me fundamentals of mathematics. I express gratitude to my wife, Sheela, and children, Shriniwas and Anjaneya, who stood behind me like a rock in difficult times of life.

Would also like to thank my students (Vishnu Potty, S R Yoganandan, Sharat Sinha, Santosh Gupta, Rajesh Arora, M V Rao, Vikas Wadhwani and Sameer Agarwal) who dared to do their M Tech theses in MRP systems and spent long frustrating hours before computer screen debugging the MRP Simulation Program.

List of Contributors

R R K Sharma
Industrial and Management Engineering Department
Indian Institute of Technology, Kanpur, India

V S Potty
Industrial and Management Engineering Department
Indian Institute of Technology, Kanpur, India

S R Yoganandan
Tata Iron and Steel Company, Jamshedpur, India

Sharat Sinha
Industrial and Management Engineering Department
Indian Institute of Technology, Kanpur, India

Sameer Agarwal
Industrial and Management Engineering Department
Indian Institute of Technology, Kanpur, India

S Gupta
Industrial and Management Engineering Department
Indian Institute of Technology, Kanpur, India

R Arora
Industrial and Management Engineering Department
Indian Institute of Technology, Kanpur, India

M V Rao
Industrial and Management Engineering Department
Indian Institute of Technology, Kanpur, India

Vikas Wadhwani
Industrial and Management Engineering Department
Indian Institute of Technology, Kanpur, India

S Shahi
Industrial and Management Engineering Department
Indian Institute of Technology, Kanpur, India

1 Material Requirement Planning (MRP) System : An Introduction

R R K Sharma

1. INTRODUCTION

This chapter provides a general overview of Material Requirement Planning (MRP) system. It mainly deals with the objectives, purpose, assumptions and prerequisites of MRP, its inputs and outputs and its role in manufacturing, planning and control system. We briefly review its working, mathematical models available for analysis of the decisions to be taken that greatly affect the system performance.

MRP is a formal, computerised information system that integrates the scheduling and control of materials. Through a set of logically related records, procedures and rules for decision making, MRP translates a Master Production Schedule (MPS) into time-phased net requirements for each inventory item needed to implement the schedule and spells out the plan for covering these requirements. The system specifies materials to be procured and the actions to be taken and determines when they are needed during the planning period.

2. MRP OBJECTIVES

MRP is necessary because of the volume of materials, supplies and components involved in producing a company's product line and the speed with which management needs to react to the constant dynamic changes of the economy. An MRP system has the following objectives:

- Improve customer service, increase sales and lower prices
- Reduce inventories
- Provide a change-sensitive, reactive manufacturing system
- Improve efficiency through:
  - ➢ Reduced idle time
  - ➢ Reduced set-up costs
  - ➢ Avoidance of unplanned delays
  - ➢ Fewer cancelled orders and changes in order quantities

 - ➢ Information for schedule planning before actual release of orders
- Aiding in capacity planning

3. PURPOSE OF THE MRP SYSTEM

The main purpose of an MRP is to control the inventory levels, assign appropriate priorities and plan capacity of the manufacturing system. Controlling inventory means ordering the right part at the right quantity and time. While assigning priorities among different assemblies, it is required to consider due dates and inventory-carrying costs. Capacity planning is to decide on machine capacities with reasonable capacity utilisation for a schedule of due dates and throughput. Thus, an MRP system is designed to answer the question as to what needs to be produced (i.e., what capacity is required and what is to be subcontracted) to meet a given MPS.

4. ASSUMPTIONS AND PREREQUISITES OF MRP

MRP is effective for companies with the following production characteristics of manufacturing operations:

- Products produced by using a defined sequence of materials (components, parts and sub-assemblies)
- Existence of a dependent demand
- Demand for components variable and/or discontinuous in nature

Proper use of an MRP system depends on the following:

- The final product's component parts that are uniquely identified
- Existence of an MPS stated in bill of material terms
- Existence of computerised bill of materials at the planning stage
- Inventory records that provide data on the status of each item
- Lead times known for the individual items
- Accurate and up-to-date file data
- All components that go in to and out of inventory stock
- Discrete disbursement and component material's usage required
- Final product's component needed during assembly order release
- Independent processing of manufactured items

The above requirements are critical for setting up an MRP. Implementing an MRP requires that MRP data files, shop floor control and data integrity be well established. In addition, the bill of material files must be computerised, which in itself a major task.

5. ROLE OF MRP IN MANUFACTURING PLANNING AND CONTROL SYSTEMS

The field of Manufacturing Planning and Control (MPC) is concerned with management problems and techniques for their solution, as well as with the linkages or interactions among particular problem areas. This full system includes all data inputs, system modules and feedback connections. The front end section of the MPC system is the set of activities and systems for the overall direction settings, which produces MPS. The back end or execution section of the system deals with the detailed scheduling of the factory and with managing materials coming from vendor plants.

MRP is the central system in the engine portion. It has the primary purpose of taking a period-by-period (time-phased) set of MPS requirements and producing a resultant time-phased set of components/raw material requirements. In addition to MPS inputs, MRP has two other basic inputs. A bill of material (BoM) shows what other part numbers are required as direct component for each part number. The second basic input to MRP is inventory status.

The MRP system serves a central role in MPC. It acts as a translator of the overall plans for production into the detailed individual steps necessary to accomplish those plans. It provides information for developing capacity plans and it links to the systems that actually get the production accomplished. Due to this, the MRP process is where many companies have chosen to start the development of their formal MPC systems.

6. MASTER PRODUCTION SCHEDULE

MRP is a scheme for converting Master Production Schedule (MPS) into a planned schedule of raw materials, components and sub-assemblies orders. Based on inputs from sales (demand and forecast) and inventory and backlog levels (management input) a production plan or the MPS is prepared. MRP system takes this as input and prepares the purchase orders for the raw materials and the shop production orders (for assemblies and sub-assemblies).

Just In Time(JIT) system, in its purest form, tends to break down (loses its agility) when there is too much variability in demand. Faced with these circumstances, even Toyota (inventor of the JIT system) set-up its factory in 1996 in Japan that was based on MRP. JIT is a 'pull' system that pulls the product from the production system. However, MRP system is a robust system that is a 'push' system that retains its agility under extreme variability in demand. Maintenance of 'inventory' is essential to the MRP system.

7. PRODUCT STRUCTURE

A product has a 'product structure' (see Appendix 1). A product is made up of several sub-assemblies and components. Refer to sample product structure 1 (in Appendix 1). In this, components/sub-assemblies 10,9 and 13 can be procured from outside. In this, assembly/component 13 goes through a specified sequence of operations to get converted to assembly number 12. Assembly number 13, in order to get converted to assembly number 12 goes through a set of general purpose machines. In contrast, sub-assemblies 12 and 7 go to a specified assembly machine that uses quantities of 12 and 7 in certain (prespecified) proportions to get converted to assembly number 5.

Thus, in a shop using MRP system, there are assembly machines and general purpose machines. General purpose machines process a variety of assemblies and hence, there are issues of set-up times (when machine processes a different component/sub-assembly/assembly) and queues before them (as many assemblies will be waiting to get processed at a general purpose machine). Thus, the shop is composed of general purpose machines and the assembly machines.

In the product structure 1, we have not shown the proportion of lower sub-assemblies required to produce a higher level assembly. These could be as follows. For example, 3 units of assembly 3 (in product structure 1 : Appendix 1), 4 units of assembly 4, 5 units of assembly 5 and 6 units of assembly 6 could be required for producing 1 unit of higher level assembly number 2. These numbers are determined by the technological considerations.

8. BILL OF MATERIALS

All these information about a product (in the form of product structure) is kept in computers and is called the 'Bill of Materials' (BoMs). It is real challenge to an organisation to maintain correct information of its 'Bill of Materials'. An aircraft manufacturer typically has product structures with nearly 1,50,000 levels and nearly 7,00,000 assemblies/sub-assemblies. Maintaining a high fidelity BoMs is challenging. The problem is even more serious in the regime of design changes. Many MRP implementations fail because of failure to maintain accurate BoMs.

9. TIME PERIOD

If time horizon is one year, then this is further divided into smaller time periods typically either a 15-day slot or a month or a week or even a day. Demand vector of say (30, 20, 10, 5, 25, 50) corresponds to demand of an end item for month 1, 2, 3, 4, 5, and 6. This could also be a weekly demand for next six weeks or even next six days depending upon what is the chosen time period (due to convenience) by the production planning persons. Concept of time period is introduced so that now a 'dynamic' demand (as opposed to a constant demand rate usually expressed when conventional Economic Order Quantity (EOQ) formula is used for lot sizing) can be expressed for all the assemblies and sub-assemblies for all the time periods.

10. MECHANICS OF MRP

The MRP is a technique or a set of systematic procedures for managing inventory in a manufacturing operation. There are four basic steps to the MRP process:

1. **Net** Netting is subtracting of on-hand and on-order quantities, from gross requirements.
2. **Lot** Lot sizing is determination of individual batch or order quantities for manufacturing based on the calculated time-phased net requirements. There are many lot-sizing models or techniques which will be discussed later. Some of the techniques involve economic balancing of set-up and inventory-carrying cost and others are simpler rules such as using a fixed number of period requirements.
3. **Offset** Offsetting is the determination of the appropriate time for release of planned orders so that they will be completed in time to satisfy demand. The planned order release data is determined by subtracting the lead time from the date of the earliest net requirement which it is intended to satisfy.
4. **Explode** Explosion is the calculation of gross requirements for the next lower level components which result from planned orders. Explosion may take into consideration shrinkage or yield of the components in the manufacture of the higher level item and the quantity of each component

required to make the higher level item. The 'quantity per' factors for the components are multiplied by the planned order quantities for the parent item and then, if appropriate, the result is divided by the yield factor for the component to give the requirements for the components.

The process of determining net requirements, lot sizing and offsetting of planned orders is then performed for the lower level components. If the lower level components are also manufactured items, their planned orders are exploded into gross requirements for their components and so on until planned orders are generated for purchased parts and materials.

In an on-going situation, each MRP planning cycle re-evaluates and adjusts the plans generated in the previous cycle. It is this ability to re-evaluate plans in light of changing conditions and signal appropriate corrective actions which makes MRP such a valuable tool in manufacturing control. This adjustment capability is an important part of the MRP methodology. Frequent adjustment procedures cause frequent changes in plants which cause "nervousness" also.

11. DECISION PROBLEM ONE: LOT SIZING

Production specialists prefer MRP when demand fluctuations are large and JIT tends to fail. In JIT system, the lot-size is nearly one. But this is not so in MRP system. MRP is recommended when there are large fluctuations in demand and the producing company is forced to produce stock and manage its inventories.

In MRP, lot sizing is an activity of translating into an order quantity the net unfilled requirements for a given item (while ignoring scheduling decisions). Order quantity is a question of minimising the costs of ordering (or set-up) plus the cost of carrying the item in stock. Certainly, it is desirable in MRP to generate the least-cost purchasing and manufacturing orders.

There are many approaches to selecting the least-cost order quantity, which are discussed extensively in the MRP literature (Orlicky;[17] Wagner-Whitin[26]). Among these approaches, Wagner-Whitin algorithm is an optimising technique based on dynamic programming model. It is popularly used as it has been proved to be computationally efficient. It is described below in brief for the sake of completeness.

11.1 Wagner-Whitin Algorithm

Wagner-Whitin algorithm[26] evaluates all possible ways of ordering to cover net requirements in each period of the planned horizon. Its objective is to arrive at the optimum ordering strategy for the entire net requirements schedule. The Wagner-Whitin algorithm is elegant since it reaches this objective without actually having to consider, specifically, each of the strategies that are possible. The algorithm is as follows:

Let d_t = quantity needed,

i_t = interest per unit of inventory carried forward to period t +1,

S_t= ordering (or set-up cost),

X_t= quantity ordered (or manufactured)

where t denotes period, t = 1, 2,....., N.

It is assumed that all period demands and costs are non-negatives. The problem is to find a program $X_t \geq 0$; t = 1, 2,...., N, such that all demands are met at a minimum total cost,

$$\text{Let } F(t) = \min_{t}\left\{\min_{1\leq j\leq t}\left[s_j + \sum_{h=j}^{t-1} \sum_{k=h+1}^{t} i_h d_k + F(j-1)\right], s_t + F(t-1)\right\}$$

The algorithm is based on 'dynamic programming' which uses various properties of the optimal solution (given in list of References[26]). This is still a popular algorithm among the researchers.

11.2 Economic Order Quantity (EOQ)

Under certain well known conditions, ordering the EOQ minimises the total of set-up and inventory-holding costs. Once computed, every order release is for the fixed quantity of EOQ units. The EOQ rule often generates a relatively high level of average inventory in a dynamic demand setting because it creates inventory remnants. A remnant is an inventory carried into a week, but is too small to prevent a shortage. This is because the EOQ does not exactly match the requirements.

11.3 Lot for Lot (LFL)

This rule simply specifies that components are ordered in the quantity needed by the parent order. The LFL rule minimises inventory investment, but maximises the number of orders placed. This rule is most applicable to expensive items or items with small ordering and set-up costs. It is usually better suited for make-to-order than for make-to-stock items.

11.4 Fixed Period Requirements (FPR)

The lot 'size' is equal to the demand during a predetermined, constant number of periods. The FPR reduces the amount of on-hand inventory because it better matches requirements. It adjusts lot-sizes as requirements increase or decrease. Even though the fixed period requirements improve the inventory-holding cost performance by allowing the lot-sizes to vary, it ignores much of the information in the requirement schedule, i.e., the orders are constrained to occur at fixed time intervals and therefore rule out the possibility of combining orders in periods with low demand.

11.5 Period Order Quantity (POQ)

The POQ model computes the number of periods of average demand that an EOQ would supply. It is simply the EOQ divided by the average demand per period rounded to its nearest integer. Thereafter, POQ orders the total demand expected for this integer number of periods. If demand is less or more than average, POQ will order less or more, respectively, and make a better trade-off between set-up and inventory-holding costs than the ordinary EOQ would. Thus, POQ finds an economic time interval between set-ups.

11.6 Silver-Meal algorithm (S&M)

The Silver-Meal algorithm selects the order quantity so as to minimise the cost per period over the time periods that the order quantity lasts. Therefore, as a parallel model to least total cost (LTC) and least unit cost (LUC), the Silver-Meal algorithm can be referred to as least period cost (LPC).

12. DECISION PROBLEM TWO: SCHEDULING

MRP provides component due dates by the expected lead time from each parent item. Once the due dates have been determined, it is left to the shop floor control (SFC) system to meet these deadlines. The sequencing rule is used to select the next job to be processed from a set of jobs awaiting service. Sequencing rules are normally used to minimise total inventory cost. The nature of the dispatching rule employed influences delay costs, in-process and final inventory costs and set-up costs. Due date-based sequencing rules are the best performers in the multi-stage job shop.[1,4,7,8] Critical Ratio Rule (CRR), a member of the family of due date based rules, performs well in MRP environment. Biggs[5] has considered the following rules in MRP environment:

1. **Dollar Volume Rule (DVR)** Process that component first that is a component of the final product(s) with highest dollar value of total sales (forecast).
   This rule is a variation of ABC analysis. It is dynamic in that it is updated weekly as the forecast changes. This could also mean greater difficulty in making the necessary calculations.
2. **Dollar Unit Rule (DUR)** Process that component first that is a component or sub-assembly of the final product with the highest unit cost.
   This too is based on ABC analysis, but it is a static rule in that the information needed should remain the same from week to week.
3. **Unit Volume Rule (UVR)** Process that item first that is a component of most successor items.
   This is similar to rule of 2 and can be determined with the bills of material.
4. **Dollar Cost Rule (DCR)** Process that component first that has the largest unit cost. This is similar to rule 2.
5. **Shortest Processing Time Rule (SPT)** Process that component lot first has the shortest standard processing time. This rule is dynamic in the sense that the time requirement is based on the current lot-size and standard operating time. It should be easy to calculate, as the necessary information in most firms is generally at hand.

12.1 Critical Ratio Rule (CRR)

A good discussion of several CRRs (including some in actual use at Black and Decker, Hughes Archoff and Western electric) is provided by Putnam et al.[19] In its most general form, it is computed as:

$$\text{Critical Ratio} = \frac{[\text{time remaining} - \text{work remaining}]}{[\text{work remaining}]}$$

If CRR value of a job is less than one, then it is behind the schedule and it has to be given high priority. If CRR value is greater than one, then it is ahead of schedule and it can be delayed. Simply, it means, the least the CRR value, higher the priority and vice versa.

13. DECISION PROBLEM THREE: DETERMINATION OF LEAD TIMES

Lead time determination is done by a level at which the assembly is located in the product structure, amount of processing to be done on it and the safety lead time. However, constant lead times (for assemblies) are also used in MRP systems.

14. MRP II: MANUFACTURING RESOURCES PLANNING

When the 'capacity planning problem' is added to the list of problems, then one gets the 'MRP II' or the manufacturing resources planning systems. Here, the lot sizing, scheduling, lead time determination and the capacity planning are done in series and many times over to converge to a set of common decision values. In MRP I, the first three decisions are taken into account (lot sizing, scheduling and lead time determination) and required capacity over the available one is simply outsourced. In MRP II, we go over these four decisions many times over and fix decision variables after considering many options. This is also known as the 'closed loop' MRP. It is also known to date that these decisions (lot sizing, scheduling, lead time determination and capacity planning) interact with each other to affect performance criteria, Billington et al.[6]

15. CAPACITY PLANNING PROBLEM

Another important issue that is not treated explicitly by MRP is the capacity of the production facility. Capacity Requirement Planning (CRP) is the process by which the capacity requirements placed on a work centre or group of work centres is computed by using the output of the MRP planned order releases. If the planned order releases result in an infeasible requirements schedule, there are several possible actions. One is to schedule overtime at the bottleneck locations. Another is to revise the MPS so that the planned order releases at lower levels can be achieved with the current system capacity. This is clearly a cumbersome way to solve the problem, requiring an iterative trial and error process between the CPP and the MRP.

16. MRP NERVOUSNESS

According to Steele,[24] nervousness in schedules is mainly in single-level MRP systems. 'Nervousness' is measured using various methods, in either of terms the frequency or the magnitude of changes in order quantity. A number of studies have been reported that evaluated schedule nervousness under more realistic conditions, such as in multi-level MRP systems under uncertain demand conditions. This paper discusses the shortcomings of existing methods for measuring schedule nervousness and presents a new metric for measuring schedule nervousness in multi-level MRP environments.

Uncertainties about supply and/or demand and dynamic lot-sizing combined with rolling planning are major causes for nervousness in schedules. Some of the undesirable effects of nervousness are increased costs, reduced productivity, low morale and lower customer service levels. Many strategies have been recommended to dampen nervousness, including freezing the MPS, time-fencing, using lot-sizing procedures selectively, forecasting beyond the planning horizon, incorporating the cost of changing the schedule into the lot-sizing process, using lot-for-lot ordering below level zero and using buffer stock at the end-item level.

A more robust measure is needed to evaluate strategies for combating schedule nervousness in a multi-item, multi-level MRP system operating under demand uncertainty.

Researchers who studied schedule nervousness defined instability in various ways like the number of times an unplanned order is made in period 1 when the schedule is rolled forward (BKM metric). Measuring instability in this fashion, i.e., counting only the unplanned orders in the first period of the horizon, artificially reduces instability as the horizon length is increased. Thus, this approach could potentially lead to erroneous conclusions. Changes in the timing or quantity of orders occurring in any period within the planning horizon could potentially have a major impact on the shop floor. Therefore, the changes that take place beyond the imminent period must also be considered in measuring instability. Another deficiency of the BKM metric concerns open order changes which is an important aspect of system instability in most manufacturing companies.

Many researchers investigated the issue of open order instability, which represents schedule nervousness in the execution stage. They measured MRP system nervousness in terms of the number of notices to change open orders. Because this approach counts only the frequency of the changes, ignoring their magnitude, all changes are considered equal in their severity and the adverse effects of changes in order quantity are masked.

Some researchers defined instability as the weighted average of changes in the MPS over subsequent planning cycles. Their definition emphasises not only the changes in order quantity but also the number of times that changes take place. The metric permits changes that take place in successive periods of the planning horizon to be weighed differently by means of a weight parameter, the value of which can be varied to assign rapidly or slowly declining weights. This approach is attractive because it is easier to implement changes in future periods rather than imminent periods.

Some researchers employed the SBU metric to study the impact of safety stock on schedule instability in a single level system. In addition to the weighted average measure, they reported several additional measures to assess both the magnitude and the frequency of changes. They measured changes in order size, including the average size of unplanned new orders, the average size of cancelled orders, the average increase and decrease in order quantity. Frequency of change was measured in terms of the number of times an unplanned new order was made, an existing order was cancelled and an existing order was increased or decreased.

17. REGENERATIVE/NET CHANGE MRP

The complete netting, lot sizing, scheduling, lead times and simulation is done and the day-to-day plans are prepared. This consumes a lot of computing power. The MRP system is prone to changes and these changes are normally reflected by cheap (in terms of computing power) 'Net Change MRP' where only the deviations from the main is plan is reported. Over a period of time, the systems accumulate many changes that it adds to confusion and management becomes difficult. Then the system does the netting, explosion, lot sizing, scheduling routines again and prepares a fresh plan by discarding earlier 'change notes'. This is called 'regeneration'. Firm has to balance the cost of too many change notes to operations persons and the cost of preparing the fresh plan. This is used to determine the frequency of 'regeneration'. It is expensive to provide the 'net change' feature in MRP that is implemented in a firm.

18. PEGGING

It is very common to have same part/sub-assembly being absorbed by two or more higher level assemblies. Then when one has inventory of these parts, it is a common question to be asked: To which higher level assembly it must go into? MRP systems provide a feature that let us know 'where to' this part goes. This is known as the 'pegging' feature.

19. SETTING OF SAFETY STOCKS/TIMES

The demand is uncertain. Hence, it is required to keep safety stocks. Thus, inventory is inflated to the extent of safety stocks.

The long product structure chains require that we also need some safety time build into the release of jobs into the shop so that there are no excessive delays. We may keep variable safety times or lead times, that is different lead times for different assemblies or one may keep it constant. It is research problem to find out which one is better in MRP context.

20. SHORTCOMINGS OF MRP

Many of the assumptions made in MRP are unrealistic. In this section, we will discuss some of these assumptions, the problems that arise as a result of them and the means for dealing with these problems.

20.1 Uncertainty

Underlying MRP is the assumption that all required information is known with certainty. However, uncertainties do exist. The two key sources of uncertainty are the forecasts for future sales of the end item and the estimation of the production lead times from one level to another. Safety stock can be included to protect against the uncertainty of demand. The manner in which the uncertainty transmits itself through a complex multi-level production system is not well understood. For that reason, it is not recommended to include independent safety stock at all levels of the systems. Rather suitable safety levels can be built into the forecasts for the end item. These will automatically be transmitted down through the system to the lower levels through the explosion calculus.

20.2 Rolling Horizon and System Nervousness

In practice, production planning environment is dynamic. The MRP system may have to be re-run each period and the production decisions are re-evaluated. Often, it is the case that only the lot-sizing decisions for the current planning period need to be implemented. Rolling horizon is used to refer to the situation in which only the first-period decision of an N-period problem is implemented. The full N-period problem is re-run each period to determine a few first-period decision.

Another common problem that results when using MRP is nervousness. The term was coined by Steele,[24] who used it to refer to the changes that can occur in a schedule when the horizon is moved forward one period. Some of the causes of nervousness include unanticipated changes in the MPS because of updated forecasts, late deliveries of raw materials, failure of key equipment or absenteeism of key personnel and unpredictable yields.

20.3 Factors Affecting the Computation of Requirements

The computation of requirements is complicated by six factors:

1. The structure of the product, containing several manufacturing levels of materials, component parts and sub-assemblies.
2. Lot sizing, i. e., the ordering of inventory items in quantities exceeding net requirements, for reasons of economy or convenience.
3. The different individual lead times of inventory items that make up the product.
4. The timing of the end-item requirements across a planning horizon of, typically, a year's span or longer, and the recurrence of these requirements within such a time span.
5. Multiple requirements for an inventory item due to its so-called commonalty, i.e., usage in the manufacture of a number of other items.
6. Multiple requirements for an inventory item due to its recurrence on several levels of a given end item.

21. PREVIOUS RESEARCH

The recent growth in the use of (MRP) systems resulted in increased interest in the topic of decision making in multi-stage, multi-product systems. MRP has been subjected to extensive research. Particularly, there is hardly a scarcity of research in the area of lot sizing and dispatching rules, their interaction and their impact of MRP system.

Biggs[4] reported that the effect of lot sizing and sequencing rules and the interaction between these is significant at the level of 0.01 significance. He has argued that a particular sequencing rule may work in opposite direction to particular lot-sizing rule or vice versa.

Blackburn and Millan[7] have modelled a multi-stage problem analytically to indicate the potential errors inherent in the commonly purposed single-pass, stage-by-stage approaches. Then, based on this analysis, several simple cost modifications are suggested.

Biggs,[5] Billington et al[6] and Collier[10] studied the effect of using various priority scheduling rules to capacity management and SFC in a multi-stage, multi-product system which uses MRP. He found that CRR performs consistently well over different levels of capacity.

Grasso and Taylor[11] studied main effects and interaction effects among four factors, namely, lead time, buffering alternatives, lot-size rule and cost value on total cost and reported that main effects of each factor and the interaction between lead time distribution and lot size and that between buffering alternative and cost value on total cost are significant.

South and Steward[23] reported their experience at Hix Corporation wherein 50 per cent increase in lot sizes and planned manufactured lead time resulted in low system tardiness without increase in work-in-process (WIP) inventory costs.

As already discussed, lot sizing, sequencing, determination of planned lead times and capacity planning are important decisions in the effective use of MRP. Bedworth and Baily,[3] Gutzman and Wysk,[14] Magad and Amos,[15] Vollman et al[25] and Sharma and Potty.[22]

Panwalkar Iswander[18] classified over 100 scheduling rules and made an attempt to explain the general idea behind different rules.

Blackstone, Philips and Hoggs[8] discussed the state of the art in the study of dispatching rules, listed 34 dispatching rules and compared them. They concluded that no single dispatching rule developed so far consistently produces lower total cost than all other rules under a variety of shop configurations and operating conditions.

Goodwin and Weeks[13] showed that the performance of various sequencing rules do not generalise the multi-stage job shop.

In a recent study, Russell and Taylor[20] evaluated the performance of various dispatching rules in two different product structures. The authors constructed a BoM representing a tall product structure having four levels and a BoM representing a flat product structure having three levels. They concluded that as the BoM gets taller, the probability that the job will finish after its due date increases.

In another study Goodwin and Weeks[13] studied the effect of sequencing rule and frequency of priority updating. They concluded that due date-based sequencing rules were the best performers in the multi-stage job shop.

Fry, Philipoom and Markland[12] evaluated the performance of selected dispatching rules in an unbalanced multi-stage job shop to determine whether the performance is consistent for jobs which are rated through the bottleneck and for jobs which by-pass the bottleneck. They concluded that sequencing rules which are based on job due date tends to be[17] the overall better performers. They also concluded that the results for jobs which pass through the bottleneck were not the same for jobs which by-pass the bottleneck.

But, sequencing in a multi-stage, multi-product system requires a coordinated flow of materials throughout the various stages to assure components needed for assembly are available when planned. Coordination is vital since shortage of a single item can halt the assembly process, resulting in sharply diminishing productivity and increased inventory costs.

But, surprisingly, no work has been done in this area to question the uncoordinated scheduling. Also, little work is done on multi-pass heuristics in MRP systems that secures coordination between lot sizing and scheduling heuristics.

22. SIZE OF THE SHOP

When Baker and Dzielinski[2] tested some of the dispatching rules in shops of various sizes, they found that size of the shop does not affect the relative performance of the rule. This finding is convenient to state that it is cheaper to simulate a small shop. Buffa[9] concluded: Since shop size has never appeared as a major variable, it seems that we may be able to experiment with small shops and generalise the resulting conclusion.

23. THE SIMULATION MODEL

24. MRP AS A PART OF ERP

Now-a-days, MRP is a part of ERP (Enterprise Resource Planning) System implemented in organisations. ERP seeks to integrate information within an organisation. Almost all the issues related to MRP implementation are covered in ERP implementation and are discussed below.

24.1 ERP Implementation Chronologies

There are six phases of technology implementation. Pre-adoption is the stage at which organisations begin to consider the need to change technologies, identify technology options and consider strategic directions. The result is an adoption. The adoption point marks the beginning of the pre-implementation phase. This involves such activities as planning for the technology introduction, deciding on the role of the vendor and in-house resources in managing the introduction, providing preliminary training, planning the logistics of the change, deciding whether a pilot study will be used and deciding whether everything will be changed at once or whether a gradual phase-in will be used. If a pilot study is used, it represents a distinct stage in the process. In the pilot study stage, employees see the technology for the first time, talk to their colleagues about it and form opinions of how things are likely to change in the future. The next stage is the actual implementation, which may take of lot of time and identifying when it ends may benefit the organisation. The post-implementation stage or "routinisation" represents a return to equilibrium the new technology has been implemented, it is being used and people are reaching whatever accommodation to it that they are likely to reach. Over time, employee attitudes are likely to converge on a consensus or agreement about the use and value of the new technology.

24.2 Pre-Implementation Phase

24.2.1 Effect of Pre-implementation Attitudes of Employees on Implementing an ERP

Employee attitudes toward ERP systems in the pre-implementation age are important determinants of implementation behaviours and these can either hinder or facilitate implementation success. The variables that shape attitudes towards an ERP system (capability, value, acceptance and timing) in the pre-implementation stage are:

- Job tenure
- Job type
- Levels of involvement with the early implementation process

Sue Abdinnour-Helm,[28] Mark L Lengnick-Hall and Cynthia A Lengnick-Hall, in their study in a large aircraft manufacturing organisation in the Midwest, presented the effect of these variables on attitudes towards ERP system. Job tenure is an important factor shaping attitudes towards the implementation of a new ERP system. Employees with less tenure (i.e., newer employees) are more optimistic about the potential capabilities and the potential value of the new ERP system than those employees who had been with the organisation for longer periods of time. Employees with less tenure show greater acceptance of the new ERP system than employees with more tenure. Newer employees appear to be more receptive to new information technologies than those who have been employed by the firm for a longer period of time. Additionally, newer employees have not experienced previous management and IT initiatives, so they have not formed negative attitudes about their potential capabilities or value.

Job type is also an influential factor in shaping attitudes towards ERP implementation. Managers appear to be significantly higher on the capability variable than production workers. Managers are significantly higher than supervisors, production workers and others on the value variable, but not significantly different from professionals/engineers on this variable. Managers are more positive than professionals/engineers, supervisors, production workers and others on acceptance of the new ERP system. Perhaps, managers saw the new ERP system as both inevitable and likely to enhance their control over operations. As with job tenure, a consensus developed across all job types that the timing of the implementation was not satisfactory. Effect of levels of involvement with the early implementation process: level of involvement in pre-implementation training appears to have little influence on attitudes toward ERP. Exposure to the ERP/IT system and greater levels of involvement in its implementation does not seem to dramatically change the attitudes of employees. Across all levels of involvement, the capabilities and value and acceptance of the ERP system were rated more positively than the timing of the implementation. How these attitudes in pre-implementation phase can play a role in actual implementation of ERP system are presented below.

Organisational demography is an important factor determining attitudes toward ERP implementation and its ultimate effectiveness. Organisations with a higher proportion of relatively new employees may find it easier to implement ERP systems than organisations with a higher proportion of older employees who have higher levels of tenure. Firms with large proportions of long-tenured employees may need to find creative ways to ensure that employees attitudes developed through their experience with previous technology initiatives. Conversely, firms are likely to find it easier to convince their managerial and professional employees of the value and potential contributions of ERP to organisational effectiveness than to convince their operations level employees of these benefits. This suggests that firms which have a history of trust and collaboration across hierarchical levels are likely to experience a smoother implementation experience than organisations which have a tradition of adverse relationship between managers/professionals and other employees.

An exceptionally quick implementation approach may not provide the time necessary for employees to learn about the system and appreciate its potential value. The consistent dissatisfaction with implementation timing across demographic and involvement segments may signal the need to give employees time to absorb the change as well as learn how the system works.

24.2.2 ERP System Selection

Since an ERP system, by its very nature, will impose its own logic on a company strategy, organisation and culture, it is imperative that the ERP selection decision be conducted with great care. The greatest enterprise system implementation failures seem to occur when the new technology capabilities and needs are mismatched with the organisation existing business processes and procedures. An organisation should try to select and implement a system that underscores its unique competitive strengths while helping to overcome competitive weaknesses. The ultimate goal should be to improve the business not to implement software.

Umble, Haft and Michael[27] recommended a 13-step selection process which is summarised below.

1. Create the vision. Define the corporate mission, objectives and strategy. Use cross-functional teams and executive-level input to identify, examine and rethink existing business processes. This helps to ensure the necessary buy-in of both executive management and the process owners. Define clearly why the ERP system is to be implemented. If multiple plants are involved, the process must include participants from all plants.
2. Create a feature function list, identifying the features and functions required for the software to effectively support each functional area as well as the overall company vision.
3. Create a software candidate list.
4. Narrow the field to four to six serious candidates. This can be accomplished by a preliminary analysis of the strengths and weaknesses of each supplier and the "goodness of fit" of the software.
5. Create the Request for Proposal (RFP).
6. Review the proposals.

7. Select two or three finalists.
8. Have the finalists demonstrate their packages.
9. Select the winner. Based on cost, supplier support, ease of impleme tation closeness of fit to the company business, flexibility when the company business changes, technological risk and value (total implemented cost versus total value to the company).
10. Justify the investment. Based on the specific ERP software that has been selected, the potential tangible and intangible benefits of the implementation can be compared to the costs.
11. Negotiate the contract.
12. Run a pre-implementation pilot. The purpose of a pre-implementation pilot is to uncover major surprises, both good and bad, about the software as quickly as possible so as to facilitate the overall implementation.
13. Validate the justification.

24.2.3 Critical Factors in Pre-implementation Phase for a Successful ERP System Implementation

Umble, Haft and Michael[27] examined the factors that, to a great extent, determine whether the implementation will be successful.

The most prominent of these success factors are given below:

1. **Clear Understanding of Strategic Goals** ERP implementations require that key people throughout the organisation create a clear, compelling vision of how the company should operate in order to satisfy customers, empower employees and facilitate suppliers for the next three to five years. There must also be clear definitions of goals, expectations and deliverables. Finally, the organisation must carefully define why the ERP system is being implemented and what critical business needs the system will address.
2. **Commitment by Top Management** Successful implementations require strong leadership, commitment and participation by top. Since executive level input is critical when analysing and rethinking existing business processes, the implementation project should have an executive management planning committee that is committed to enterprise integration, understands ERP, fully supports the costs, demands payback and champions the project. Moreover, the project should be spearheaded by a highly respected executive level project champion.
3. **Excellent Project Management** A clear definition of project objectives and a clear plan will help the organisation avoid the all too common

'scope creep' which can strain the ERP budget, jeopardise project progress and complicate the implementation. The project scope must be clearly defined at the outset of the project and should identify the modules selected for implementation as well as the affected business processes. If management decides to implement a standardised ERP package without major modifications. This will minimise the need to customise the basic ERP code. This, in turn, will reduce project complexity and help keep the implementation on schedule.

4. **Organisational Change Management** The existing organisational structure and processes found in most companies are not compatible with the structure, tools and types of information provided by ERP systems. Thus, implementing an ERP system may force the re-engineering of key business processes and/or developing new business processes to support the organisation goals. And redesigned processes require corresponding realignment in organisational control to sustain the effectiveness of the re-engineering efforts. This realignment typically impacts most functional areas and many social systems within the organisation. The resulting changes may significantly affect organisational structures, policies, processes and employees.

   Clearly, ERP implementations may trigger profound changes in corporate culture. If people are not properly prepared for the imminent changes, then denial, resistance and chaos will be predictable consequences of the changes created by the implementation.

   However, if proper change management techniques are utilised, the company should be prepared to embrace the opportunities provided by the new ERP system and ERP will make available more information and make amenable improvements than at first seemed possible. The organisation must be flexible enough to take full advantage of these opportunities.

5. **A Great Implementation Team** ERP implementation teams should be composed of top people who are chosen for their skills, past accomplishments, reputation and flexibility. These people should be entrusted with critical decision-making responsibility. Management should constantly communicate with the team, but should also enable empowered rapid decision making. The implementation team is important because it is responsible for creating the initial, detailed project plan or overall schedule for the entire project, assigning responsibilities for various activities and determining due dates. The team also makes sure that all necessary resources will be available as needed.

6. **Data Accuracy** Educating users on the importance of data accuracy and correct data entry procedures should be a top priority in an ERP implementation.
7. **Extensive-Education and Training** Education/training is probably the most widely recognised critical success factor because users understanding and buy in are essential. The full benefits of ERP cannot be realised until end users are using the new system properly. To make end user training successful, the training should start early, preferably well before the implementation begins. Top management must be fully committed to spend adequate money on education and end user training and incorporate it as part of the ERP budget. It has been suggested that reserving 15 per cent of the total ERP implementation budget for training will give an organisation an 80 per cent chance of implementation success. A designated individual (preferably the project leader) should maintain ongoing contact with all system users and monitor the use of and problems with the new system. There is also a need for post-implementation training. Periodic meetings of system users can help identify problems with the system and encourage the exchange of information gained through experience and increasing familiarity with the system.
8. **Focussed Performance Measures** Performance measures that assess the impact of the new system must be carefully constructed. But the measures must also be designed so as to encourage the desired behaviours by all functions and individuals. Such measures might include on-time deliveries, gross profit margin, customer order-to-ship time, inventory turns, vendor performance, etc. Project evaluation measures must be included from the beginning. If system implementation is not tied to compensation, it will not be successful. Management, vendors, the implementation team, and the users must share a clear understanding of the goal. If someone is unable to achieve agreed-upon objectives, he/she should either receive the needed assistance or be replaced. When teams reach their assigned goals, rewards should be presented in a very visible way. The project must be closely monitored until the implementation is completed. The system must be forever monitored and measured. Management and other employees often assume that performance will begin to improve as soon as the ERP system becomes operational. But since the new system is complex and difficult to master, organisations must be prepared for the possibility of an initial decline in productivity. As familiarity with the new system increases, improvements will occur. Thus, realistic expectations about performance and time frames must be clearly communicated.

9. **Multi-Site Issues** The manner in which these concerns are addressed may play a large role in the ultimate success of the ERP implementation. The desired degree of individual site autonomy may be a critical issue which depends on two factors: (1) the degree of process and product consistency across the remote sites and (2) the need or desire for centralised control over information, system set-up and usage. Another complexity in dealing with multi-site implementations is the degree to which the culture of the organisation differs between sites. The fundamental issue here is one of corporate standardisation versus local optimisation. Corporate standardisation brings with it simplified interfaces among diverse parts of the organisation, ability to move people and products between sites with minimal disruption and relative ease in consolidating data across the entire organisation. On the other hand, local optimisation may result in more effective and efficient operation and may reduce costs. Perhaps the most difficult decision to be made in a multi-site implementation is the question of cutover strategy. The organisation must choose between an approach where the implementation takes place simultaneously in all facilities or a phased approach by module, by product line or by plant with a pilot implementation at one facility. With a large outlay of cash up front for software, hardware and the project team, the company may want a simultaneous implementation in order to recoup its investment as quickly as possible. In a multi-site implementation, a phased approach is generally considered to be preferable. This is partly because the success or failure experienced in the first attempt, at implementation, often decides the fate of the entire project. Thus, the management team can gain momentum by selecting a pilot site that has a high likelihood of success. If ERP is installed in a phased approach module-by-module department-by-department or plant-by-plant, the lessons learned at early sites can make the implementations at later sites go smoother.

24.3 Pre-Implementation (Planning) Strategies

Mandal and Gunasekaran[16] in their paper offered suggestions in resolving the issues of implementing ERP during pre-implementation phase.

- Incorporate the risk and quality management plans in the change management.
- Breakdown the project into natural phases or sub-systems for modular planning and for development of cross-functional communications.

- Consider a phase-based approach for gradual implementation rather than radical approach.
- Use appropriate planning styles for different tasks, detailed task plans for tangible tasks, iterative plans for evolving tasks and personal communications plans for change management.
- Prepare plans for the recruitment, selection and training of the necessary personnel for the project team.

24.4 Implementation Phase

24.4.1 Implementation Strategies

- Formulate a network for collecting user requirements and feedback.
- Set-up monitoring and feedback network for collecting control information at each stage of the implementation process.
- Prepare to handle expected or unexpected crises and deviations.
- Provide a strong leadership with concerns for the welfare of people and resource commitment.
- Provide a professionally stimulating work environment.
- Obtain top management support for the project and plan for an adequately resourced and proficiently executed launch.
- Promote client consultation and user participation and obtain approval from parties for what is being undertaken throughout the project.
- Use pro-active communications to establish more realistic expectations about the technology capabilities while communicating in tailored way to each division or unit.
- Promote collaborative system development between the users and the developers.
- Use multi-functional project teams to bring complementary capabilities together during the total life of the project.
- Familiarise the staff about the incoming technology and train the people involved with the system.
- Use intra-project teams and intra- and inter-industry networking for technology transfer.
- Provide stake holders with a detailed plan of the implementation process, explain how it achieves business objectives and keep them informed about the system and progress of its implementation.
- Propose possible ways for restructuring personnel and systems to accommodate the new technology including maximising of system integration and interfacing.

24.5 Post-Implementation Phase

Post-implementation activities are critical for the acceptance (adoption) of ERP systems. Requirements to fit systems and structures tend to change continuously even after the completion of a project. Post-project evaluation strategy could be followed by measuring the effectiveness of an ERP system, where questions such as listed below could be used for further improvement:

- Whether the objectives of the ERP system were realised fully?
- Whether the scheme options were considered adequately?
- Whether the estimates and project information were accurate?
- Whether the agreed practices and techniques were complied with?
- Which other factors which are considered appropriate?

Such evaluations could concentrate on, firstly, cost estimates against actual and reasons for variations. Secondly, the evaluation could suggest any possible improvements to the IT system. Thirdly, the degree of staff consultation could be assessed and improvements suggested. Finally, post-implementation evaluation can suggest improved procedures in avoiding failure in future similar projects in the organisation.

24.6 A Survey of Implementation of ERP Systems in Swedish Manufacturing Firms

Jan and Erik Selldin[29] present results of a survey of implementation of ERP systems in Swedish manufacturing firms. The survey was done with PLAN members employed within manufacturing firms in Sweden. The questionnaire focussed on six areas: characteristics of the firm and the respondent including ERP system penetration, pre-implementation process, ERP system configuration, implementation experience benefits observed and future directions planned. With a response rate of 37.2 per cent of the contacted companies, this survey provided a fairly accurate overview of the status of ERP system implementation issues. Some interesting findings are summarised below.

First, Swedish manufacturing firms are broadly adopting ERP systems, 83.6 per cent have implemented such systems or are in the process of implementing. Second, the cost for implementing ERP systems range from an average of 0.5 per cent of annual revenues for large enterprises up to an average of 3.5 per cent for smaller companies. Thus, the ERP system cannot be considered to be an overwhelming investment for the enterprise. Third, Swedish firms often choose to implement ERP systems from Swedish vendors. Fourth, the modules that are implemented tend to be the core production management modules involved in the customer order process; these modules are also the modules requiring the most customisation. Financial accounting and control come next as the most implemented modules. Thus, ERP systems primarily support the material and information flows and secondarily the financial flows. Fifth, the most cited improvements related to ERP systems are concerned with information access and improved intra-organisational interaction. Sixth, given that the ERP penetration is high, most Swedish companies plan to extend their ERP systems with functional support for upstream and downstream supply chain operations.

25. BENEFITS OF MRP

- MRP lowers inventory levels by reducing the safety stocks.
- MRP helps in tracking material requirements over the planning horizon.
- MRP continuously monitors capacity requirements and uses load-reporting capability to reschedule the operations at work centres.
- MRP gives the purchasing department a better handle on acquisition activities and allows purchasing in quantity over time at a discount.
- Since MRP uses a longer planning horizon, the manufacturer is able to issue long-run contracts with suppliers of component materials. Suppliers, in turn, are able to plan longer, more efficient production runs that can reduce production costs.
- Various other purchasing and logistical savings will also accrue with such contracts, e.g., back-orders can be eliminated and less costly modes of transportation can be selected.
- MRP also allows better scheduling of production runs for improving production efficiency. A properly implemented system insures that component materials are routed to the proper points during assembly and that sufficient supplies will be available.
- Through careful planning, MRP can eliminate labour idle time and the need for overtime production and finally through MRP scheduling, cost estimates of materials and labour can be calculated at any point during the production process.

REFERENCES

1. Baker KR, Introduction to Sequencing and Scheduling, John Wiley & Sons, New York, 1974.
2. Baker CT and Dzielinki BP, Simulation of a Simplified Job Shop, Management Science, Vol. 6,311, 1960.
3. Bedworth AB and Baily TH, Integrated Production Systems: Management, Analysis, Design, John Wiley & Sons.
4. Biggs JR, Heuristic Lot Sizing and Sequencing Rules in a Multi-stage Production Inventory System, Decision Science, Vol 10, 96-115, 1979.
5. Biggs JR, Priority Rules for Shop Floor Control in a Material Requirements Planning System Under Various Levels of Capacity, International Journal of Production Research, Vol 23, No I, 33-46, 1985.
6. Billington P, McClain J and Thomas LJ, The Interaction of Lead Time Determination, Lot Sizing Decisions and Capacity Planning in MRP Systems, Proceedings, American Institute of Decision Sciences, Eleventh Annual Meeting, 1979.
7. Blackburn JD and Millan RA, Improved Heuristics for Multi-stage Requirements Planning Systems, Vol 28, No I, 44-56, 1982.
8. Blackstone JH, Philips DT and Hogg, GL, A State-of-the-Art Survey of Dispatching Rules for Manufacturing Job Shop Operations, International Journal of Production Research, Vol 20, No I, 27-45, 1982.
9. Buffa ES, Production-Inventory Systems: Planning and Control, HomeWood, Illenios: Richard D Irwin, Inc, 1968.
10. Collier DA, A Comparison of MRP Lot Sizing Methods considering Capacity Change Costs, Journal of Operation Management, August, 1980.
11. Grasso ET and Taylor, BW, A Simulation Based Experimental Investigation of Supply Timing Uncertainty in MRP Systems, International Journal of Production Research, Vol 22, No 3, 485-467, 1984.
12. Fry TD, Philipoom PR and Markland RE, Dispatching in a Multi-stage Job Shop where Machine Capacities are Unbalanced, International Journal of Production Research, Vol 26, No 7, 1193-1223, 1988.
13. Goodwin JS and Weeks JK, Evaluating Scheduling Policies in a Multi-level Assembly System, International Journal of Production Research, Vol 24, No 2, 247-257, 1986.
14. Gutzmann KM and Wysk RA, Capacity Control Policies for MRP systems, International Journal of Production Research, Vol 24, No 2, 359-374, 1986.
15. Magad EL and Amos JS, Total Material Management The Frontier for Maximising Profit in the 1990s, Competitive Manufacturing Series, Van Nostrand Reinhold, New York.

16. Mandal P and Gunasekharan A, Issues in Implementing ERP: A Case Study, 146 (2), pp 274-283, 2003.
17. Orlicky J, Material Requirement Planning, McGraw-Hill Book Company, New York, 1975.
18. Panwalker SS and Iskander W, A Survey of Scheduling Rules, Operation Research, Vol 25, No I, January-february, 45-61, 1977.
19. Putnam AO, Everdell R, Dornam GH, Cronen RR and Lindgren LH, Updating Critical Ratio and Slack-time Priority Scheduling Rules, Production-Inventory Management, Vol 12,51, 1971.
20. Russell RS and Taylor BW, An Evaluation of Sequencing Rules for an Assembly Shop, Decision Science, Vol 16,196-212, 1985.
21. Selldin JE, Enterprise Resource Planning: Survey of Swedish Manufacturing Firms, 146 (2), pp 365-373, 2003.
22. Sharma RRK and Potty VS, Multi-pass Heuristic for Improved Stockout Performance, Design Automation and Computer Integrated Manufacturing, Tata-McGraw-Hill, New Delhi, 1991.
23. South JB and Steward RJ, A Increase in Lot-size and Planned Manufactured Lead Time with No Increase in Work-in-Process Inventory, Production and Inventory Management. Vol 27, No 1 19-25, 1986.
24. Steele DC, The Nervous MRP System-How to Battle, Production & Inventory Management, Vol 16, 81-85, 1973.
25. Vollman TE, Berry WL and Whybark DC, Manufacturing Planning and Control Systems, Galgotia Publications Pvt Ltd, New Delhi, 1989.
26. Wagner HM and Whitin TM, Dynamic Version of Economic Lot Size Model, Management Science, October. 89-96, 1958.
27. Umble EJ, Haft RR and Michael M, Enterprise Resources Planning: Implementation Procedures and Critical Success Factors, European Journal of Operational Research, V146 (2), pp 241-257, 2003.
28. Abdinnour-Helm S, Lengnick-Hall, M L and Lengnick-Hall, C A, Pre-implementation attitudes and organization readiness for implementing an Enterprise Resource Planning system. European Journal of Operational Research, vol 146(2),258-273, 2003.
29. Jan and Erik Selldin. Enterprise resource planning survey of Swedish manfacturing firms. European Journal of Operational Research, Vol 146(2), 365-373, 2003.

2 Multi-pass Heuristic for Improved Stockout Performance in MRP System

R R K Sharma, V S Potty

ABSTRACT

Different decision problems in MRP systems, such as lot sizing, sequencing, capacity planning and planned lead times are interdependent. Multi-pass heuristics attempt to initiate communication among these decision problems in some manner. We present here a simple multi-pass heuristic which improves the stockout performance substantially. This heuristic is computationally attractive to use.

1. INTRODUCTION

Lot sizing, sequencing, determination of planned lead times and capacity planning are important decisions in the effective use of MRP. These decisions are interdependent, however, a few operating procedures are available which consider these interactions.

In this chapter, we give a multi-pass heuristic to improve the due date performance. Due date becomes an important criteria when machine capacities are tight. General product structure with known routing pattern over various processing centres is considered. Demand by time period for end items are assumed known (but not constant) over a finite horizon. The performance criteria considered in this chapter are the number of stockouts, units stockouts (which indicate the extent to which customer demands have been successfully met), inventory costs and the set-up costs.

2. INTERACTIONS BETWEEN IMPORTANT DECISIONS IN MRP

Biggs[1] showed that main effects of lot sizing and sequencing rules and the interaction between these are significant at the level of 0.01 significance and argued that it is possible that a particular sequencing rule may work in 'opposite direction' to a particular lot sizing rule and vice versa. Biggs[2] studied the interaction of priority rules with the capacity levels and reported that these are significant. He found that the Critical Ratio Rule (CRR) performed consistently well over different levels of capacity. Collier[3] and Billington et al[4] pointed out that certain lot sizing rules may hurt the capacity utilisation. Grasso and Taylor[5] studied main effects and interaction effects among four factors, namely lead time, buffering alternative, lot-size rule and cost value on total cost and reported that main effects of each factor and the interaction between lead time distribution and lot-size rule and that between buffering alternative and cost value on total cost are significant. Potty[6] reported that the choice of a lot-size rule has significant impact on the total costs and the choice of a sequencing rule has significant effect on the number of stockouts and the units stockouts.

Bahl and Ritzman[7] presented an integrated model for master scheduling, lot sizing and Capacity Requirement Planning (CRP) and gave a heuristic procedure to minimise the sum of capacity costs, set-up costs and inventory-carrying costs. South and Stewart[8] reported their experience at Hix Corporation wherein 50 per cent increase in lot sizes and planned manufacturing lead time resulted in low system tardiness without increase in work-in-process (WIP) inventory costs. An intuitive explanation could be that the increase in lot sizes reduces the number of set-ups while releasing the shop capacity and hence leads to reduction in queue length before the processing centres which leads to low tardiness. In the case of Hix Corporation, the effects balanced in such a manner that it did not increase the WIP inventory. Billington et al[9] formulated capacity/lot-size/lead time problem as mixed integer linear programming problem and have suggested product structure compression to reduce problem size. Models which include lot sizing and sequencing together become large and are intractable to the conventional integer programming techniques. Single-stage optimisation procedures, such as Wagner-Whitin[10] and Silver-Meal[11] are used due to its simplicity, are likely to yield sub-optimal solutions as stage wise interactions are ignored. Afentakis et al[12] developed computationally efficient procedures to give optimal solutions to lot sizing problems in multi-stage pure assembly systems with infinite capacity.

In literature, very few multi-pass heuristic have been reported, see Graves.[13] This heuristic modifies the variable production cost in each iteration and is shown to perform better than the single-pass heuristic due to McLaren[14] which modifies the set-up costs but tends to become more complex as the number of stages increases. We present here two simple multi-pass heuristics which aim to improve stockout performance under fixed capacity and permit exchange of information between lot sizing and sequencing problems.

3. HEURISTICS

If the production capacity is finite and the sub-assemblies have a varied routing sequence across the work centres, then for some parts and sub-assemblies, the delay is likely to be more due to the queue length before the work centres. In the heuristic described below, higher flow time of an item or sub-assembly is accounted for in the lot sizing problem by increasing its holding cost.

3.1 Heuristic 1

Let R be the set of parts with difference in actual and theoretical holding costs exceeding 10 per cent and S be the set of parts already considered twice in the iterative procedure. Let K(j) denote the number of times the part 'j' has been considered in the iteractive procedure, and BestSol denote the best solution arrived at with respect to stockouts. The steps of the heuristic are described below.

Step 1: Initialisation. Set K(j) to zero for all j. Using Wagner-Whitin algorithm for the lot sizing and the CRR (Lead time remaining-Work remaining/Work remaining) for sequencing, simulate the MRP system to prepare the set R and initialise the following:
$S \leftarrow 0$, $K(j)\ 0 \leftarrow$ for all j, BestSol$\leftarrow \infty$

Step 2: Select part 'j' from set R which has the highest percentage difference in theoretical and actual holding costs. Increase the holding cost of part 'j' in steps of 0.2 until the lot size changes. Set $K(j) = K(j) + 1$ and if $[K(j) = 2]$, then update $S = S + (j)$. If the current solution is better than the BestSol with respect to stockouts then update BestSol $\leftarrow$ Current solution.

Step 3: Simulate and prepare the set R afresh and let $R \leftarrow R — S$.

Step 4: If R = { }, then stop, else go to step 2.

An increase in the holding costs is likely to reduce the lot size to improve the stockout performance but an exscessive decrease in lot sizes may increase the number of set-ups and adversely affect the due date performance (as more capacity may be lost in set-ups now), hence the number of times a part or a sub-assembly may be considered for holding cost modification is limited to two. Results of empirical investigation described in the next section showed that Heuristic 1 improved the stockout performance. In Heuristic 1, the planned manufacturing lead times were kept constant. It is also possible to improve delivery schedule by increasing the lead times. Heuristic based on these ideas is presented below.

3.2 Heuristic 2

Step 1: Initialisation. Set K(j) to zero for all j. Using Wagner-Whitin algorithm for the lot sizing and the CRR (Lead time remaining – Work remaining/Work remaining) for sequencing, simulate the MRP system to prepare the set R and initialise the following:

$$S \leftarrow 0, K(j)\ 0 \leftarrow \text{for all } j, \text{BestSol} \leftarrow \infty$$

Step 2: Select part 'j' from set R which has the highest percentage difference in theoretical and actual holding costs. Increase the lead time of part 'j' by one time unit and set [K(j) = K(j) + 1] and if [K(j) = 2], then update S = S + (j). If the current solution is better than the BestSol with respect to stockouts then update BestSol ← Current solution.

Step 3: Simulate and prepare the set R afresh and let R = R — S.

Step 4: If R = { }, then stop, else go to step 2.

4. EMPIRICAL INVESTIGATION AND RESULTS

At each step of the iteration, heuristics require the flow time details of all parts and sub-assemblies and also the stockout details. A computer based model was prepared to see the effect of the Heuristics 1 and 2. Eight different problems having product structures 1-13 (given in Appendix 1) were solved. Multiple end item product structures were considered. The problem instances were carefully chosen to keep the shop utilisation at 70–75 per cent. CRR was chosen for sequencing as it was reported to do consistently better, see Biggs.[2] Wagner-Whitin[10] algorithm was chosen as the lot-size rule as it gives the optimal solution for the single-stage lot-size problem and is easier to implement. Simulation was run for 50 time periods.

The computational performance of the heuristics is given in Table 2.1. It can be seen that improvement in number of stockouts and units stockouts is significant for both heuristics. On an average, Heuristic 1 improved the number of Stockouts by 39.36 per cent and units stockouts by 32.81 per cent while increasing the total costs by 2.05 per cent, whereas, Heuristic 2 improved the number of stockouts by 29.65 per cent and units stockouts by 23.70 per cent while increasing the total costs by 7.33 per cent.

Mann-Whitney Test was carried out to compare the performance of the two heuristics and results are summarised in Table 2.2. In Table 2.2 denotes the means of a performance criteria due to Heuristic 1 and Heuristic 2 respectively. It may be inferred from Table 2.2 that, Heuristic 1 performed better than Heuristic 2 on the criteria of total costs and that both heuristics gave comparable performance on the number of stockouts and units stockouts. Thus, the results seem to suggest that it may be better to change lot sizes than the lead time for improvement in stockout performance for the case when shop utilisation is high. For solving one problem, heuristics took less than half an hour on an IBM-386 personal computer and terminated in just under 20 iterations.

5. CONCLUSIONS

Biggs[2] has shown that CRR performed consistently better on a variety of performance criteria like stockouts, units stockouts, set-ups and dollar inventory. Our multi-pass heuristic significantly improved the performance on the number of stockouts and the units stockouts by an iterative interaction with the lot-size rule. The heuristics are computationally attractive and are simple to implement on any existing MRP package.

Table 2.1 Summary on Mann-Whitney Test Improvement in Number of Stockouts

Problem Number	No. of Set-ups	No. of Stockouts	Units Stockouts	Set-up Costs	Inventory Costs	Total Costs
Problem 1						
Starting Solution	1314.00	129.00	4280.00	522933.00	307480.00	830413.00
Soln. of Heuristic 1	1559.00	80.00	2767.00	612667.00	278014.00	890681.00
% Improvement of Heuristic	−18.65	37.98	35.35	−17.16	9.50	−7.26
Soln. of Heuristic 2	1533.00	67.00	2351.00	602417.00	322808.00	925225.00
% Improvement of Heuristic 2	−16.67	48.00	45.07	−15.20	−4.99	−11.42
Problem 2						
Starting Solution	129.00	29.00	684.00	419461.00	317566.00	737027.00
Soln. of Heuristic 1	3234.00	20.00	482.00	431594.00	307561.00	739155.00
% Improvement of Heuristic 1	−3.36	31.03	29.53	−2.89	3.15	−0.29
Soln. of Heuristic 2	3143.00	19.00	453.00	421673.00	324104.00	745777.00
% Improvement of Heuristic 2	−0.45	34.48	33.77	−0.53	−2.06	−1.19

Contd...

Summary on Mann-Whitney Test Improvement in Number of Stockouts

Problem Number	No. of Set-ups	No. of Stockouts	Units Stockouts	Set-up Costs	Inventory Costs	Total Costs
Problem 3						
Starting Solution	2723.00	41.00	1492.00	35851.00	420655.00	746506.00
Soln. of Heuristic 1	2861.00	31.00	1160.00	331672.00	422172.00	753844.00
% Improvement of Heuristic 1	–5.07	24.39	22.25	–1.79	–0.36	–0.98
Soln. of Heuristic 2	2731.00	35.00	1223.00	324254.00	454518.00	778772.00
% Improvement of Heuristic 2	–0.29	14.63	18.03	0.49	–8.05	–4.32
Problem 4						
Starting Solution	1865.00	51.00	1153.00	281973.00	252727.00	534700.00
Soln. of Heuristic 1	1878.00	44.00	936.00	282355.00	247201.00	529556.00
% Improvement of Heuristic 1	–0.70	13.73	18.82	–0.14	2.19	0.96
Soln. of Heuristic 2	1872.00	47.00	1041.00	274645.00	277186.00	551831.00
% Improvement of Heuristic 2	–0.38	7.84	9.71	2.60	–9.68	–3.20
Problem 5						
Starting Solution	1345.00	79.00	2253.00	223601.00	222107.00	445708.00
Soln. of Heuristic 1	1622.00	38.00	1320.00	256250.00	197823.00	454073.00
% Improvement of Heuristic 1	–20.59	51.90	41.41	–14.60	10.93	–1.88
Soln. of Heuristic 2	1393.00	58.00	1742.00	226013.00	258137.00	484150.00
% Improvement of Heuristic 2	–3.57	26.58	22.68	–1.08	–16.22	–8.62
Problem 6						
Starting Solution	1895.00	39.00	814.00	115235.00	171627.00	286882.00
Soln. of Heuristic 1	2381.00	14.00	308.00	126618.00	170665.00	297283.00
% Improvement of Heuristic 1	–25.65	64.10	62.16	–9.88	0.56	–3.63
Soln. of Heuristic 2	1855.00	17.00	516.00	112181.00	233714.00	345895.00
% Improvement of Heuristic 2	2.11	56.41	36.61	2.65	–36.18	–20.58
Problem 7						
Starting Solution	1560.00	81.00	1800.00	301197.00	281904.00	583101.00
Soln. of Heuristic 1	1660.00	41.00	1203.00	320004.00	268190.00	588194.00
% Improvement of Heuristic 1	–6.41	49.38	33.17	–6.24	–4.86	–0.87
Soln. of Heuristic 2	1614.00	51.00	1567.00	300090.00	310987.00	611077.00

Contd...

Summary on Mann-Whitney Test Improvement in Number of Stockouts

Problem Number	No. of Set-ups	No. of Stockouts	Units Stockouts	Set-up Costs	Inventory Costs	Total Costs
% Improvement of of Heuristic 2	−3.46	37.04	12.94	0.37	−10.32	−4.80
Problem 8						
Starting Solution	2800.00	33.00	1514.00	318759.00	425754.00	744513.00
Soln. of Heuristic 1	2957.00	19.00	1214.00	320140.00	428140.00	748280.00
% Improvement of Heuristic 1	−5.61	42.42	19.82	−0.43	−0.56	−0.51
Soln. of Heuristic 2	2859.00	29.00	1347.00	317980.00	460004.00	777984.00
% Improvement of Heuristic 2	−2.11	12.12	11.03	0.24	−8.04	−4.50

Table 2 .2 Summary Mann-Whitney Test Improvement in Number of Stockouts

Problem Number	1	2	3	4	5	6	7	8	Mean	Std. Dev	Rank Sum
% Improverovement of Heuristic 1 (H1)	37.98	31.03	24.39	13.73	51.90	64.10	49.38	42.42	39.36	16.17	–
Combined rank (for H1)	10.00	7.00	5.00	3.00	14.00	16.00	13.00	11.00	–	–	79.00
% Improvement of Heuristic 2 (H2)	48.06	34.48	14.63	7.84	26.58	56.41	37.04	12.12	29.65	17.53	–
Combined rank (for H2)	12.00	8.00	4.00	1.00	6.00	15.00	9.00	2.00	–	–	57.00

$H_o : \mu_1 = \mu_2$; $H_1 : \mu_1 \neq \mu_2$;$U = 21$; $P(V \leq 21) = 0.139$; $\alpha = 0.05$ $2P \leq \alpha \Rightarrow$ accept H_o

Improvement in Units Stockouts											
Problem Number	**1**	**2**	**3**	**4**	**5**	**6**	**7**	**8**	**Mean**	**Std. Dev**	**Rank Sum**
% Improverovement of Heuristic 1 (H1)	35.65	29.53	22.25	18.82	41.41	62.16	33.17	19.82	32.81	14.28	–
Combined rank (for H1)	12.00	9.00	7.00	5.00	14.00	16.00	10.00	6.00	–	–	79.00
% Improvement of Heuristic 2 (H2)	45.07	33.57	18.03	9.71	22.68	36.61	12.94	11.03	23.70	12.37	–
Combined rank (for H2)	15.00	11.00	4.00	1.00	8.00	13.00	3.00	2.00	–	–	57.00

$H_o : \mu_1 = \mu_2$; $H_1 : \mu_1 \neq \mu_2$; $V = 21$; $P(V \leq 21) = 0.139$; $\alpha = 0.05$ $2P \leq \alpha \Rightarrow$ accept H_o

Contd...

Summary Mann-Whitney Test Improvement in Number of Stockouts

Increase in Total Costs											
Problem Number	1	2	3	4	5	6	7	8	Mean	Std. Dev	Rank Sum
% Improverovement of Heuristic 1 (H1)	7.26	0.29	0.98	0.96	1.88	3.63	0.87	0.51	2.05	2.36	–
Combined rank (for H1)	13.00	1.00	5.00	4.00	7.00	9.00	3.00	2.00	–	–	44.00
% Improvement of Heuristic 2 (H2)	11.42	1.19	4.32	3.20	8.62	20.62	4.80	4.50	7.33	5.84	–
Combined rank (for H2)	15.00	6.00	10.00	8.00	14.00	16.00	12.00	11.00	–	–	92.00

$H_o : \mu_1 \geq \mu_2; H_1 : \mu_2 > \mu_1; U = 8; P(V \leq 8) = 0.005; \alpha = 0.05\ P \leq \alpha \Rightarrow H_{o \text{ is rejected}}$

REFERENCES

1. Biggs, JR, Heuristic Lot sizing and Sequencing Rules in a Multi-Stage Production Inventory System, *Decision Sciences*, 10, 1979, 96-115.
2. Biggs, JR, Priority Rules for Shop Floor Control in a Material Requirements Planning System under Various Levels of Capacity, *International Journal of Production Research*, 23(1), 1985, 33-46.
3. Collier, DA, A Comparison of MRP Lot sizing Methods Considering Capacity Change Costs, *J Oper Management, August* 1980.
4. Billington P, McClain J and Thomas L J, The Interaction of Lead Time Determination, Lot sizing Decisions and Capacity Planning in MRP System, *Proceedings, American Institute of Decision Sciences, Eleventh Annual Meeting*, 1979.
5. Grasso ET and Taylor BW, A Simulation Based Experimental Investigation of Supply Timing Uncertainty in MRP Systems, *International Journal of Production Research*, 22(3), 1984, 485-497.
6. Potty VS, Simulation of Heuristics, Lot sizing and Sequencing Procedures in MRP, unpublished *M Tech dissertation*, Indian Institute of Technology, Kanpur, 1990.
7. Bahl HC and Ritzman L, An Integrated Model for Master Scheduling, Lot sizing and Capacity Requirements Planning, *Journal of Operations Research Society*, (UK), 35(5), 1984, 389-399.
8. South JB and Stewart RJ, A 50% Increase in Lot Size and Planned Manufacturing Lead Time with No Increase in Work-in-Process Inventory, *Production and Inventory Management, First Quarter*, 27(1), 1986, 19-25.
9. Billington P, McClain J and Thomas LJ, Mathematical Approaches to Capacity Constrained MRP Systems: Review, Formulation and Problem Reduction, *Management Science* 29(10), 1983, 1126-1141.
10. Wagner MH and Whitin TM, Dynamic Version of the Economic Lot sizing Model, *Management Science*, 5, 1958, 89-96.
11. Silver EA and Meal HC, A Heuristic for Selecting Lot sizing Quantities for the Case of a Deterministic Time Varying Demand Rate and Discrete Opportunities for Replenishment, Production and Inventory Management, 2nd Quarter, 1973.
12. Afentakis, A, Gavish, B and Karmarkar U, Çomputationally Efficient Optimal Solutions to the Lot sizing Problem in Multi-Stage Assembly Systems, *Management Science*, 30(2), 1984, 222-239.
13. Graves SC, Multi-Stage Lot sizing: An Iterative Procedure, in Schwarz, LW, (Ed): *Multi level Production/Inventory Control Systems: Theory and Practice, North Hol land Publishing Company, Amsterdam*, 1981.
14. McLaren, A Study of Multi Level Lot sizing Procedures for Material Requirements Planning System, *unpublished Ph D dissertation*, Purdue University, 1976.

3 Heuristic for Securing Coordinated Scheduling in MRP

R R K Sharma, S R Yoganandan

ABSTRACT

It has been reported by Goodwin and Weeks[1,2] and Fry et al[3] that sequencing rules which are based on due dates are overall better performers. It is possible to improve performance (lateness/tardiness) if variance of arrival times of different sub-assemblies at an assembly centre is reduced. This means, in other words, that efforts made to improve the coordinated arrival of jobs at various assembly centres can be made fruitful. A heuristic, which seeks to achieve a better coordinated arrival at assembly centre, is developed. Its performance is compared with the multi-pass heuristic (Chapter 2) which seeks to improve the performance by modifying the holding cost of the lots whose actual inventory-carrying cost is much higher than the theoretical inventory-carrying cost. Finally, a combination heuristic is developed, which combines the ideas of the above two heuristics. A comparative analysis is arrived at and some interesting results are presented.

1. INTRODUCTION

Lot sizing, sequencing, determination of planned lead time and capacity planning are important decisions in the effective use of MRP system. While little work is available that considers the interactions between these decisions (see Grasso and Taylor[4]), almost no work is available that considers coordinated sequences in multi-stage systems such as MRP (see Sharma and Yoganandan[5]). We make an effort to develop a sequencing-based heuristic to secure a more coordinated arrival of components and sub-assemblies at an assembly centre. We also present empirical results which at least show that efforts made to achieve better coordination improve the lateness performance substantially reduce inventory-carrying costs.

2. LITERATURE REVIEW

Grasso and Taylor[4] studied main effects and interaction effects among four factors, namely; lead time determination, buffering alternative, lot-size rule and cost value on total cost and reported that main effects of each factor and interaction between lead time determination and lot-size rule and that between buffering alternative and cost value on total costs are significant. Biggs[6] showed that the main effects of lot-sizing rule and sequencing rule and interaction between these are significant at the level of 0.01 significance and has argued that it is possible that a particular sequencing rule may work in opposite direction to a particular lot-sizing rule and vice versa. Bahl and Ritzman[7] have presented an integrated model for master scheduling, lot sizing and CRP and have developed a heuristic procedure to minimise the sum of capacity costs, set-up costs are inventory-carrying costs.

In literature, very few multi-pass heuristics have been reported, (see Graves[8]). This heuristic modifies the variable production costs in each interation and is shown to perform better than the single-pass heuristic due to McLaren[9] which modifies set-up costs but tends to become more complex as the number stages increase. The multi-pass heuristic (Chapter 2) modifies holding costs in each iteration to perform better than the best combination of Lot-sizing Rule (Wagner-Whitin algorithm) and Sequencing Rule (CRR, see Biggs[6]).

In literature, almost no heuristic is available that attempts to improve the coordinated arrival of components and assemblies at an assembly centre. It has been reported by Goodwin and Weeks[1,2] and Fry et al[3] that sequencing rules that are based on due dates are overall better performers. It has also been reported by Fry et al[3] that dispatching rules, based on look ahead, do not perform better in a multi-stage production scheduling in context to fixed sequences of operations such as MRP systems. This would imply that any kind of look ahead in securing coordinated scheduling may not perform better. However, dispatching rules based on look ahead have been reported to do well in the real time control of flexible manufacturing systems (Zeestraten[10]).

It probably implies that the sequencing rule based on 'look ahead' is successful only if it is 'knowledgeable'. Recently, Ow et al[11] have suggested the use of 'filtered beam search' scheduling. This rule stores other rules in the 'knowledge base' and develops many solutions in parallel to minimise the search effort to reach a good solution. The performance of these rules is impressive. Application of 'filtered beam search' technique to multi-stage scheduling problems may lead to difficulties as it would require a very large knowledge base which may further require a lot of effort. The chapter seeks to develop 'knowledge' about the status of various components and sub-assemblies in the shop through repeated simulations and use it for rescheduling components and sub-assemblies for achieving better coordinated arrival. An attempt is made through a simple heuristic that prepares improved schedules by reducing the variance of arrival times of different sub-assemblies at an assembly centre.

3. DEVELOPMENT OF HEURISTIC

Normally, single-pass heuristics are used in MRP systems for simplicity. That is, a single lot-sizing procedure is applied to determine the lots and next a single scheduling heuristic is applied. This procedure is popular due to its simplicity. But such a procedure is not able to communicate between the lot sizing and the scheduling sub-problem. Biggs[6] has established that lot sizing and sequencing rules interact. For example, it may be found that after scheduling is done, some sub-assemblies are spending more time in the shop than theoretically estimated by the lot-sizing rule. Hence, there may be scope to improve solutions by using multi-pass heuristic. One such effort can be found in the heuristic discussed in Chapter 2 , where it increases the inventory-holding costs for items as sub-assemblies which spend substantially more inventory-carrying costs than the theoretical costs as determined by the lot -sizing rules. The heuristic does not change the schedules in any way (but uses CRR for scheduling).

While using CRR, if some assembly has to wait for a substantial length of time at an assembly centre, no loss (in the form of aggregate lateness) will be experienced if it is given a lower priority while processing on machines before this assembly centre as other assemblies will get speeded up. Similar benefits are expected, if a job that arrives later at an assembly centre is expedited while processing on machines before this assembly centre. These ideas are combined to develop the heuristic that attempts to improve the aggregate lateness performance by altering the priority of the sub-assemblies.

3.1 Heuristic 1

Let L_i be the set of sub-assemblies/components that arrive late compared to at least 50 per cent of the sub-assemblies arriving at the assembly centre 'i' and let E_i be the set of sub-assemblies/components that arrive early compared to at least 50 per cent of the sub-assemblies arriving at the assembly centre 'i'. Let BestSol denote the best solution arrived at with respect to aggregate lateness. The steps of the heuristic are given below.

Step 1: Set BestSol ←infinity

Step 2: Using Wagner-Whitin algorithm for the lot sizing the CRR (lead time remaining-work remaining/work remaining) for sequencing, simulate the MRP system to compute aggregate lateness.

Step 3: Prepare sets L_i and E_i for each of the assembly in the shop. Add 0.1 to the critical ratio of that lot belonging to set L_i of the sub-assembly, and subtract 0.1 from the critical ratio of the lot belonging to set E_i for the same lot sizes prepared, reschedule the lots by simulation using the revised critical ratios, obtain the current value of aggregate lateness. If current solution is better than BestSol with respect to aggregate lateness, then set BestSol ← current solution.

Step 4: Repeat step 3 twenty times.

An increase in the value of critical ratio for a component results in it getting higher priority and arrives early at an assembly centre. The opposite happens when the critical ratio is decreased. So it is expected that aggregate lateness is reduced and a better coordination results, hence, inventory-carrying cost also reduces. We compare the performance of the above Heuristic H1 with other multi-pass heuristic in the previous chapter.

3.2 Heuristic 2

Let R be the set of parts with difference in actual and theoretical holding costs exceeding 10 per cent and S be the set of parts already considered twice in the iterative procedure. Let K(j) denote the number of times the part 'j' has been considered in the iterative procedure and BestSol denote the best solution arrived at with respect to stockouts. The steps of heuristic are described below.

Step 1: Initialisation. Set K(j) to zero for all j. Using Wagner-Whitin algorithm for the lot sizing and the CRR (lead time remaining -work remaining/work remaining) for sequencing, simulate the MRP system to prepare the set R and initialise the following set the following, iteration-counter = 0,

S← {}, K(j) ← 0 for all j, BestSol ←infinity

Step 2: If iteration-counter = 20, then stop, else go to step 3.

Step 3: Select part 'j' from set R which has the highest percentage difference in the theoretical and actual holding costs. Increase the holding cost of part 'j' in steps of 0.2 until the lot size changes. Set [K(j)=K(j)+1] and if [K(j)=2], then update S=S+{j}. If the current solution is better than the BestSol with respect to aggregate lateness then update the following.
BestSol ← Current solution,
iteration-counter = iteration-counter + 1.

Step 4: Simulate the MRP system to prepare set R afresh and let R ← R – S.

Step 5: If R = { }, then stop, else go to step 2.

3.3 Heuristic 3

Heuristic 2 makes no effort to improve the coordination among arrival components/assemblies at an assembly centre, but it improves the costs and lateness by modifying the holding costs for those assemblies that have higher actual inventory-carrying cost as compared to theoretical inventory-carrying cost. This improves the lateness as some shop capacity is released due to changes in the lot-sizing schedule. It is possible to reduce the aggregate lateness by (i) changing the lot size and arriving at the best solution using the Heuristic 2. (ii) finding the components/assemblies at any assembly centre which have poor coordination and application with Heuristic1. It is expected that simultaneous changes in the lot sizes and the priorities may reduce the aggregate lateness and the components are expected to arrive in coordination with one another. The steps of heuristics are described below.

Step 0: Set counter = 0.

Step 1: Simulate the MRP system and apply Heuristic 2 to arrive at a best solution with respect to aggregate lateness.

Step 2: Starting with this BestSol, apply the Heuristic 1 to get an updated solution.

Step 3: If counter = 20, then stop, else go to step 1.

4. EMPIRICAL INVESTIGATION AND RESULTS

A computer-based model was prepared to see the effects of Heuristics 1, 2 and 3 on performance criteria such as number of set-up, number of stock-outs, aggregate lateness, set-up costs, inventory-carrying costs and the total of set-up and inventory-carrying costs. A total of 23 product structures were created (product structures 14-36 given in Appendix 1) and an effort was made to ensure, as far as possible, that problems contained a mix of structures such as tall, short and broad.

Problem instances were chosen carefully to keep shop utilisation relatively at a higher level of about 70 per cent. While preparing problem instances demand, processing times on machines and so on, were altered to come up with a good problem that gave relatively uniform shop utilisation. This was done to ensure that shop had no obvious bottlenecks. It also involved simulation several times and scanning the machine utilisation each time. It took about 10 days to develop a problem instance.

The computational performance of heuristics is given in Table 3.1. It can be noted by visual inspection that Heuristic 1 improved simultaneously the aggregate lateness and inventory-carrying costs, whereas Heuristic 2 improved only the inventory-carrying costs. Only in two instances out of eight, the performance of Heuristic 2 was better than that of Heuristic 1 in terms of aggregate lateness. Since the sample size is relatively small, we apply Mann-Whitney Test to check the statistical difference in performance. The results of the test are given in Tables 3.2 and 3.3.

It can be seen in Table 3.2 that Heuristic 1 produces significantly better performance at 0.05 significance level on the criteria of aggregate lateness as compared to Heuristic 2 and that Heuristic 1 and 2 produce comparable performance on the criteria of number of stockouts and total cost (sum of inventory-carrying cost and the set-up cost). It may be seen that the coordinated schedules improve aggregate lateness and total cost much better than Heuristic 2 (Chapter 2) which brings about improvement by modifying the holding costs. Thus, it may be better to have a coordinated schedule than to change lot sizes.

It may be seen in Table 3.3 that performance of Heuristic 3 is as good as that of Heuristic 1 on all the criteria considered here (e.g., aggregate lateness, number of stockouts and total costs) at 0.05 significance level. It means after Heuristic 1 is applied there is apparently little or no room for improvement for Heuristic 2. Although the above inference is tentative due to smaller sample size taken in this research, it is an interesting hypothesis for further research.

It may be pointed out that in case of Problem 2, the Heuristic 1 has failed to improve aggregate lateness although it has improved the total cost substantially. It was found out that product structures of Problem 2 were relatively flat. Hence, It may mean that it is difficult to secuPurdueUniversity, 1976 re-coordination when product structures are flat. More research needs to be done in this direction.

Biggs[6] had earlier shown that CRR rule performed constantly better on a variety of performance criteria which was later confirmed by the studies of Goodwin and Weeks[1,2] and Fry et al.[3] Sharma and Potty (Chapter 2) have shown that units stockouts performance can be improved substantially by the marginal increase in total costs by a heuristic that modifies the holding costs in the lot-sizing procedure. We have presented here a heuristic that improves the aggregate lateness and inventory-carrying costs at the same time by preparing a coordinated schedule. Our conclusion is that more benefits may be accrued by heuristics that tend to secure coordinated flow of sub-assemblies at an assembly centre. More research is needed to be done in this regard.

Table 3.1 Summary of Results

	Aggregate Lateness	Actual Inventory Cost ('000)	Total Cost ('000)	No. of Set-up	No. of Stockouts
Problem 1					
Starting Solution	8732.61	12.07	42.42	698	105
Heuristic 1 Soln	8005.35	7.62	37.38	698	101
% Improvement	8.32	39.54	11.88	0.0	4.0
Heuristic 2 Soln	8228.02	9.61	39.68	699	102
% Improvement	5.77	23.39	6.48	−0.14	3.0
Heuristic 3 Soln	8005.00	5.25	35.31	619	101
% Improvement	8.32	58.3	16.76	0.14	4.0
Problem 2					
Starting Solution	605.86	11.82	28.15	791	39
Heuristic 1 Soln	605.86	5.81	22.13	791	39
% Improvement	0.0	54.00	21.38	0.0	0.0
Heuristic 2 Soln	605.56	5.98	22.66	791	39
% Improvement	0.0	50.63	19.71	0.0	0.0
Heuristic 3 Soln	605.86	4.54	20.82	794	39
% Improvement	0.0	61.5	25.80	−0.37	0.0
Problem 3					
Starting Solution	9793.73	21.88	58.44	801.0	31.0
Heuristic 1 Soln	8055.33	17.13	44.38	801.0	29.0
% Improvement	17.75	21.72	24.0	0.0	6.45
Heuristic 2 Soln	9793.73	21.88	52.47	807.0	31.0
% Improvement	0.0	0.0	10.21	−0.74	0.0
Heuristic 3 Soln	8055.33	17.13	49.91	801	29
% Improvement	17.75	21.72	14.59	0.0	6.45

Contd...

Summary of Results

	Aggregate Lateness	Actual Inventory Cost ('000)	Total Cost ('000)	No. of Set-up	No. of Stockouts
Problem 4					
Starting Solution	21978.87	92.88	220.67	1085.0	36.0
Heuristic 1 Soln	19976.33	52.01	144.52	1085.0	36.0
% Improvement	9.11	56.93	22.04	0.0	0.0
Heuristic 2 Soln	21759.8	49.83	145.95	1125	36.0
% Improvement	1.12	46.73	21.29	-3.6	0.0
Heuristic 3 Soln	19976.7	43.6	143.06	1142.0	36.0
% Improvement	9.11	46.57	22.85	5.25	0.0
Problem 5					
Starting Solution	11104.33	85.95	280.83	758	28
Heuristic 1 Soln	10292.84	47.58	223.02	758	28
% Improvement	7.37	55.43	20.58	0.0	0.0
Heuristic 2 Soln	11098.40	49.32	246.83	777.0	28
% Improvement	0.2	42.62	12.11	0.0	0.0
Heuristic 3 Soln	10292.84	32.75	228.12	766	28
% Improvement	7.71	64.13	18.77	0.0	0.0
Problem 6					
Starting Solution	17529.48	33.74	76.50	1457	66
Heuristic 1 Soln	16980.52	18.45	61.21	1457	68
% Improvement	3.13	45.3	19.98	0.0	3.03
Heuristic 2 Soln	17529.48	33.74	76.69	1462	69
% Improvement	0.0	0.0	-0.26	-0.34	4.55
Heuristic 3 Soln	16980.52	18.45	61.21	1457	70
% Improvement	3.13	45.3	19.98	0.0	6.06
Problem 7					
Starting Solution	6293.62	72.48	129.15	716	12
Heuristic 1 Soln	6185	30.72	87.39	716	12
% Improvement	1.72	57.62	32.33	0.0	0.0
Heuristic 2 Soln	6193.62	7.86	66.86	724	12
% Improvement	0.0	73.46	48.23	-1.11	0.0
Heuristic 3 Soln	6185.00	26.68	84.02	718	12
% Improvement	1.72	63.19	65.04	-0.28	0.0
Problem 8					
Starting Solution	4756.10	21.83	89.35	482	18
Heuristic 1 Soln	4493.10	8.57	76.09	482	19
% Improvement	5.53	60.74	14.84	0.0	5.35
Heuristic 2 Soln	4756.10	13.46	80.94	498	18
% Improvement	0.0	38.34	9.41	3.33	0.0
Heuristic 3 Soln	4493.10	5.22	70.77	4.83	18
% Improvement	5.53	76.12	20.79	0.27	0.0

Table 3.2 Summary of Mann-Whitney Test Improvement in Aggregate Lateness [Heuristic 1 (H1) and Heuristic 2 (H2)]

Problem Number	1	2	3	4	5	6	7	8	Mean	Std. Dev	Rank Sum
% Improvement of Heuristic1 (H1)	8.32	0.0	17.75	9.11	7.37	3.13	1.72	5.53	6.62	5.18	–
Combined Rank (for H1)	14	3.5	16	15	13	10	9	11	–	–	91.5
% Improvement of Heuristic2 (H2)	5.77	0.0	0.0	1.12	0.2	0.0	0.0	0.0	0.89	1.88	–
Combined Rank (for H2)	12	3.5	3.5	8	7	3.5	3.5	3.5	–	–	44.5

Ho: $\mu_1 = \mu_2$; U = 8.5; P (V ≤ 8.5) = 0.007; a = 0.05 ; 2P < α ≤ reject H_o

Problem Number	1	2	3	4	5	6	7	8	Mean	Std. Dev	Rank Sum
% Improvement of Heuristic1 (H1)	4.0	0.0	6.45	0.0	0.0	3.03	0.0	5.35	2.35	2.53	–
Combined Rank (for H1)	13	5.5	16	5.5	5.5	12	15	–	–	–	78
% Improvement of Heuristic 2 (H2)	3.0	0.0	0.0	0.0	0.0	4.55	0.0	0.0	0.94	1.68	–
Combined Rank (for H2)	11	5.5	5.5	5.5	5.5	14	5.5	5.5	–	–	58

H_o: $\mu_1 = \mu_2$; U = 22; P (V ≤ 22) = 0.164; α= 0.05 ; 2P ≤ α⇒accept Ho

Contd...

Summary of Mann-Whitney Test Improvement in Aggregate Lateness [Heuristic 1 (H1) and Heuristic 2 (H2)]

Improvement in Total Cost											
Problem Number	1	2	3	4	5	6	7	8	Mean	Std. Dev	Rank Sum
% Improvement of Heuristic1 (H1)	11.88	21.38	24.0	22.04	20.58	19.98	32.33	14.84	2.88	5.70	–
Combined Rank (for H1)	5	12	14	13	10	9	15	7	–	–	85
% Improvement of Heuristic2 (H2)	6.48	19.71	10.21	21.29	12.11	–0.26	48.23	9.41	15.89	13.18	–
Combined Rank (for H2)	2	8	4	11	6	1	16	3	–	–	51

$H_o: \mu_1 = \mu_2$; U = 15; P (V ≤15) = 0.041; α = 0.05 ; 2P ≤ α ⇒is accepted

Table 3.3 Summary of Mann-Whitney Test Improvement in Aggregate Lateness [Heuristic 1 (H1) and Heuristic 3 (H3)]

Problem Number	1	2	3	4	5	6	7	8	Mean	Std. Dev	Rank Sum
% Improvement of Heuristic1 (H1)	8.32	0.0	17.75	9.11	7.37	3.13	1.72	5.53	6.62	5.18	–
Combined Rank (for H1)	11.5	1.5	15.5	13.5	9	5.5	3.5	7.5	–	–	67.5
% Improvement of Heuristic3 (H3)	8.32	0.0	17.75	9.11	7.71	3.13	1.72	5.13	6.66	5.19	–
Combined Rank (for H3)	11.5	1.5	15.5	13.5	10	5.5	3.5	7.5	–	–	68.5

$H_o: \mu_1 = \mu_3$; U = 32.5; P (V ≤32.5) = 0.520; a = 0.05 ; 2P ≤ α ⇒ accept H_o

Contd...

Summary of Mann-Whitney Test Improvement in Aggregate Lateness [Heuristic 1 (H1) and Heuristic 3 (H3)]

Improvement in Number of Stockouts											
Problem Number	1	2	3	4	5	6	7	8	Mean	Std. Dev	Rank Sum
% Improvement of Heuristic1 (H1)	4.0	0.0	6.45	0.0	0.0	3.03	0.0	5.35	2.35	2.53	–
Combined Rank (for H1)	11.5	5.0	15.5	5.0	5.0	10	5.0	13	–	–	70
% Improvement of Heuristic3 (H3)	4.0	0.0	6.45	0.0	0.0	6.06	0.0	0.0	2.06	2.74	–
Combined Rank (for H3)	11.5	5.0	15.0	5.0	5.0	14	5.0	5.0	–	–	66

H_o:$\mu_1 = \mu_3$; U = 30 ; P (V ≤30) = 0.439; α= 0.05 ; 2P ≤α⇒accept H_o

Improvement in Number of Stockouts											
Problem Number	1	2	3	4	5	6	7	8	Mean	Std. Dev	Rank Sum
% Improvement of Heuristic1 (H1)	11.88	21.38	24.0	22.04	20.58	19.98	32.33	14.84	20.88	5.7	–
Combined Rank (for H1)	1	10	13	11	8	6.5	15	3	–	–	67.5
% Improvement of Heuristic3 (H3)	16.76	25.80	14.59	27.85	18.77	19.98	65.04	20.79	25.57	15.26	–
Combined Rank (for H3)	4	14	2	12	5	6.5	16	9	–	–	68.5

H_o: $\mu_1 = \mu_2$; U = 31.5; P (V ≤ 31.5) = 0.50; a = 0.05 ; 2P ≤ a ⇒accept H_o

REFERENCES

1. Goodwin JS and Weeks JK, Evaluating Scheduling Policies in a Multi-level Assembly System. International Journal of Production Research. 24, 1986, 247-257.
2. Goodwin JS and Weeks JK, Operating Policies for Scheduling Assembled Products. Decision Sciences. 13, 1982, 585-603.
3. Fry TP, Philipoom PR and Markland RE, Dispatching in Multi-stage Job Shop where Machine Capacities are Unbalanced. International Journal of Production Research. 26, 1988, 1199-1223.
4. Grasso ET and Taylor BW, A Simulation Based Experimental Investigation of Supply Timing Uncertainty in MRP Systems. International Journal of Production Research, 22(3), 1984, 485-497.
5. Sharma RRK and Yoganandan SR, Heuristic for Securing Coordination in MRP. Proceedings of 12th International Conference on Production Research held at Finland during August 16-20, 1993.
6. Biggs JR, Priority Rules for Shop Floor Control in a Material Requirements Planning System under Various Levels of Capacity. International Journal of Production Research. 23, 1985, 33-46.
7. Bahl HC and Ritzman L, An Integrated Model for Master Scheduling, Lot Sizing and Capacity Requirement Planning. Journal of Operations Research Society (UK). 35(5), 1984, 389-399.
8. Graves SC, Multi-stage Lot Sizing: An Iterative Procedure. Ed Schwarz, Multi-level Production/Inventory Control Systems: Theory and Practice. North Holland Publishing Company, Amsterdam, 1981.
9. McLaren BJ, A Study of Multi-level Lot Sizing Procedures for Material Requirement Planning Systems. Unpublished PhD dissertation, Purdue University, 1976.
10. Zeestraten MJ, The Look Ahead Dispatching Procedure. International Journal of Production Research. 28, 1990, 369-384.
11. Ow PS and Maron TE , Filtered Beam Search in Scheduling. International Journal of Production Research, 26, 1988, 35-62.

4 A Sequencing-based Multi-pass Heuristic for Improved Performance in MRP Context

R R K Sharma, Sharat Sinha

ABSTRACT

Different decision problems in MRP, such as, lot sizing, sequencing, capacity planning and planned lead times are inter-dependent. As shown earlier (Chapter 2) multi-pass heuristic which modifies lot size does better than the best known single-pass heuristic which uses CRR for sequencing and Wagner-Whitin algorithm for lot sizing. It was shown by Sharma and Yoganandan[1] that a multi-pass heuristic that attempts to secure coordinated flow of sub-assemblies in a MRP situation produces better performance than the multi-pass heuristic discussed in Chapter 2. Here, we extend the ideas of Sharma and Yoganandan[1] to develop a multi-pass heuristic based on the idea of coordination index which allows more 'uniform' rescheduling to produce an improvement in performance on many criteria.

1. INTRODUCTION

Lot sizing, sequencing, determination of planned lead times and capacity planning are important decisions in the effective use of MRP systems. These decisions are inter-dependent. However, few operating procedures are available which consider these interactions. To develop operating schedules for MRP, various single-pass heuristics have been popular due to their simplicity, where a simple decision rule is chosen for each of the sub-problems i.e., lot sizing, sequencing, determination of lead times and capacity planning. The purpose of this chapter is to develop a multi-pass heuristic that changes schedules that seek to achieve coordinated flow of materials. Here, we provide the relevant literature review and further develop a multi-pass heuristic that seeks to alter the schedules to produce coordinated flow of lots at assembly centres. Here, we also provide the other multi-pass heuristics in the literature. We provide the results of the experimental investigation carried out to determine the efficacy of various multi-pass heuristics available. Finally, we give our conclusions and suggest a few topics for further research.

2. LITERATURE REVIEW

Biggs[2] has studied the interaction of priority rules with the capacity levels and has reported that these are significant. He found that the Critical Ratio Rule (CRR) performed consistently well over different levels of capacity. Grasso and Taylor[3] studied main effects and interaction effects among four factors, namely, lead time, buffering alternative, lot size rule on total cost and reported that main effects of each factor and the interaction between lead time distribution and lot size rule and that between buffering alternative and cost value on total cost were significant. Potty[4] has reported that the choice of a lot size rule has significant impact on the choice of sequencing rule and both taken together have a significant effect on the number of stockouts and the units stockouts.

South and Stewart[5] report their experience at Hix Corporation wherein 50 per cent increase in lot size and planned manufacturing lead time resulted in low system tardiness without increase in WIP inventory costs. An intuitive explanation for this could be that increase in lot size reduces the number of set-ups while releasing the shop capacity and hence leads to reduce in queue length before processing centres which leads to low tardiness. In the case of Hix Corporation, the effects balanced in such a manner that it did not increase the WIP inventory. Billington et al[6] formulated the capacity/lot size/lead time problem as mixed integer linear programming problem and have suggessted product structure compression to reduce problem size. Models which include lot sizing and sequencing together become large and are traceable to the conventional integer programming techniques.

In literature, very few multi-pass heuristics have been reported. Graves[7] has suggested a multi-pass heuristic that modifies the variable production cost in each iteration, which performs better than the single-pass heuristic due to McLaren,[8] which modifies the set-up cost. In Chapter 2, we have developed multi-pass heuristics where holding cost and planned lead times for assemblies having greater difference in actual and theoretical holding costs has been modified. This has been observed that it is better to change lot size than to change the planned lead times and that both heuristics did better than the single-pass heuristic that uses Wagner-Whitin algorithm for lot sizing and CRR for sequencing which was shown to produce better performance among the various single-pass heuristics considered (Biggs[2]). Finally, Sharma and Yoganandan[1] (Chapter 3) have presented a multi-pass heuristic that identifies those assemblies that arrive late compared to 50 per cent of sub-assemblies at an assembly centre and increase their priority value at machines that are prior to the assembly centre to expedite them and reduce priority of those assemblies which come early, causing further delay. It was observed that this heuristic performed better than the one discussed in Chapter 2 on all performance criteria.

Encouraged by the work of Sharma and Yoganandan,[1] the idea of coordination index at an assembly centre is used to alter the priority value of assemblies at previous processing centres. The Rescheduling thus done leads to better performance compared to the performances of the heuristics developed by Sharma and Potty (Chapter 2) and Sharma and Yoganandan.[1]

3. DEVELOPMENT OF HEURISTIC

If scheduling causes delays in increasing the actual inventory-carrying costs, then it is communciated to the lot sizing problem by increasing the holding cost so that lot size are changed in accordance with the heuristic mentioned in Chapter 2. This one does not make any modifications in the schedules.

Actually, if lots are made to arrive at assembly centres such that variance of arrival time is as less as possible, then it could lead to coordinated arrival of lots at assembly centres and improve the performance. After scheduling is done, assemblies arriving late/early compared to the 50 per cent of sub-assemblies at an assembly centre are identified and for subsequent scheduling their criticality in previous processing centres is increased/decreased.

An increase in the value of critical ratio for a component results in it getting higher priority and it arrives early at an assembly centre. The opposite happens when the critical ratio is decreased. So it is expected that when aggregate lateness is reduced, a better coordination results. Hence, inventory carrying cost also reduces. Details of this heuristic (Heuristic 2 here) are given in Sharma and Yoganandan[1] and in Chapter 3 of this book.

The Heuristic 2 alters the critical ratios of all the lots coming early or late by the same factor. It was reasoned that if the criticality is altered more uniformly, then it could lead to better performance. This idea formed the core of the heuristic developed here. We define coordination index for a sub-assembly or as component as follows.

At the end of simulation,

Let a = reaching time for lot at an assembly centre,

b = mean time of reaching an assembly centre.

Coordination index = 1+(a-b)/b.

Modify the priority of the lot for subsequent runs at processing centres before this assembly centre as a product of (-1), coordination index and critical ratio and is used for sequencing in the subsequent simulation run. We kept the lead times of lots same as before. The details of the heuristic are given below.

3.1 Heuristic H3

The coordination index for job 'j' is denoted by c(j). BestSol is the best solution obtained so far with respect to the criteria of aggregate lateness.

- Step1: Initialisation. Set c(j) =1 for all lots. Using Wagner-Whitin algorithm for lot sizing and CRR for sequencing simulate the MRP system. Set BestSol to the solution obtained so far.
- Step 2: Compute coordination index = (1+ (a – b)/b), where a = Reaching time for lot at an assembly centre, b = Mean time of reaching an assembly centre. Modify the priority of the lot for subsequent runs at processing centres before this assembly centre, as a product of (-1), coordination index and critical ratio, is used for sequencing in the subsequent simulation run.
- Step 3: Use the priority indices calculated in step 2 and again simulate the MRP system. Update BestSol if a better solution is obtained.
- Step 4: Perform steps 2 and 3 twenty times. The Heuristic 3 computes the range of arrival of assemblies at an assembly centre and uniformly alters the priority values of the lots/components. Hence, it is expected that it performs better than the Heuristic 2 mentioned above. We conduct an experimental investigation to verify our prior expectations about the performance of various heuristics.

4. EXPERIMENTAL INVESTIGATION AND RESULTS

A computer based model was prepared to generate empirical experience about the performances of Heuristics 1, 2 and 3. A number of performance criteria were used, i.e., total units lateness, total aggregate lateness, total cost (sum of total inventory carrying costs and total set-up costs), average utilisation of machines and the average coordination range. A total of 20 product structures were created and effort was made to ensure that problems contained a mix of structures such as tall, short and broad (product structures 37-56 mentioned in the Appendix 1 were used). Problem instances were chosen carefully to keep shop utilisation at a relatively higher level of about 70 per cent.

Computational performance of the Heuristic 3 is mentioned in Sinha.[12] We give the percentage improvements due to Heuristics 1, 2 and 3 over the starting solution (starting solution uses the single-pass heuristic using Wagner-Whitin algorithm for lot sizing and CRR for sequencing) in Table 4.1, 4.2 and 4.3 respectively.

Since the sample size is reasonable, we conducted 't' test on the percentage improvements achieved over the starting solution obtained by the best known single-pass heuristic for different performance criteria. The results of the 't' tests are given in Table 4.4.

For Total Aggregate Lateness

Heuristic 1 and 2 are as good as each other at 0.05 significance level. Heuristic 3 is better than Heuristic 2 at 0.005 significance level and Heuristic 3 is better than Heuristic 1 at 0.005 significance level.

For Total Units Lateness

Heuristic 1 and 2 are as good as each other at 0.05 significance level. Heuristic 3 is better than Heuristic 2 at 0.005 significance level and Heuristic 3 is better than Heuristic 1 at 0.005 significance level.

For Total Cost

Heuristic 2 is better than Heuristic 1 at 0.005 significance level. Heuristic 2 and 3 are as good at 0.05 significance level and Heuristic 3 is better than Heuristic 1 at 0.005 significance level.

For Average Utilisation of Machine

Heuristic 1 and 2 are as good as each other at 0.05 significance level. Heuristic 3 is better than Heuristic 2 at 0.0005 significance level and Heuristic 3 is better than Heuristic 1 at 0.0005 significance level.

For Average Coordination Range

Heuristic 1 is better than Heuristic 2 at 0.0005 significance level. Heuristic 3 is better than Heuristic 2 at 0.0005 significance level and Heuristic 3 is better than Heuristic 1 at 0.0005 significance level.

Based on the results of empirical investigation it can be concluded that Heuristic 3 attempts to produce coordinated schedules and also achieves much better performance on the criteria of total units lateness, total aggregate lateness machine utilisation and average coordination range while achieving insignificant decrease in total costs. It appears that it is better to achieve coordinated schedules than to change the lot size as per the Heuristic 1(Chapter 2). It is true that Heuristic 3 produces a much better average performance. But, we may focus our attention on the individual problems where Heuristic 1 produces a better performance than Heuristic 2 or 3. In the case of Problem 7, it is found that Heuristic 1 produces a 42 per cent improvement in total units lateness which is better than the improvement produced by Heuristics 2 and 3 on the same criteria. Similarly, in case of Problem 6, the heuristic produces maximum improvement in total costs. In case of Problem 17, Heuristics 1 and 3 produce comparable performance on the criteria of total units lateness. Thus, it appears that there could be a unique situation which may require application of either Heuristic 1, 2 or 3. Thus, there is the need to develop a framework which diagnoses the prevailing situation in the MRP context and enable us to determine which heuristic to use to bring improvement on a given performance criteria.

5. CONCLUSIONS

Biggs[2] had earlier shown that CRR performed better on a variety of performance criteria which was later confirmed by the studies of Goodwin and Weeks[9,10] and Fry et al,[11] Sharma and Potty (Chapter 2 of this book) have improved the performance further by changing lot size by modifying holding costs. Sharma and Yoganandan[1] have attempted to modify in one step the priority of lots coming early or late and have produced better performance. Here, we modify priorities of lots in a more uniform manner and obtain a much better performance. We note that the heuristic developed here performs better on all the criteria in average, but Heuristic 1 which changes lot size also produces improvement for specific problem instances. Hence, there is the need to develop a framework which will be able to tell us when to use Heuristic 1 and/or Heuristic 3 to produce better performance on a given criteria. This could be a topic for future research. The Heuristic 3 does not modify the lot size at all. Some innovation is necessary if it is required to change lot size after application of Heuristic 3 while retaining the essence of coodinated scheduling. This is also a topic for further research.

Table 4.1 % Improvement due to Heuristic 1

Problem Number	Total Aggregate Lateness	Total Unit Lateness	Total Cost	Average Utilisation	Average Coord. Range
1	-0.04	0.40	-11.45	0.58	0.34
2	-1.74	19.01	-10.92	15.98	34.86
3	-0.01	0.0	0.0	0.0	39.22
4	8.15	-28.10	0.53	1.84	29.25
5	8.28	-59.50	-50.85	3.94	-4.03
6	-0.45	8.08	4.27	4.42	44.53
7	2.8	42.81	36.13	-1.11	30.28
8	-0.01	0.0	0.0	0.0	1.43
9	-5.42	11.26	-33.91	5.12	31.58
10	-6.08	5.82	-12.29	1.81	47.96
11	0.0	0.0	0.0	0.0	84.50
12	0.0	0.0	0.0	0.0	79.50
13	1.92	24.62	-15.11	-2.55	75.52
14	0.0	0.0	0.0	0.0	35.62
15	16.52	-135.72	-8.36	0.91	-5.64
16	-10.36	-18.55	-25.47	-0.36	44.85
17	-8.61	14.07	-3.60	-1.70	32.81
18	-0.72	-5.66	-76.18	-11.17	49.07
19	-3.96	-27.20	-22.38	1.53	36.21
20	-7.33	4.53	-15.70	12.40	30.02
MEAN	**-0.35**	**-7.21**	**-15.88**	**1.58**	**35.88**

Table 4.2 % Improvement due to Heuristic 2

Problem Number	Total Aggregate Lateness	Total Unit Lateness	Total Cost	Average Utilisation	Average Coord. Range
1	23.87	33.28	-29.00	39.44	-0.86
2	-0.60	7.51	0.0	2.82	41.75
3	-5.52	7.23	0.0	3.49	0.0
4	0.07	0.0	0.0	-1.45	-0.62
5	2.37	-4.63	3.42	-2.34	-2.60
6	-2.50	8.08	-3.55	2.49	-0.25
7	0.0	0.0	0.0	0.0	0.0
8	-0.53	5.69	-1.90	0.61	-0.26
9	-4.25	22.53	-9.35	5.42	0.0
10	1.79	0.0	0.0	0.0	0.0
11	0.0	0.0	0.0	0.0	0.0
12	0.0	0.0	0.0	0.0	0.0
13	1.06	14.76	56.03	-1.40	-2.23

Contd...

% Improvement due to Heuristic 2

Problem Number	Total Aggregate Lateness	Total Unit Lateness	Total Cost	Average Utilisation	Average Coord. Range
14	−0.57	8.53	0.81	8.83	−0.26
15	7.36	−42.34	23.79	−10.86	−8.15
16	0.56	−12.37	0.0	−14.75	−6.17
17	−1.06	7.03	0.0	9.17	−5.28
18	0.01	0.0	0.0	0.0	0.0
19	−0.83	0.0	4.10	−2.15	−1.45
20	−0.24	0.0	0.0	−0.09	−1.63
MEAN	**1.14**	**2.76**	**2.21**	**1.96**	**0.59**

Table 4.3 % Improvement due to Heuristic 3

Problem Number	Total Aggregate Lateness	Total Units Lateness	Total Cost	Average Utilisation	Average Coord. Range
1	26.41	34.70	31.35	32.09	73.65
2	3.52	26.76	1.68	8.67	61.58
3	−2.61	12.96	4.97	14.53	58.78
4	12.30	11.95	10.21	0.0	31.35
5	13.01	0.0	2.36	0.0	31.81
6	−1.94	30.25	31.27	−4.44	45.00
7	7.37	5.38	−20.43	1.44	42.47
8	5.36	11.39	−10.07	−4.58	70.93
9	2.45	22.53	16.84	0.41	67.08
10	4.79	7.27	7.37	4.09	60.25
11	1.55	8.63	−3.68	−7.47	85.57
12	11.15	13.02	−1.72	10.25	87.43
13	15.13	26.79	99.99	1.53	88.02
14	14.30	12.79	−4.09	9.18	50.05
15	26.99	70.68	10.03	4.45	65.03
16	4.03	5.84	0.0	7.24	71.10
17	2.97	14.07	3.60	18.36	57.36
18	1.90	11.33	−67.61	−2.34	66.98
19	2.97	24.16	−3.50	10.62	58.11
20	2.01	18.12	9.42	17.39	57.52
MEAN	**7.68**	**18.43**	**2.77**	**6.07**	**61.50**

Table 4.4 Calculated 't' values

	H1 Vs H2	H2 Vs H3	H1 Vs H3
Total Units Lateness	1.15	3.41 (**)	2.94 (**)
Total Agg. Lateness	0.81	2.97 (**)	4.33 (**)
Total Inv Cost	3.24 (**)	0.07	3.35 (**)
Av M/c Utilization	0.47	4.24 (***)	5.55 (***)
Av Co-ordination Range	5.79 (***)	14.34 (***)	4.21 (***)

(*) Significant at 0.05 level. ('t' value from table (with df =38) 1.686)
(**) Significant at 0.005 level. ('t' value from table (with df =38) 2.713)
(***) Significant at 0.0005 level. ('t' value from table (with df =38) 3.570)

REFERENCES

1. Sharma RRK and Yoganandan SR, Heuristic for Securing Coordination in MRP. Proceedings of 12th International Conference on Production Research held at Finland during August 16-20, 1993.
2. Biggs JR, Priority Rules for Shop Floor Control in a Material Requirements Planning System under Various Levels of Capacity. International Journal of Production Research. 23, 1985, 33-46.
3. Grasso ET and Taylor BW, A Simulation Based Experimental Investigation of Supply Timing Uncertainty in MRP Systems. International Journal of Production Research. 22, 1984, 485-497.
4. Potty VS, Simulation of Heuristic Lot Sizing and Sequencing Procedures in MRP. Unpublished M Tech dissertation, Industrial and Management Engineering Department, IIT Kanpur, 1990.
5. South JB and Stewart RJ, A 50% Increase in Lot Size and Planned Manufacturing Lead Time with No Increase in Work-in-Process Inventory. Production and Inventory Management 27, 1986, 19-25.
6. Billington P, McClain J and Thomas LJ, Mathematical Approaches to Capacity Constrained MRP Systems: Review, Formulation and Problem Reduction, Management Science 29, 1983, 1126-1141.
7. Graves SC, Multi-stage Lot Sizing: An Iterative Procedure. Ed Schwarz, Multi-level Production/Inventory Control Systems: Theory and Practice. North Holland Publishing Company, Amsterdam, 1981.
8. McLaren BJ, A Study of Multi-level Lot Sizing Procedures for Material Requirement Planning Systems. Unpublished PhD dissertation, Purdue University, 1976.

9. Goodwin JS and Weeks JK, Evaluating Scheduling Policies in a Multi-level Assembly System. International Journal of Production Research 24, 1986, 247-257.
10. Goodwin JS and Weeks JK, Operating Policies for Scheduling Assembled Products. Decision Sciences. 13, 1982, 585-603.
11. Fry TP, Philipoom PR and Markland RE, Dispatching in Multi-stage Job Shop Where Machine Capacities are Unbalanced. Internal Journal of Production.
12. Sinha Sharat, Development of Improved Sequencing-based Heuristic and Comparison of Its Performance with Other Lot Sizing and Sequencing-based Heuristics in MRP Context. Unpublished M Tech dissertation, Department of Industrial and Management Engineering, IIT Kanpur, 1994.

5 Heuristic to Modify Lot Sizes to Improve Performance in MRP Context*

R R K Sharma, V S Potty, S R Yoganandan, Sameer Agarwal, Sharat Sinha

ABSTRACT

Lot sizing, sequencing, lead time and capacity planning are important sub-problems of MRP systems. Due to computational attractiveness single-pass heuristics which use one procedure for each of the sub-problems are most popular. In these heuristics no provision exists for sharing information between these sub-problems to revise decisions. Potty[13] has developed a multi-pass heuristic that attempts to initiate feedback between lot sizing and sequencing problems to revise lot sizes to bring about improvement in criteria of lateness with insignificanzt improvements in total costs. Later Yoganandan[17] and Sinha[15] verified these claims. We report here the collective computational experience which verifies the claim of improved performance of the multi-pass heuristic.

1. INTRODUCTION

Lot sizing, sequencing, determination of planned lead times and capacity planning are important decisions in the effective use of MRP systems. These decisions are interdependent, however, few operating procedures are available which consider these interactions. Currently, operating decisions in an MRP system are developed through use of simple heuristics for each of the sub-problems i.e., lot sizing, sequencing, determination of planned lead times and capacity planning. These could be Wagner-Whitin algorithm or the lot for lot heuristic for multi-stage lot-sizing problem, due date-based rule for sequencing decisions and fixed lead times for introduction of lots in the shop. These heuristics are popular due to their simplicity and computational attractiveness. Very few heuristics are available which consider interactions between various sub-problems to improve operating schedule on some criteria. In this chapter we report substantial computational experience of a multi-pass heuristic that considers interactions between

* Reproduced with written permission from International J of Industrial Engineering, USA

lot sizing and sequencing sub-problems while keeping capacity and lead time decisions as constant.

2. LITERATURE REVIEW

Biggs[3] has shown that main effects of lot sizing and sequencing rules and the interaction between these are significant at the level of 0.01 significance and has argued that it is possible that a particular sequencing rule may work in 'opposite direction' to a particular lot-sizing rule and vice versa. Biggs[4] has studied the interaction of priority rules with the capacity levels and has reported that these are significant. He found that the CRR performed consistently better over different levels of capacity. Collier[7] and Billington et al[5] have pointed out that certain lot-sizing rules may hurt the capacity utilisation. Grasso and Taylor[10] studied main effects and interaction effects among four factors, namely; lead time, buffering alternative, lot-size rule and cost value on total cost and reported that main effects of each factor and the interaction between lead time and lot-size rule and that between buffering alternative and cost value on total cost are significant. Bahl and Ritzman[2] have presented an integrated model for master scheduling, lot sizing and CRP and have given a heuristic procedure to minimise the sum of capacity costs, set-up costs and inventory-carrying costs. South and Stewart[16] report their experience at Hix Corporastion wherein 50 per cent increase in lot sizes and planned manufacturing lead time resulted in low system tardiness without increase in WIP inventory costs. An intuitive explanation could be that the increase in lot sizes reduces the number of set-ups while releasing the shop capacity and hence leads to reduce in queue length before the processing centres which leads to low tardiness. In the case of Hix Corporation, the effects are balanced in such a manner that they do not increase the WIP inventory costs. Billington et al[6] formulated capacity/lot size/lead time problem as mixed integer linear programming problem and have suggested product structure compression to reduce problem size. Mathematical models which include lot sizing and sequencing together become large and are intractable to the conventional integer programming techniques. Single-stage optimisation procedures, such as Wagner-Whitin algorithm[18] and Silver-Meal procedure[14] are used due to its simplicity, but are likely to yield sub-optimal solutions as stagewise interactions are ignored. Afentakis et al[1] have developed computationally, efficient procedures to give optimal solutions to lot-sizing problems in multi-stage pure assembly systems with infinite capacity.

In literature, very few multi-pass heuristics have been reported, see Graves.[11] This heuristic modifies the variable production cost in each interaction and is shown to perform better than the single-pass heuristic due to McLaren[12] which modifies the set-up costs but tends to become more complex as the number of stages increase. We present here a simple multi-pass heuristic which aims to improve stockout performance under fixed capacity and permit exchange of information between lot sizing and sequencing problems and report extensive computational experience.

We give a heuristic that initiates feedback from sequencing sub-problem to modify lot sizes to achieve on improvement in performance.

3. HEURISTIC

If the production capacity is finite and the sub-assemblies have a varied routing sequence across the work centres, then for some parts and subassemblies the delay is likely to be more due to the queue length before the work centres. In the heuristic described below, higher flow time of an item or sub-assembly is accounted for in the lot-sizing problem by increasing its holding cost.

3.1 The Heuristic

Let R be the set of parts with difference in actual and theoretical holding costs exceeding 10 per cent and S be the set of parts already considered twice in the iterative procedure. Let K (j) denote the number of times the part 'j' has been considered in the iterative procedure and BestSol denote the best solution arrived at with respect to stockouts. The steps of the heuristic are described below.

Step 1: Initialisation. Set K(j) to zero for all j. Using Wagner-Whitin algorithm for lot sizing and CRR for sequencing simulate the MRP system to prepare the set R and initialise the following.

$$S = \{\ \},\ K(j) = 0 \text{ for all } j,\ \text{BestSol} = \infty$$

Step 2: Select part 'j' from set R which has the highest percentage difference in theoretical and actual holding costs. Increase the holding cost of part 'j' in steps of 0.2 until the lot sizes change. Set [K(j) = K(j) + 1] and if [K(j) = 2], then update S = S + {j}. If the current solution is better than the BestSol with respect to stockouts then update BestSol = Current solution.

Step 3: Simulate and prepare the set R afresh and let R = R – S.
Step 4: If R = { }, then stop else, go to step 2.

In Step 1 we had used CRR for sequencing as it is reported in literature by Biggs[4] and Goodwin and Weeks[8,9] that it performs better on a variety of performance criteria.

An increase in the holding costs is likely to reduce the lot sizes and improve the stockout performance but an excessive decrease in lot sizes may increase the number of set-ups and adversely affect the due date performance (as more capacity may be lost in set-ups now), hence the number of times a part or a sub-assembly may be considered for holding cost modification is limited to two.

4. EMPIRICAL INVESTIGATION AND RESULTS

Three different computer-based models were prepared, one each by Potty,[13] Yoganandan[17] and Sinha.[15] A variety of product structure were randomly created (these are product structures 1-56 and are given in Appendix 1) and problems with uniform capacity utilisation were prepared. Capacity utilisation was set at 70-75 per cent for these problems. Lead times for introduction of all assemblies into the shop was kept constant for all the problems. Eight problems were developed by Potty[13] and Yoganandan[17] while Sinha[15] prepared 20 problems. It took approximately 10 days to develop one problem as one had to ensure capacity utilisation at 70-75 per cent for all the machines in the shop. Hence, it took substantial time to generate 36 problems which were solved. Simulation was run for at least 50 time periods and computational performance was recorded. It took about half an hour to complete the simulation for one problem on a PC-AT.
Percentage improvement obtained by heuristic given in Section 3 for the criteria of aggregate lateness, units lateness and total cost (sum of set-up and inventory-carrying costs) is given in Table 5.1. It was observed that there was significant improvement in aggregate lateness (at 0.001 significance level) with no significant change in total costs. Hence, heuristic proposed in this book holds good promise.

Table 5.1 Performance of Heuristic H1

Problem No.	% Improvement in Aggregate Lateness	% Improvement in Units Lateness	% Improvement in Total Costs
1	37.98	35.53	–7.26
2	31.03	29.53	–0.29

Contd...

Performance of Heuristic H1

Problem No.	% Improvement in Aggregate Lateness	% Improvement in Units Lateness	% Improvement in Total Costs
3	24.39	22.25	−0.98
4	13.73	18.82	−0.96
5	51.90	41.41	−1.88
6	64.10	62.16	−3.63
7	49.38	33.17	−0.87
8	42.42	19.82	−0.51
9	8.32	4.00	11.88
10	0.00	0.00	21.38
11	17.75	6.75	24.00
12	9.11	0.00	22.04
13	7.37	0.00	20.58
14	3.13	3.83	19.98
15	1.72	0.00	32.33
16	5.53	5.35	14.84
17	−0.04	0.40	−11.45
18	−1.74	19.01	−10.92
19	−0.01	0.0	0.0
20	8.15	−28.10	0.53
21	8.28	−59.50	−50.85
22	−0.45	8.08	4.27
23	2.8	42.81	36.13
24	−0.01	0.0	0.0
25	−5.42	11.26	−33.91
26	−6.08	5.82	−12.29
27	0.0	0.0	0.0
28	0.0	0.0	0.0
29	1.92	24.62	−15.11
30	0.0	0.0	0.0
31	16.52	−13.72	−8.36
32	−10.36	−18.55	−25.47
33	−8.01	14.07	−3.60
34	−0.72	−5.66	−76.18
35	−3.96	−27.20	−22.38
36	−7.33	4.53	−15.70
Mean	10.02	3.839	−2.62
Estimated Std. Dev.	18.45	32.39	21.7
z table value at 0.001 sig.level	3.10	3.10	3.10
Calculated z value	3.258	0.453	−0.724

5. CONCLUSION

Earlier works, Biggs[4] and Goodwin and Weeks,[8,9] suggested that in MRP context one should use due date-based rules such as CRR for sequencing with suitable lot-sizing rule for better results on a variety of criteria. This work suggests that by using the heuristic that modifies lot sizes after intiating feedback from sequencing sub-problems, one may significantly improve performance on the criteria of aggregate lateness with insignificant worsening of total costs. These solutions exist and will be of practical value as demonstrated in this work.

REFERENCES

1. Afentakis A, Gavish B and Karmakar U. Computationally Efficient Optimal Solutions to the Lot Sizing Problem in Multi-stage Assembly System, Management science, 30(2), 1984,222-239.
2. Bahl HC and Ritzman L. An Integrated Model for Master Scheduling, Lot Sizing and Capacity Requirements Planning, Journal of Operations Research Society, (UK), 35(5), 1984, 389-399.
3. Biggs JR. Heuristic Lot Sizing and Sequencing Rules in a Multi-stage Production Inventory Systems, Decision Sciences, 10, 1979, 96-115.
4. Biggs JR. Priority Rules for Shop Flow Control in A Material Requirements Planning System under Various Levels of Capacity, International Journal of Production Research 23(1), 1985, 33-46.
5. Billington P, McClain J and Thomas L J. The Interaction of Lead Time Determination, Lot-sizing Decisions and Capacity Planning in MRP Systems, Proceedings, American Institute of Decision Sciences, Eleventh Annual Meeting, 1979.
6. Billington P, McClain J and Thomas LJ. Mathematical Approaches to Capacity Constrained MRP Systems: Review, Formulation and Problem Reduction, Management Science 29(10), 1983, 1126-1141.
7. Collier DA. A Comparison of MRP Lot-sizing Methods Considering Capacity Change Costs, J Oper. Management, August, 1980.
8. Goodwin JS and Weeks JK. Operating Policies for Scheduling Assembled Products. Decision Sciences, 13, 1982, 585-603.
9. Goodwin JS and Weeks JK. Evaluating Scheduling Policies in A Multi-level Assembly System. International Journal of Production Research, 24, 1986, 247-257.
10. Grasso ET and Taylor BW. A Simulation Based Experimental Investigation of Supply Timing Uncertainty in MRP Systems, International Journasl of Production Research, 22(3), 1984, 485-497.

11. Graves SC. Multi-Stage Lot Sizing: An Iterative Procedure, in Schewarz, LW, (Ed): Multi Level Production/Inventory Control Systems: Theory and Practice, North Holland Publishing Company, Amsterdam, 1981.
12. McLaren BJ. A Study of Multi-level Lot-sizing Procedures for Material Requirements Planning System, unpublished PhD dissertation, Purdue University, 1976.
13. Potty VS. Simulation of Heuristics: Lot Sizing and Sequencing Procedures in MRP, unpublished M Tech dissertation, Indian Institute of Technology, Kanpur, 1990.
14. Silver EA and Meal Holding Cost: A Heuristic for Selecting Lot Size Quantities for The Case of A Deterministic Time Varying Demand Rate and Discrete Opportunities for Replanishment, Production and Inventory Management, 2nd quarter, 1973.
15. Sinha, Sharat. Development of Improved Sequencing Based Heuristic and Comparison of Its Performance with Other Lot Sizing and Sequencing Based Heuristic in MRP Context. Unpublished M Tech dissertation, Department of Industrial and Management Engineering, IIT Kanpur, India,1994.
16. South JB and Stewart, RJ. A 50% increase in Lot Size and Planned Manufacturing Lead Time with No Increase in Work-in-Process Inventory, Production and Inventory Management, First Quarter, 27(1), 1986, 19-25.
17. Yoganandan SR. Heuristic for Coordinated Scheduling in Material Requirement Planning System, Unpublished M Tech dissertation, Indian Institute of Technology, Kanpur, India, 1992.
18. Wagner MH and Whitin TM. Dynamic Version of The Economic Lot-sizing Model, Management Science, 5, 1958, 89-96.

6

Multi-pass Heuristic for Improved Performance in MRP Systems with Capacity Imbalance

R R K Sharma, S Gupta

ABSTRACT

Multi-pass heuristics that modify lot sizes and modify schedules have been shown to give better performance that the best known combination of single-pass heuristics suggested in MRP literature, see Chapters 2 to 5 of this book and Biggs.[1,2] It has been reported by Yoganandan[7] and Sinha[6] that their heuristics show improvement only when capacity utilisation of machines is uniform and that when variance in machine utilisation is high, then, these heuristics tend to become ineffective. However, no such evidence is documented. Here, we explore the case of MRP systems where variance in machine capacity utilisation is high and find that a combination of lot-size modification rule and a modified multi-pass scheduling based rule performs best.

1. INTRODUCTION

Lot sizing, sequencing, determination of planned lead times and capacity planning are important decisions in the effective use of MRP systems. Biggs[2] has shown that these decisions are interdependent, however, few operating procedures are available which consider these interactions. The heuristics developed in these chapters are reported to work only for the case when there is very little variation in machine capacity utilisation in the shop and it has been reported that these heuristics tend to become ineffective when there is large variation in machine capacity utilisation in the shop. However, computational experience is not documented.

In this chapter, we consider the case of MRP system with wide variation in machine capacity utilisation and report the performances of heuristics that modify only lot sizes or only schedules or both the lot sizes and schedules.

General product structure with known routing pattern over various processing centres is considered. Demand by time period for end items are assumed known (but not constant) over a finite horizon. The performance criteria considered in this paper are the number of stockouts, units stockouts (which indicate the extent to which customer demands have been successfully met), inventory costs and the set-up costs.

2. LITERATURE REVIEW

Lot sizing, sequencing, lead time of introduction and capacity planning are important problem areas in MRP systems. Appropriate decisions in each of the problem areas can affect MRP system performance with respect to criteria such as units lateness, aggregate lateness, inventory- carrying costs, set-up costs, total costs. It has been shown by Biggs[1,2] that these decisions made in these problems areas interact with each other. Hence, there is need to develop a decision/solution procedure that considers interaction between these sub-problems (i.e. lot sizing, sequencing, lead time determination and capacity planning). However, MRP literature has concentrated on making one time (single-pass) decisions in each of these sub-problems. Goodwin and Weeks[4,5] and Fry et al[3] have reported that due date-based sequencing rule such as CRR performs better over most of the criteria multi-stage and multi-level job shop situation such as MRP systems. Recently, Sharma and Potty (Chapter 2), Sharma and Yoganandan (Chapter 3), Sharma and Sinha (Chapter 4) and Sharma, et al (Chapter 5) have suggested different multi-pass heuristics and documented computational experience to show that these give better performance than the best known single-pass heuristic available in MRP literature.

However, these works are limited to those cases where machine utilisation in shops is nearly constant. It has been reported by Yoganandan[7] and Sinha[6] that their heuristics become ineffective when there is substantial variance in machine capacity utilisation in shop. However, they have not documented their findings. In this chapter, we investigate the case of MRP systems, when there is substantial variation in machine utilisation.

3. HEURISTICS

Here, we consider the heuristic due to Sharma and Potty (Chapter 2), which is reproduced below for the sake of completeness.

3.1 Heuristic H1

Let R be the set of parts with difference in actual and theoretical holding costs exceeding 10 per cent and S be the set of parts already considered twice in the iterative procedure. Let K(j) denote the number of times the part 'j' has been considered in the iterative procedure, and BestSol denote the best solution arrived at with respect to stockouts. These steps of heuristic are described below.

Step 1: Initialisation. Set K(j) to zero for all j. Using Wagner-Whitin algorithm for the lot sizing and the CRR (lead time remaining-work remaining/work remaining) for sequencing, simulate the MRP system to prepare the set R and initialise the following, iteration-counter = 0.
$S \leftarrow \{\ \}$, $K(j) \leftarrow 0$ for all j, BestSol = infinity

Step 2: If iteration counter = 20, then stop, else go to step 3.

Step 3: Select part 'j' from set R which has the highest percentage difference in the theoretical and actual holding costs. Increase the holding cost of part 'j' in steps of 0.2 until the lot size changes. Set [K(j) = K(j) + 1] and if [K(j) = 2], then update S = S + {j}. If the current solution is better than the BestSol with respect to aggregate lateness then update the following.
BestSol $\leftarrow$ Current solution,
iteration-counter = iteration-counter +1.

Step 4: Simulate the MRP system to prepare set R afresh and let
$R \leftarrow R - S$.

Step 5: If R = { }, then stop else, go to step 2.

Now, we give the rationale of modification in the scheduling heuristics. If an assembly is routed to bottleneck machines, then its priority is increased so that it gets a higher priority. Priority for components/assemblies that are children of critical assemblies is also increased by a factor that is proportional to its depth in the product structure. Scheduling is also affected by its depth in the tree structure. These ideas form the basis of heuristic that modifies the schedules.

3.2 Heuristic H2

Step 1: Initialisation. Using Wagner-Whitin algorithm for lot sizing and CRR (lead time remaining-work remaining)/work remaining for scheduling, simulate the MRP system and prepare set R (set of critical assemblies as in H1) and set M (set of bottleneck machines: A machine is bottleneck if its capacity utilisation is more than 70 per cent). And initialise the following.
BestSol $\leftarrow \infty$ and

Step 2: ∀ j ∈ R, modify the critical ratio value as given below if j is routed through bottleneck machines from modified $CRR_j = CRR_j + 0.1$ else Modified $CRR_j = CRR_j$. Also for all i : i is a child of assembly j : j ∈ R, then modified critical ration for assembly I=earlier critical ratio + 0.1*(absolute value of level difference of I and j in the product structure).
Simulate the MRP system again and if current solution is better than BestSol with respect to to aggregate lateness then
Let BestSol←current solution, Prepare set R afresh

Step 3: Repeat step 2 twenty times.

3.3 Heuristic H3

Step 1: Use Heuristic H1and simulate MRP system

Step 2: Using results of Heuristic H1 as initialisation, use Heuristic H2 and simulate the MRP system.

Step 3: Repeat step 1 and step 2 for 10 times.

4. ANALYSIS

We developed a MRP simulation model in PASCAL and prepared nine test problems with wide variation structures (i.e., tall, broad and combination of the two were considered). The necessary information on product structure like (processing times, set-up times, holding cost, processing cost, set-up cost etc.) where randomly generated. Later, they were suitably modified to have as large variation in machine capacity utilisation as possible. Details of product structures 57-65 are given in Appendix 1.

4.1 Comparison of Results

For comparing the results of the three heuristics, test of significance ("t" test) was performed over the data of percentage improvement given by each heuristic over the original solution (original solution is the solution obtained by the best known single-pass heuristics which uses Wagner-Whitin rule for lot sizing and CRR for scheduling). We compared the performance of each heuristic with original solution for different performance criterion. Also, we compared the relative performance of Heuristics H1, H2 and H3. The criteria considered are:total units lateness, total aggregate lateness, total inventory-carrying cost and total cost. Percentage improvement of these heuristics over the original solution is given in Table 6.1.

The three heuristics are H1 (Potty's heuristic), H2 (sequencing-based heuristic developed) and H3 (combined heuristic). The results of "t" test are given in Tables 6.2 to 6.5.

4.2 Discussion

On the basis of results obtained by performing the "t" test on percentage improvement of different performance criterion over original solution the following inference can be drawn.

1. **Total Units Lateness** We find that for this criterion all heuristics give better results when compared to original one and are statistically significant at 5 per cent significance level. Heuristic H3 gives significant result at 1 per cent significance level over original solution. Results given by Heuristic H3 are significantly better than both Heuristics H1 and H2 at 2.5 per cent significance level. (Appendix B.1).
2. **Total Aggregate Lateness** The results obtained by Heuristic H2 are better than original solution at 5 per cent significance level. Though Heuristic H3 improves the result for this criterion but it is not statistically significant at 5 per cent significance level. Potty's Heuristic (H1) neither improves nor worsens three test problem out of nine and it worsens three out nine. So we can say that over this performance criteria Heuristic H1 does not work as the test also supports this findings. Heuristics H2 and H3 give better results than Heuristic H1 though results are not statically significant.
3. **Total Inventory-Carrying Cost** All heuristics perform better than original solution at 5 per cent significance level. Also, Heuristic H3 works better than original solution at 5 per cent significance level. By comparing Heuristic H3 with Heuristics H1 and H2, it is found that Heuristic H3 gives significantly better performance than Heuristics H1 and H2 at 5 per cent (also at 2.5 per cent) significance level.
4. **Total Cost** By test data we find that, for this performance parameter, Heuristics H1 and H3 perform better than original solution at 5 per cent significance level. Also, we found that Heuristic H3 works better at 5 per cent significance level. By comparing Heuristic H3 with Heuristics H1 and H2 at 5 per cent (also at 2.5 per cent) significance level.

So, from the above discussion, it becomes clear that the combined Heuristic (H3) improves performance most significantly. Since our sample size is limited, its generalisability is tentative even though its performance is impressive.

5. CONCLUSION

One of the primary aims of this research was to develop an approach by which the shop performance could be improved in the case of capacity imbalance. It was observed that by reducing the variance in arrival times of components (by giving priority to critical assemblies at non-bottleneck machines for ensuring better coordination) with lot-size modification, system performance could be improved.

Bigg[2] had earlier shown that CRR performed better on a variety of performance criteria which was letter confirmed by the studies of Goodwin and Weeks.[4,5] We have found that the combined heuristic performed significantly better on all criteria on average for the case when there is large variation in machine capacity utilisation in a shop using MRP system.

Table 6.1 Percentage Change in Parameters Over Original Solution

Parameter/Problem	TAL	TUL	TSC	TICC	TC	ACU
Problem 1						
Original Solution	2691650	55550	4592	797304	801896	0.65
H1 Solution	2624880	52160	4800	754151	758951	0.65
% Improvement of H1	+2.48	+6.10	−4.53	+5.41	+5.36	0.00
H2 Solution	2500480	53830	4592	803237	807829	0.66
% Improvement of H2	+7.20	+3.10	0.00	−0.7	−0.74	+1.54
H3 Solution	2603840	49500	4748	781358	786106	0.65
% Improvement of H3	+3.30	+10.90	-3.40	+2.00	+1.97	0.00
Problem 2						
Original Solution	2771750	54540	4346	770448	774794	0.72
H1 Solution	2639910	54220	4737	740700	45437	0.72
% Improvement of H1	+4.76	+0.59	-9.00	+3.86	+3.79	0.00
H2 Solution	2766070	54470	4346	766998	771344	0.74
% Improvement of H2	+0.21	+0.13	+0.00	+0.45	+0.45	2.78
H3 Solution	2831650	50260	4737	739630	744367	0.74
% Improvement of H3	−2.16	+7.85	-9.00	+4.00	+3.93	2.78
Problem 3						
Original Solution	5770980	109420	6362	3255850	3262212	0.71
H1 Solution	5596300	108690	6401	3254270	3260671	0.69
% Improvement of H1	+3.03	+0.67	−0.61	0.05	+0.05	−2.82
H2 Solution	5551860	107520	6362	3040700	3047130	0.81
% Improvement of H2	+3.80	+1.74	0.00	+6.61	+6.59	14.09

Contd...

Percentage Change in Parameters Over Original Solution

Parameter/Problem	TAL	TUL	TSC	TICC	TC	ACU
H3 Solution	5489340	85310	6515	2897700	2904215	0.76
% Improvement of H3	+4.88	+22.03	−2.41	+11.00	+10.97	+7.04
Problem 4						
Original Solution	3024560	84890	7002	1710990	1717992	0.69
H1 Solution	3024640	84890	7040	1702960	1710000	0.69
% Improvement of H1	0.00	0.00	−0.54	+0.47	+0.47	0.00
H2 Solution	3070680	84890	7002	1687550	169452	0.83
% Improvement of H2	−1.53	0.00	0.00	+1.37	+1.36	+20.24
H3 Solution	3046880	74650	7112	1622780	1629892	0.84
% Improvement of H3	−0.74	+12.06	−1.57	+5.16	+5.13	+21.74
Problem 5						
Original Solution	3205970	78580	6899	488123	495022	0.71
H1 Solution	3206050	78580	6942	481006	494948	0.73
% Improvement of H1	−0.002	0.00	−0.63	+0.024	+0.01	+2.82
H2 Solution	3207060	78580	6899	488052	494951	0.71
% Improvement of H2	−0.034	0.00	0.00	+0.15	−0.01	0.00
H3 Solution	3204660	77910	7139	473480	480619	0.71
% Improvement of H3	+0.041	+0.85	−3.45	+3.0	+2.91	0.00
Problem 6						
Original Solution	3913220	41940	5405	392281	397686	0.62
H1 Solution	3979580	39450	5467	384668	390135	0.64
% Improvement of H1	−1.70	+5.94	−1.15	+1.94	+1.90	+3.23
H2 Solution	3821700	39450	5405	389575	394980	0.71
% Improvement of H2	+2.34	+5.94	0.00	−0.69	+0.68	+19.36
H3 Solution	3784420	39450	5480	360898	366378	0.74
% Improvement of H3	+3.29	+5.94	−1.39	+8.0	+7.87	+19.36
Problem 7						
Original Solution	2317930	55040	4195	716781	720976	0.73
H1 Solution	2317930	55040	4195	716781	720976	0.73
% Improvement of H1	0.00	0.00	0.00	0.00	0.00	0.00
H2 Solution	2357500	53430	4195	713128	717323	0.71
% Improvement of H2	−1.71	+2.93	0.00	+0.51	+0.51	−2.74
H3 Solution	2357500	53430	4317	708896	713213	0.71
% Improvement of H3	−1.71	+2.93	−2.91	+1.10	+1.08	−2.74
Problem 8						
Original Solution	3129450	72360	7520	475653	483173	0.68
H1 Solution	3139640	71370	7619	462383	470002	0.68
% Improvement of H1	−0.33	+1.37	−1.32	+2.79	+2.73	0.00
H2 Solution	2981440	73420	7520	475257	482777	0.80

Contd...

Percentage Change in Parameters Over Original Solution

Parameter/Problem	TAL	TUL	TSC	TICC	TC	ACU
% Improvement of H2	+4.73	−1.46	0.00	+0.08	+0.08	+17.65
H3 Solution	2996110	70440	7617	468043	475660	0.80
% Improvement of H3	+4.26	+2.65	−1.29	+1.6	+1.55	+17.65
Problem 9						
Original Solution	5387890	99135	6361	3318800	774794	0.78
H1 Solution	5487240	97435	6526	3318330	745437	0.78
% Improvement of H1	−1.84	+1.72	−2.60	+0.02	+3.79	0.00
H2 Solution	5281050	97425	6361	3110440	771344	0.77
% Improvement of H2	+2.0	−1.73	0.00	+6.30	+0.45	−1.30
H3 Solution	5223100	75950	6498	2933730	744367	0.74
% Improvement of H3	+3.10	+22.10	−2.20	+11.60	+3.93	−5.13

Abbreviations:

TAL –Total Aggregate Lateness
TUL–Total Units Lateness
TSC–Total Set-up Cost
TICC– Total Inventory-carrying Cost
TC–Total Cost
ACU– Average Capacity Utilisation

Table 6.2 Results of "t" test for Total Units Lateness

Original Vs H1			
α	Degrees of Freedom	Calculated value (t)	Value from table (t_α)
0.05	8	2.223	1.860

$H_0 : \mu = 0, H_1 : \mu > 0$; $(t > t_\alpha)$ H_0 rejected.

Original Vs H2			
α	Degrees of Freedom	Calculated value (t)	Value from table (t_α)
0.05	8	2.117	1.860

$H_0 : \mu = 0, H_1 : \mu > 0$; $(t > t_\alpha)$ H_0 rejected.

Original Vs H3			
α	Degrees of Freedom	Calculated value (t)	Value from table (t_α)
0.05	8	3.290	1.860

$H_0 : \mu = 0, H_1 : \mu > 0$; $(t > t_\alpha)$ H_0 rejected.

H1 Vs H2			
α	Degrees of Freedom	Calculated value (t)	Value from table (t_μ)
0.05	16	0.229	1.746

$H_0 : \mu_2 - \mu_1 = 0, H_1 : \mu_2 - \mu_1 > 0$; $(t < t\alpha)$ H_0 accepted.

H2 Vs H3			
α	Degrees of Freedom	Calculated value (t)	Value from table (t_α)
0.05	16	2.468	1.746

$H_0 : \mu_3 - \mu_2 = 0, H_1 : \mu_3 - \mu_2 > 0$; $(t < t\alpha)$ H_0 rejected.

H1 Vs H3			
α	Degrees of Freedom	Calculated value (t)	Value from table (t_α)
0.05	16	2.336	1.746

$H_0 : \mu_3 - \mu_1 = 0, H_1 : \mu_3 - \mu_1 > 0$; $(t < t\alpha)$ H_0 rejected.

Table 6.3 Data of "t" test for Total Aggregate Lateness

Original Vs H1			
α	Degrees of Freedom	Calculated value (t)	Value from table (t_α)
0.05	8	0.956	1.860

$H_0 : \mu = 0, H_1 : \mu > 0$; $(t < t\alpha)$ H_0 accepted.

Original Vs H2			
α	Degrees of Freedom	Calculated value (t)	Value from table (t_α)
0.05	8	1.902	1.860

$H_0 : \mu = 0, H_1 : \mu > 0$; $(t > t\alpha)$ H_0 rejected.

Contd...

Original Vs H3			
α	Degrees of Freedom	Calculated value (t)	Value from table (t_α)
0.05	8	1.750	1.860

$H_0 : \mu = 0, H_1 : \mu > 0$; ($t < t\alpha$) H_0 accepted.
(however at $\alpha = 0.06$ H_0 can be rejected.)

H1 Vs H2			
α	Degrees of Freedom	Calculated value (t)	Value from table (t_α)
0.05	16	0.947	1.746

$H_0 : \mu_1 - \mu_2 = 0, H_1 : \mu_1 - \mu_2 > 0$; ($t < t\alpha$) H_0 accepted.

H2 Vs H3			
α	Degrees of Freedom	Calculated value (t)	Value from table (t_α)
0.05	16	0.220	1.746

$H_0 : \mu_2 - \mu_3 = 0, H_1 : \mu_2 - \mu_3 > 0$; ($t < t\alpha$) H_0 accepted.

H1 Vs H3			
α	Degrees of Freedom	Calculated value (t)	Value from table (t_α)
0.05	16	0.746	1.746

$H_0 : \mu_1 - \mu_3 = 0, H_1 : \mu_1 - \mu_3 > 0$; ($t < t\alpha$) H_0 accepted.

Table 6.4 Data of "t" test for Total Inventory Carrying Cost

Original Vs H1			
α	Degrees of Freedom	Calculated value (t)	Value from table (t_α)
0.05	8	2.413	1.860

$H_0 : \mu = 0, H_1 : \mu > 0$; ($t < t\alpha$) H_0 rejected.

Original Vs H2			
α	Degrees of Freedom	Calculated value (t)	Value from table (t_α)
0.05	8	1.870	1.860

$H_0 : \mu = 0, H_1 : \mu > 0$; ($t < t\alpha$) H_0 accepted.

Original Vs H3			
α	Degrees of Freedom	Calculated value (t)	Value from table (t_α)
0.05	8	3.944	1.860

$H_0 : \mu = 0, H_1 : \mu > 0$; ($t < t\alpha$) H_0 rejected.

H1 Vs H2			
α	Degrees of Freedom	Calculated value (t)	Value from table (t_α)
0.05	16	0.648	1.746

$H_0 : \mu_2 - \mu_1 = 0, H_1 : \mu_2 - \mu_1 > 0$; ($t < t\alpha$) H_0 accepted.

Contd...

H2 Vs H1			
α	Degrees of Freedom	Calculated value (t)	Value from table ($t_α$)
0.05	16	2.197	1.746

$H_0 : \mu_3 - \mu_2 = 0, H_1 : \mu_3 - \mu_2 > 0$; $(t > t\alpha)$ H_0 rejected.

H1 Vs H3			
α	Degrees of Freedom	Calculated value (t)	Value from table ($t_α$)
0.05	16	2.444	1.746

$H_0 : \mu_3 - \mu_1 = 0, H_1 : \mu_3 - \mu_1 > 0$; $(t > t\alpha)$ H_0 rejected.

Table 6.5 Data of "t" test for Total Cost

Original Vs H1			
α	Degrees of Freedom	Calculated value (t)	Value from table ($t_α$)
0.05	8	2.402	1.860

$H_0 : \mu = 0, H_1 : \mu > 0$; $(t > t\alpha)$ H_0 rejected.

Original Vs H2			
α	Degrees of Freedom	Calculated value (t)	Value from table ($t_α$)
0.05	8	1.846	1.860

$H_0 : \mu = 0, H_1 : \mu > 0$; $(t < t\alpha)$ H_0 accepted.

OriginalVs H3			
α	Degrees of Freedom	Calculated value (t)	Value from table ($t_α$)
0.05	8	3.909	1.860

$H_0 : \mu = 0, H_1 : \mu > 0$; $(t < t\alpha)$ H_0 rejected.

H1 Vs H2			
α	Degrees of Freedom	Calculated value (t)	Value from table ($t_α$)
0.05	16	0.09	1.746

$H_0 : \mu_2 - \mu_1 = 0, H_1 : \mu_2 - \mu_1 > 0$; $(t < t\alpha)$ H_0 accepted.

H2 Vs H3			
α	Degrees of Freedom	Calculated value (t)	Value from table ($t_α$)
0.05	16	2.180	1.746

$H_0 : \mu_3 - \mu_2 = 0, H_1 : \mu_3 - \mu_2 > 0$; $(t > t\alpha)$ H_0 rejected.

H1 Vs H3			
α	Degrees of Freedom	Calculated value (t)	Value from table ($t_α$)
0.05	16	2.438	1.746

$H_0 : \mu_3 - \mu_1 = 0, H_1 : \mu_3 - \mu_1 > 0$; $(t > t\alpha)$ H_0 rejected.

REFERENCES

1. Biggs JR, Heuristic Lot Sizing and Sequencing Rules in a Multi-stage Production Inventory System, Decision Sciences, 10, 1979, 96-115.
2. Biggs JR, Priority Rules for Shop Floor Control in a Material Requirements Planning System under Various Levels of Capacity, International Journal of Production Research, 23(1), 1985, 33-46.
3. Fry TP, Philipoom PR and Markland RE, Dispatching in Multi-stage Job Shop where Machine Capacities are Unbalanced. International Journal of Production Research.
4. Goodwin JS and Weeks JK. Operating Policies for Scheduling Assembled Products. Decision Sciences, 13, 1982, 585-603.
5. Goodwin JS and Weeks JK. Evaluating Scheduling Policies in a Multi-level Assembly System. International Journal of Production Research, 24, 1986, 247-257.
6. Sinha Sharat. Development of Improved Sequencing-based Heuristic and Comparison of Its Performance with Other Lot Sizing and Sequencing-based Heuristic in MRP Context. Unpublished M Tech dissertation, Department of Industrial and Management Engineering, IIT Kanpur, India, 1994.
7. Yoganandan SR. Heuristic for Coordinated Scheduling in Material Requirement Planning System, Unpublished M Tech dissertation, IIT Kanpur, India, 1992.

7 Lot-size Rule for Improved Performance in Pure Assembly System Incorporating Set-up, Holding and Shortage Costs

R R K Sharma, R Arora

ABSTRACT

In the present work, lot sizing algorithms without capacity constraints is considered in pure assembly Material Requirement Planning (MRP) systems. The objective is to minimise the set-up, holding and the shortage cost. A heuristic is developed for solving the problem. The heuristic assumes that the items can be shifted to some other period as a lot only. Both types of shifts—forward and backward—are taken while moving the items from one period to another. The heuristic solutions are compared with the solutions given by traditional Wagner-Whitin Algorithm which does not consider the shortage cost. Twenty problems have been solved and it was found that the percentage improvement by the heuristic is significant.

1. INTRODUCTION

An important area of the MRP is inventory management. The objective of inventory management is to have the appropriate amount of raw material, supplies and finished goods in the right place, at the right time and at a low cost. Inventory costs are associated with the operation of an inventory system and result either from action or lack of action on the part of management in establishing the system. They are the basic economic parameters to any inventory decision model and the more relevant ones to systems are itemised as follows:

1. **Order Cost** The order cost of an item is the unit purchase price if it is obtained from an external source and the set-up cost is the unit production cost if it is produced internally. The unit cost should always be taken as the cost of the item as it is placed in the inventory. For purchased items, it is the purchase price plus freight cost if any. For manufactured items, the unit cost includes direct labour, direct material and factory overhead.

2. **Holding Cost** The holding cost synonymous with carrying cost, subsumes the cost associated with investing in inventory and maintaining the physical investment in inventory and maintaining in physical investment in storage. It incorporates such items as capital costs, taxes, insurance, handling, storage, shrinkage, obsolescence and deterioration. Capital cost reflects lost earning or opportunity cost. If the funds were invested elsewhere, a return on the investment would be expected. Capital cost is a charge that accounts for this unreceived return. Obsolescence is the risk that an item will lose value because of shifts in styles or consumer preference. Shrinkage is the decrease in inventory quantities over time from loss or theft. Deterioration means a change in properties due to age or environmental degradation. The usual simplifying assumption made in the inventory management is that the holding costs are proportional to the size of the inventory investment. On an annual basis, they most commonly range from 10 per cent to 30 per cent of the investment. In line with this, assumption is the practice of establishing the holding cost of inventory as percentage of its total cost.
3. **Stockout Cost** The stockout cost (depletion cost) is the economic consequence of an external or internal shortage. An external shortage occurs when a customer's order is not filled, an internal shortage occurs when an order of a group or department within the organisation is not filled. External shortages can incur backorder costs, present profit-loss (potential sale), and future profit-loss (goodwill erosion). Internal shortages can result in lost production (idle men and machines) and a delay in a completion date. The extent of the cost depends on the reaction of the customer to the out-of-stock condition. If demand occurs for an out-of-stock item the economic loss depends on whether the shortage is backordered, satisfied by substitution of another item or cancelled. In one situation, where the sale is not lost but delayed a few days in shipment. In another situation, the sale is lost. The actual cost is less identifiable in this case but ranges from the apparent profit-loss on the sale to loss of goodwill, which can be hard to specify. It can be seen that the stockout cost can vary considerably from item to item, depending on customer response or internal practice. It can be extremely high if the missing item either forces a production line to shut down or causes customer to go elsewhere in the future.

The quantification of these costs has long been a difficult and unsatisfactorily resolved issue. The central idea of inventory management (though not the sole objective) is usually minimisation of the costs. Only those costs which change as level of inventory changes should be considered in any analysis. For example, amounts expended on heating, lighting and security services should be disregarded if they do not change as the stock levels vary. As it is stated above, the objective of inventory management is minimisation of the cost. Therefore, there are various methods available, such as Wagner-Whitin, Silver Meal and Part-Period Heuristic, which are extensively being used in the industries.

But all these methods which are used to minimise the cost are applicable at the single-level and they do not optimise the total cost of the production when the production is done at various stages as the minimum cost of the all stages is not the sum of the cost of the different stages optimised separately. For example, to optimise the total cost of the multi-level production, in industries first the explosion is done and then the Wagner-Whitin algorithm is applied at all the levels for each assembly separately and the total cost is calculated as the summation of the costs for all the assemblies and no interaction is taken between production schedules of all the assemblies in minimisation of the cost. So, this procedure produces the sub-optimal schedule. But due to high complexity of the multi-level lot-sizing problem, the above procedure is still being widely used in the industries as a result the high cost of production is being incurred. Therefore, methods which improve the multi-level lot-sizing problem are in great demand.

2. LITERATURE REVIEW

Lots of literature are available on the lot-sizing techniques with which the present work deals with. A detailed review of literature was undertaken. First, the research was done to understand the lot-sizing techniques for multi-level multi-period case and then it was diverted to specific problem of the above type.

Since the problem undertaken is uncapacitated, lot-sizing problem for multi-level multi-period with shortage cost in addition to set-up and inventory-carrying costs, the papers by Afentakis and Gavish[1] and Axaster and Nuttle[10] were of considerable help. In this, they discussed the scheduling of lot sizes in multi-stage production environments for the minimisation of the set-up and holding costs and a new mathematical formulation of the lot-sizing problem in multi-stage assembly system which leads to an effective optimisation algorithm for the problem was done. They then used the Lagrangian Relaxation Method to solve their formulation by incorporating the 'echelon stock', which simplifies their method of solution. They also developed the 'Branch and Bound' algorithm which uses the bounds obtained by the relaxation and used it in their mathematical formulation.

Initially, they solved only assembly product structure but, later on they incorporated the general product structure also. A good summary of various models used for lot sizing in MRP systems, can be found in Johnson and Montgomery,[6] Tersine,[11] Plossal and Wight,[4] Riggs[8] and Vollman and Whybark.[13]

The case of infinite horizon, stationary demand, is considered in Crowsten et al[2,3] and Love.[5] In addition, a number of heuristic procedures which can be employed to generate optimal or near optimal solutions for assembly and/or serial systems have been developed (Early references include Crowston et al[2,3] Vollman and Whybark,[13] Graves[4]).

As the focus of this chapter is multi-level and multi-period production, the book by Stefan F Love[9] gave some insight to the problem. In this book, the author combined two or more items satisfying some properties of set-up and holding cost. In this way, he tried to reduce the complexity of problem by combining various items as a single item. But, as it is mentioned above, the greater benefit of optimisation was achieved in a serial type of structures only. It may be seen that various works listed above do not consider shortage costs in multi-level multi-period assembly systems. Hence, we choose this problem for study here.

An important conclusion from the literature is that the generation of optimal production plans is generally quite difficult for these lot-sizing problems.

3. DEVELOPMENT OF THE MODEL

As it is evident from the literature review that a lot of work has already been done on multi-level multi-period lot-sizing problem, but the costs considered were only holding and order (set-up) costs and no literature was available which considers the shortage cost also. So, we decided to incorporate the shortage cost also in already built algorithms for multi-level multi-period lot-sizing problem. Before the mathematical formulation of the problem, the following assumptions and notations were made for the development of the model.

3.1 Assumptions

1. Inventories at the beginning/end of the planning horizon are zero.
2. There is no capacity restriction during production. We can produce as much as we want. So, with this assumption, our problem becomes uncapacitated lot-sizing problem.

3. The lead time is assumed to be zero. The time lag between production and delivery is assumed to be zero.
4. Sufficient inventory of all the immediate child assemblies should be there, if the production of the parent assembly has to take place, without this the production of parent assembly cannot take place.
5. The demands of all the assemblies in all the time periods are known with certainty.
6. The shortage cannot continue beyond last period. The production has to take place at least once in the planning period.

The notations, the constants and the variables of the formulation are explained as follows:

3.2 Notations

n = assembly number varies from 1 to N
t = time period varies from 1 to T.
m = assembly machine number varies from 1 to M.
Child (n) = set of child assemblies of assembly number n.
Parent (n) = set of all parents of assembly number n.
M = a large number.

3.3 Constants

C_n = Cost of assembly 'n'.
D_{nt} = Demand for assembly 'n' in period 't'.
V_{nm} = Value added by machine 'm' while processing assembly number 'n'.
I = Inventory carrying charge per period
r_{rk} = Quantity of assembly 'k' used in manufacturing of one unit of assembly 'n'.
S_{nm} = Set-up cost incurred on machine 'm' for producing assembly 'n'.
$(SC)_n$ = Shortage cost per period incurred for having one unit of shortage of asembly 'n'.

3.4 Variables

X_{nt} = the quantity produced of assembly 'n' in period 't'.
I_{nt} = the ending inventory in period 't' of assembly 'n'.

S_{nt} = the shortage of assembly 'n' in period 't'.
Y_{nmt} = the production variable = {1 if the machine m pr duces product n = {0 otherwise
Z_{nt} = the inventory variable = { 1 if the inventory is there at the end of the period t = {0 if the inventory is not there at the end of the period t.

3.5 Formulation

minimise

$$\sum_{n=1}^{n=N}\sum_{m=1}^{m=M}\sum_{t=1}^{t=T} S_{nm}\,Y_{nmt} + \sum_{n=1}^{n=N}\sum_{t=1}^{t=T}(IC_n)(I_{nt}) + \sum_{n=1}^{n=N}(SC)_n\left(\sum_{t=1}^{t=T} S_{nt}\right)$$

subject to

$$\sum_{t=1}^{t=t1} X_{nt} - I_{ntl} + S_{ntl} - \sum_{n=1}^{n=N}\left(\sum_{t=1\;k\in Parent(n)}^{t=t1} r_{kn}\,X_{kt}\right) = \sum_{t=1}^{t=t1} D_{ntl}, \text{.............}(1)$$

$X_{nt} - MY_{nmt} \le 0$.................(2)

$\forall n = 1,2...N\; t = 1,2...T\; m = 1,2...M;$

$I_{k,t-1} - r_{nk}X_{nt} \ge 0$............(3)$\forall t = 1.2...T; n = 1,2...N$

$k \in Child(n)$

$S_{nl}=0;$...............................(4)$\forall n=1,2.....N;$

$I_{nt}-MZ_{nt} \le 0$..................(5)$\forall n=1,2...,N, t=1,2,....,T;$

$S_{nt}-MG_{nt} \le 0$.................(6)$\forall n=1,2....,N, t=1,2,...,T;$

$Z_{nt}+G_{nt} \le 1$......................(7)$\forall n=1,2......,N, t=1,2.....,T;$

$Y_{nmt}, G_{nt}, Z_{nt} \in \{0,1\}$ variables.

All the variables are integers and ≥0.

The objective function minimises the set-up cost (only for those which require the processing on the machine), holding cost (for the periods in which ending inventories are not zero) and the shortage cost for all the assemblies.

The first constraint allows sufficient production or shortage to take place, production to meet the external as well as internal demands of the assembly and shortage if the external demands are not met. The external demand is the demand due to the external sources and the internal demand is the demand due to the production of the parent assembly. As it is already assumed that the production is uncapacitated, there is no limit to the quantity manufactured in any period.

The second constraint assures the incurring of the set-up cost associated with those assemblies which require manufacturing on the machine.

The third constraint assures sufficient quantity of all immediate child assemblies to be there if the production of any assembly is to take place.

The fourth constraint restricts shortages not to extend into the final period. It makes it necessary to do production at least once in the planning horizon if not in any other period, then in the last period itself.

The fifth, sixth and seventh constraints allow either shortage or inventory to be there at a time. Both cannot exist simultaneously.

4. HEURISTIC DEVELOPMENT

4. 1 Terminology

Before describing the heuristic, the following terms are explained which give better idea of the heuristic.

4.4.1 Level-Period

It is the time period equal to the level of the assembly in the product structure. The significance of the level-period is that the production of the assembly cannot take place before the level-period because of the initial inventory constraint.

4.1.2 Modified External Demand

It is the demand of the assembly obtained by rightward shifting of demands to level-period that will be having demand equal to its own demand plus the summation of all the previous period's demands.

4.1.3 Modified Demand

It is the summation of the modified external demand and the internal demand of the assembly (internal demand due to the production of the parent assembly). For example, if the production quantity of the parent assembly in period T is X and one unit of parent quantity requires Y units of child assembly (having external demand Z in period T – 1), then the internal demand of the child assembly will be X*Y in period T – 1 (due to initial inventory constraint) and the modified demand of the child assembly will be X*Y – Z.

4.1.4 Wagner-Whitin Algorithm

It is the lot-sizing algorithm used when the demand is dynamic. The algorithm uses dynamic programming to calculate the lot-sizes. It has characterised several forms of an optimal solution which substantially reduces the search space. Its objective is to arrive at the ordering strategy for the entire net requirements schedule. The Wagner-Whitin[12] algorithm minimises the total cost of set-up and carrying inventory.

4.1.5 Wagner-Whitin Algorithm (Conventional)

This is the conventional method by which the lot-sizes of various assemblies and sub-assemblies are calculated in an MRP system. Here, first the explosion is done and then the total demand of all the assemblies and sub-assemblies are calculated. After this, the Wagner-Whitin algorithm is applied at each level for all the assemblies and the lot-sizes are calculated. Essentially, this is a repeated application of Wagner-Whitin algorithm to all levels.

4.1.6 Wagner-Whitin Algorithm (Modified)

It is the Wagner-Whitin algorithm modified to satisfy the constraints of the formulation. Here, the demand for the assemblies are their modified demands. That is, first the lot sizes of the parent assembly is calculated and from it the modified demands of the child assembly is calculated and then the Wagner-Whitin algorithm is applied for the child assemblies and this process continues till the lot sizes of all the assemblies are calculated.

4.2 Developed Heuristic (H2)

Multi-level lot-sizing problem becomes too complex with the increase in the number of levels, periods and the increase in the number of assemblies. We know that change in the production schedule of topmost assembly has considerable impact on the production schedules of all the assembly due to which the total cost is affected. If we imagine the product structure as a tree, then the topmost assembly will be at its root. It implies that if we change the order schedules of the assemblies which are root assemblies (i.e., those assemblies which are having some child assemblies), then there can be considerable change in the total cost can result. Even for those assemblies which are not the root assemblies, the change in the total cost can result because shortage cost is not considered in the Wagner-Whitin algorithm. The order schedule of the assembly is changed by shifting the demand either forward or backward. With forward shift, there will be increase in the shortage cost of the assembly, but there may or may not be, an increase in the holding or shortage cost. With backward shift, there will be a reduction in the shortage cost but there may or may not be an increase in the holding and order cost. First, we make the heuristic with forward shifts of the external demands of the assemblies, but it works with only small number of problems and in most of the cases, the improvement is either not significant or there is no improvement at all. So, we decide to incorporate both types of shifts (backward and forward). The steps in the heuristic are explained below:

Step 1: Run the Wagner-Whitin (Modified) to get the initial solution. Note the total cost of the Wagner-Whitin (Modified) as cost (original) and the order-schedule of all the assemblies as the initial order schedule, start with the topmost assembly.

Step 2: Take the order schedule of the assembly as its modified demand. Start with the level-period (here only forward shift is possible).

Step 3: Shift the modified external demand of this period to the one period forward. Run the Wagner-Whitin (Modified) program to calculate the total cost. Let this cost be cost 1.

Step 4: If the cost (original) is less than the cost 1, modify value of the cost (original) with that of the cost 1 and also modify the order schedules obtained earlier with this new order schedules. The cost (original) has now become cost 1 if this condition holds. Time period after this shift is level-period +1.

Step 5: Apply the forward shift and note the cost obtained after this shift as cost 2. If cost 2 is less than cost, change the value of the cost with that of the cost 2 and the schedule with the schedule obtained after this shift. Therefore, if this condition holds, the original schedule will become the schedule obtained after this step.

Step 6: Apply the backward shift and note the total cost obtained in this shift as, cost 3. If the cost 3 is less than cost, modify the value of the cost with that of cost 3 and change the value of the order schedule with that of the schedule obtained after this shift. Keep on doing the backward shift till the benefit is obtained i.e., cost 3 comes out to be lesser than the cost or till the level-period has reached.

Step 7: Increase the time-period in step 5 by 1. If the time-period is less than last period, go to step 5, else go to step 6. If the time-period is greater than the last period, increase the assembly number by one. Go to step 8.

Step 8: If the assembly number is not the assembly number of last assembly, go to step 2, else go to step 9.

Step 9: Note down the order schedule and the total cost obtained after this shift.

4.2.1 Complexity of Heuristic

The heuristic searches at each level for each assembly. The assembly once searched is not searched again by the heuristic when it goes to next assembly. On each search, the minimum combinations that can be possible is 'T'. For example, for n assemblies, the number of searches done by the heuristic is:

$$nT + (n - 1)T + (n - 2)T + (n - 3)T + \ldots + T = n(n + 1)T/2 \cong n^2 T.$$

Therefore, the worst case complexity of the heuristic is n^2 T.

5. ANALYSIS AND RESULTS OF PROBLEMS TESTED

Twenty problems were developed using product structures 66 to 85 (see Appendix 1) and the heuristic developed in section three was tested. Details appear in Table 7.1.

The heuristic developed for the problem is N^2 T complex for the worst case. That is Wagner-Whitin (Modified) is applied at least N^2 T times in the heuristic.

When the 't' test was applied on the sample population of 20, the value of 't' calculated is coming out to be 11.783 compared to the value of '$t\alpha$' equal to 2.86 at level of significance 0.5 per cent. Therefore, the Null Hypothesis (that percentage improvement is equal to zero) is rejected and the Alternate Hypothesis (that percentage improvement is greater than zero) is accepted. As the value of t_{cal} is more than t_{α}, the results are highly significant. Details of the "t" test appear in Table 7.2.

6. CONCLUSION

It was thus found that the heuristic developed in this chapter performed better than Wagner-Whitin (Modified) algorithm (the percentage improvement was significant). Average computation time taken by this heuristic was 0.44 second for one problem whereas CPLEX package (High-performance software for mathematical programming) took average time of 1.15 seconds to solve one problem. Thus, our heuristic was on an average three times faster than the CPLEX package.

We hope in future, genetic algorithm will be applied to this problem.

Table 7.1 Results of all Test Problems

S. No.	W-W (Con.) (H0)	W-W (Mod.) (H1)	Cplex Solution (C1)	Heuristic (H2)	% Improvement of H2 over H1	% Difference Between (C1 and H2)	CPU Time Taken (H2)	CPU Time Taken (C1)
1	950250	113362	73612	87802	22.55	–19.28	0.9	0.3
2	11701450	1050640	921840	943340	10.21	–2.33	0.3	0.2
3	657000	1221458	963256.81	1013490.8	17.03	–5.22	0.3	0.2
4	6030000	1122880.75	888320.81	927920.81	17.36	–5.50	0.2	0.3
5	586950	69205	53248	63831	7.71	–19.87	0.3	0.8
6	2018750	217553	142428	167748	22.89	–6.13	0.3	1.0
7	586950	68305	47048	62931	7.87	–33.76	0.4	0.2
8	445490	59497	46410.4	54610.39	8.21	–17.67	0.3	1.1
9	588850	61629	40337.20	48372.199	21.51	19.92	0.3	0.2
10	630550	62436	42821	52059.2	16.62	–18.80	0.3	0.2
11	592450	166550	141300	154524	7.22	–9.36	0.5	3.9
12	647750	186953	171296	175012	17.35	–2.17	0.6	3.0
13	1795850	150427	130502	136720	9.11	–4.70	0.7	1.2
14	1469480	165922	132276	141706	14.59	–7.13	0.2	3.4
15	4118250	157782	138562	146805.2	12.18	–5.95	0.3	1.0
16	343110	127739.39	92275.80	99807.50	21.87	–8.17	0.3	1.0
17	808680	91146.20	74413.4	80936.20	11.20	–8.77	0.3	0.3
18	1079310	181807	157521.8	158105.79	13.04	–0.37	0.9	2.2
19	76200	276065	233691	243605	11.76	–4.21	0.5	1.5
20	950250	113362	73612	87802	22.55	–19.28	0.9	0.3

Table 7.2 Results of "t" test

Wagner-Whitin (Modified) Vs Heuristic			
α	Degrees of freedom	Calculated Value (t)	Value from Table (t_α)
0.005	19	11.783	2.861

H_0: $\mu = 0$; H_1 : $\mu > 0$; ($t_\alpha < t$) H_0 rejected
H_0– Null Hypothesis
H_1– Alternate Hypothesis

REFERENCES

1. Afentakis P, Gavish B and Karmarkar U, Computationaly Efficient Optimal Solutions to The Lot-sizing Problem in Multi-stage Assembly Systems. Management Sciences, 30, 222-239, 1984.
2. Crowsten WB and Wagner MH, Williams JF, Economic Lot Determination in Multi-stage Assembly Systems. Management Sciences,19, 517-524, 1973.
3. Crowsten WG and Wagner MH, Dynamic Lot-size Models for Multi-stage Assembly Systems. Management Sciences, 20, 14-21, 1973.
4. Graves SC, Multi-stage Lot-sizing: An Iterative Procedure in Multi-level, Production/ Inventory Control: Theory and Practice, edited by LB Schwarz, Chapter 5, 1981.
5. Love SF, Facilities in Series Inventory Model with Nested Schedule. Management Science, 18, 327-338, 1972.
6. Lynwood A, Johnson, Douglas C Montegomery, Operations Research in Production Planning, Scheduling and Inventory Control, Addisson Wesley, New York, 1980.
7. Plossal GW, Wight OW, Designing and Implementing A Material Requirements Planing System, Presented at APICS International Conference, Cincinnatti, OH-October, 1970.
8. Riggs LJ, Production Systems planning, Analysis and Control, Third Ed., Wiley Eastern Ltd., 1984, pp. 462-469.
9. Stephan F Love, Inventory Control, McGraw-Hill Book Company, 1984.
10. Seven Axsater and Henry LW Nuttle, Combining Items for Lot-sizing in Multi-level Assembly Systems, IJPR, 1987, Vol. 25, No.6, 79807.
11. Tersine RJ, Production/Operations Management, Elsevier North Holland Inc, New York, 1980.
12. Wagner-Whitin, Dynamic Version of The Economic Lot-size Model. Management Science, 89-96, 1958.
13. Vollman TE, Berry WL and Whybark DC, Manufacturing Planning and Control System, Richard D Irwin, Homewood, IL, 1984.

8 Application of Genetic Algorithm to Single-level Lot-sizing Problem with Shortage Costs

R R K Sharma, M V Rao

1. INTRODUCTION

This section introduces the dynamic lot-sizing problem by listing basic terms used and in the context of inventory decisions. Next, the usage of lot-sizing in Material Requirement Planning (MRP) is discussed after a brief introduction to MRP. Then, the evolution of lot-sizing problem from Economic Order Quantity (EOQ) to dynamic stage is given. The ultimate goal for all business operations is profit. The only restriction to profit making is that it should be made under good ethos. In order to make profit, the business should be efficient with minimum wastage.

Of late, materials management and thereby inventory control has become an important tool to minimise wastage of money, men and material. People have become increasingly aware that the overall efficiency of a company's operation is directly related to the inventory situation existing within the company. A practical inventory situation is bound to be reasonably mathematically complicated. Thus, there has been an increasing requirement for a knowledge of mathematical theory which can be used to analyse and control stocks. The phenomenal computational power offered by the latest chips made it possible to apply various techniques, which can be computationally-intensive but offer good results, to various problems including inventory control. In this work, an attempt has been made to apply the prevalent technique of Genetic Algorithms to the dynamic deterministic lot-sizing problem with backordering costs.

1.1 Basic Terms in a Lot-sizing Problem

The following are the costs associated with a lot-sizing problem:

1. **Ordering Costs** These are incurred because of the work involved in placing purchase orders with vendors or organising for production within a plant. For purchased items, this can include such activities as order processing forms, selecting vendors, fixed costs of handling by

vendors, processing receiving documents and inspection of goods when they arrive. If a manufactured lot is ordered within a plant, the ordering costs are called set-up costs and they include paperwork, machine set-up and start-up costs. Ordering costs do not depend on the number of items purchased or manufactured, but on the number of times that an order is placed.

2. **Inventory-holding or Inventory-carrying Costs** They include all expenses incurred because inventory is carried. These costs can include items such as rent, electricity and heat, insurance and taxes, spoilage and obsolescence, and the cost of capital. Rent, utilities, insurance, etc., are fixed costs associated with maintaining the storage facilities and are relatively easy to measure from accounting data. Spoilage and obsolescence costs apply to food and drug items, which may have only a limited shelf life, or to novelty and seasonal items. The cost of capital invested in inventory normally accounts for the largest component of inventory-holding costs. Cost of capital is the product of the value of a unit of inventory, the length of time held and an interest rate associated with the money tied up in inventory. The interest rate can often be volatile and depends upon the prime interest rate, the risk environment of the firm and management goals for rates of return on investment. If money is borrowed to finance inventory, an interest charge is incurred. If the firm's own money is used, then there is an opportunity cost associated with not being able to use the money for other productive investments. Thus, careful analysis is necessary to determine holding costs for a specific situation.
3. **Shortage Costs** These costs are represented by a backorder, in which case a customer waits until the item is available, or by a lost sale, in which case the customer purchases the item somewhere else. Backorders incur additional costs for shipping, invoicing and labour involved in handling the paper work, receiving the goods and notifying customers. Lost sales result in lost profit opportunities and possible future loss of revenues which are often referred to as goodwill costs. Shortage costs are also to be determined after careful analysis of the system.

2. LITERATURE REVIEW

Here, some of lot-sizing rules useful in MRP context are described. Also, the evolution of single level lot-sizing problem, which has a transfer value to more complex situations from EOQ through algorithms to heuristics in literature is discussed. Finally, the basic problem's extension, single-level lot-sizing problem with stockouts, is reviewed including an introduction and the applicability of genetic algorithms to this topic.

2.1 Lot-sizing Situations

Various lot-sizing situations can be summarised as follows:

- Demand is fixed and occurs at constant rate for a given period
- Demand varies with time, a dynamic demand
- Dynamic demand with stockouts

All the above situations in a single-stage are considered here. The problem gets more complex when we have a multi-stage production. The ability to solve the single level lot-sizing problem has transfer value to more complex problems. The problem also may be sufficiently close to some real manufacturing environments, which have flexible resources like workforce, equipment, considerable capacity slack.

The main concern of single level lot-sizing problems is determining production lot-sizes of a single item for several future periods that minimise the sum of set-up costs and inventory holding costs over the planning horizon, while satisfying known demand in discrete time period. In this work, we consider the possibility of stockouts also.

2.2 Development of Lot-sizing Problem

Lot-sizing model originates with the famed classical or Wilson economic lot-size formula and dates back to the year 1915. The Wilson model was seminal and has had numerous extensions. These models have two attributes in common.

'They are:

(i) The demand for the product is assumed to occur continuously over time,

(ii) Differential calculus is used to determine the optimal production schedule'.

During the late 50's, a different fundamental approach to development of economic lot size models had emerged Manne,[6] Wagner-Whitin,[10] Zangwill.[11] This approach divided time into discrete periods and postulated that the demand in each period was known and different. To determine the optimal production schedule, the techniques of mathematical programming were used. This type of model is generally said to follow the dynamic approach to economic lot-size models, as opposed to classical approach of models in the Wilson economic lot-size tradition. The classical approach assumes demand to occur continuously and uses calculus, while the dynamic approach posits demand to occur discretely in period intervals and employs mathematical programming to calculate the optimal production schedule. Now, we discuss various important algorithms and heuristics for latest work (Evans et al[4]).

2.2.1 Wagner-Whitin Algorithm

One of the simplest and most elegant dynamic economic lot-size models was developed by Wagner-Whitin.[10] A single product was considered and no backlogging of unsatisfied demand was allowed. Given the market demands in each of the next n periods and knowing the cost of producing and holding inventory in each period, Wagner-Whitin presented an algorithm for calculating the optimal production schedule by dynamic programming.

The Wagner-Whitin algorithm is an application of dynamic programming, a mathematical procedure for solving sequential decision problems. The computational effort, often prohibitive in dynamic programming formulations, is significantly reduced because of the use of some key properties derived by them, which the optimal solution must satisfy (Wagner-Whitin[10]).

2.2.2 Acceptance of the Wagner-Whitin Algorithm in Practice

Though the Wagner-Wintin algorithm provides optimum schedule of replenishment quantities, the algorithm has received limited acceptance in practice. The following are the primary reasons for this lack of acceptance.

1. The relatively complex nature of the algorithm which makes its understanding difficult for the practitioner.
2. The considerable computational effort required for each item handled by the algorithm, substantially more either for the fixed EOQ method or for the heuristics to be discussed.
3. The possible need for a well-defined ending point for the demand pattern. This would be artificial for the typical inventoried item where termination of demand is not expected in the near future. In this practical situation termed as rolling schedule environment, the Wagner-Whitin algorithm ceases to be optimal and other simpler heuristics may out perform it. Moreover, all information out to the endpoint may be needed for computing even the initial replenishment quantity.
4. The necessary assumption that replenishments can be made only at discrete intervals, namely at the beginning of each of the periods. This assumption can be relaxed by subdividing the period. However, the

computational requirements of the algorithm go up rapidly with the number of periods considered.

2.2.3 Heuristic Approaches to the Problem

Because of the above-cited reasons, various heuristics procedures have been developed and tested against the Wagner-Whitin algorithm.

These heuristic procedures are briefly described here. For a comprehensive description, Tersine[9] can be referred. All the heuristics considered are for dynamic demand problem without stockouts.

The heuristic procedures are similar in the way they arrive at lot-sizing decisions. Each starts with the present period and scans each successive period until a stopping criterion is met. Then, an order is placed to satisfy requirements up to or through the stopping period. The procedure is then repeated for periods beyond the stopping period. Orders for subsequent periods are planned by reapplying the logic. The ordering cost is charged each time an order is placed and a holding cost usually is charged for each unit carried forward from the previous period. Costs are controlled within the established criteria, but they are not necessarily minimised.

2.2.3.1 Lot-for-Lot Ordering

It is the simplest approach of all heuristics. Items are purchased in the exact quantities required for each period. There is no forward buying beyond the immediate period. This approach minimises the inventory holding cost, since no items are ever held over from period to period. However, it ignores the costs of placing an order. It is suitable for very expensive items or items with a highly discontinuous demand, where good inventory control must be maintained. It is also well suited to high volume, continuous production lines like assembly lines.

2.2.3.2 Period Order Quantity (POQ)

This approach results in varying lot sizes which encompass the demand for a fixed period of time, which is given as an Economic Order Interval (EOI) or Economic Order Quantity (EOQ) expressed as a time supply. The EOI is calculated using an average demand rate, instead of a constant demand rate per period as with continuous models. The calculated EOI is rounded to the nearest integer greater than zero, so that lot sizes obtained from its use will cover exactly an integer number of periods.

2.2.3.3 Part-period Heuristic

This heuristic selects a number of periods to be covered by the replenishment such that accumulated holding costs equal the ordering cost. Exact equality is usually not possible because of the discrete nature of requirements. So, an order size is increased as long as the accumulated holding costs are less than or equal to the ordering cost.

2.2.3.4 *Incremental Part-period Heuristic*

This heuristic increases an order as long as the incremental holding cost is less than or equal to the fixed ordering cost. Part periods are not accumulated but are stated on an incremental basis.

2.2.3.5 *Silver-Meal Heuristic*[7]

This heuristic selects a lot size that includes an integer number of period requirements such that the Total Relevant Costs (TRCs) per time period for the duration of the lot size are minimised. The TRCs are the ordering and the holding costs. If an order arrives at the beginning of the first period and it covers requirements through the end of the Tth period, the criterion function can be expressed as:

$$\frac{\mathrm{TRC(T)}}{\mathrm{T}} = \frac{\mathrm{C + Total\ holding\ costs\ to\ the\ end\ of\ period\ T}}{\mathrm{T}}$$

The objective is to select T to minimise the TRC per unit time. The heuristic evaluates increasing values of T until:

$$\frac{\mathrm{TRC(T+1)}}{\mathrm{T}} > \frac{\mathrm{TRC(T)}}{\mathrm{T}}$$

When the relevant cost per unit time starts increasing at T + 1, the associated T is selected as the number of periods supply for replenishment order.

For a complete description of this heuristic Silver-Meal[7] can be referred.

The Silver-Meal Heuristic[7] guarantees only a local minimum for the current replenishment. It is possible that larger values of T could yield even lower costs per unit time, but the likelihood of improvement in most real cases is small. The justification for using a less than optimal heuristic is a combination of simplicity and reasonable cost performance. In most cases, the average cost penalty is less than 1 per cent from the optimal Wagner-Whitin algorithm, and often there is no cost penalty. When the heuristic is tested in a rolling schedule environment, it may outperform the dynamic programming algorithm.

The Silver-Meal heuristic does not perform well when the demand rate decreases rapidly with time over several periods or when there are a large number of periods with zero demand.

2.3 Single-level Unconstrained Resources Problem with Shortages

From a customer-service viewpoint, we would never want to incur a stockout. In situations such as blood inventories, stockouts can be tragic. However, in many situations backorders may be economically justified. For instance, with very high value items, such as automobiles, one may not keep all the models and a backorder state may always exist. One of the recommended ways of smoothing demand on workforce is planned backordering situations frequent in MRP systems.

Stockouts result in external and internal shortages. External shortages can result in backorder costs, present profit or loss due to sales' loss and future profit loss due to goodwill erosion. Internal shortages can result in lost production due to idle men and machines and a delay in a completion date resulting in cost penalty.

The customer's reaction to a stockout condition can result in a backorder or a lost sale. With a backorder, the sale is not lost, but only delayed in shipment. Typically, a company will institute an emergency expediting order to get the item or the customer will be served from the next order of items to arrive. Hence, the backorder results in expediting costs, handling costs and frequently extra shipping and packaging costs. With a lost sale, the consumer's demand for the item is lost and presumably filled by a competitor. The stockout cost for a lost sale ranges between the lost profit on the sale to some unspecified loss of goodwill. A goodwill loss can result in a customer not returning to the outlet to purchase other items in the future.

When referring to stockout cost, it is necessary to be explicit in order to avoid confusion. A stockout can result in a backorder or a lost sale. In the backorder case, the customer has his demand satisfied upon initial receipt of an order. In the lost sales case, the demand is not satisfied and is lost forever. At the retail level, a stockout of an item usually results in a lost sale, since the customer will go elsewhere to make the purchase. At the manufacturing level, a supply bin stockout of an item usually result to in a backorder. In the backorder case, the customers are patient. In the lost sales case, the customers are impatient and purchase from other sources. As pointed out earlier, in case of planned backorders and the situations in which inventory-carrying costs are very high compared to stockout costs, we need a model which allows backordering in dynamic deterministic demand situations.

2.4 Backlogging models in literature

Zangwill[11] extended the Wagner-Whitin model to allow backlogging of demand, where the backorder cost is concave. His model also allows for restrictions on the maximum number of periods that orders may be backlogged. To accomplish the backlogging extension to the Wagner-Whitin model, he used the concept of piecewise concavity. Later, he showed that a number of models, including the concave cost production planning models, can be viewed as 'single source concave cost network flow problems'. He provided a useful characterisation of the extreme points of single source network flow problems which leads directly to the development of dynamic programming algorithms for a number of individual models. The property that in the optimal solution no more than one of the variables, the on-hand inventory at the end of previous period, backorder position at the end of current period and the quantity produced in a period can be greater than zero is obtained by Zangwill through the use of the following theorem about minimum cost flows in concave cost networks.

"In a minimum cost network flow problem where the objective function is a concave function of the arc flows and the network has a single source, there is an optimal solution having the property that each node has an inward flow from at most one arc."

Another approach for the inclusion of backorders was suggested by Elmaghraby and Bawle,[3] who analysed the uncapacitated problem when ordering, must be in batches greater than one with and without set-up costs. But, the basic approach is dynamic programming only.

Swoveland[8] allowed backorders under prescribed levels using dynamic programming, where production and holding-backorder cost functions are assumed to be piecewise concave.

The literature survey of lot-sizing problems with stockouts shows that the problem is solved mainly through dynamic programming approach which has the inherent drawbacks of computationally-intensive, practitioners unable to understand the model, even initial replenishment requires all information up to the endwpoint and specific end period requirement apart from some other restrictions like concavity of the objective function. So, we felt the need to solve the problem by a new technique. We used genetic algorithms in this work and there is no restriction of 'concavity' of the objection function.

Now, the technique of genetic algorithms is introduced here.

2.5 Genetic Algorithms

Here, a simple introduction outlining the operations of genetic algorithms is given followed by the details of application of genetic algorithms to operational research problems.

2.5.1 Introduction to Genetic Algorithms

Genetic algorithms work with populations of solutions and attempt to guide the search toward improvement, using a survival of the fittest principle. The quality of each solution is measured by a fitness function which is equivalent to the objective function or cost function in traditional optimisation methods, and the search proceeds through a number of generations with each individual contributing to the next generation in proportion to its fitness. This is achieved by selecting individuals randomly, using a weighted probability function, where the weights reflect actual fitness values, scaled values, or simply rank. Three standard operators used are reproduction, crossover and mutation. Reproduction copies an individual from one generation to the next, crossover combines features from two or more parents to produce one or more children and mutation makes small local changes. Reproduction and crossover of fit individuals provide pressure for improvement or exploitation, while mutation maintains population diversity and allows wider exploitation.

A classical genetic algorithm is implemented by representing individual solutions by strings and for a good number of reasons binary strings are common. Standard crossover, usually known as one point crossover of two parents, involves selecting a point on the string and then copying that part of the string before the crossover point from the first parent and that part of the string after the crossover from the second parent. If two children are to be produced, the roles of the parents are reversed for the second child. For example, given two parents:

$parent_1$	10110 110
$parent_2$	00111 001

and a crossover after bit 5, we get children:

$child_1$	10110 001
$child_2$	00111 110

Mutation usually involves flipping a single bit. For example, mutating bit 4 in $child_2$ will give:

$child_2$ (mutated) 00101110

The development of a genetic algorithm in the solution of a particular problem involves two types of decisions:

1. The way in the problem is to be modelled to fit into the genetic algorithm framework and includes the definition of the space of feasible solutions, the form of fitness function and the way in which individuals are to be represented as string.
2. Selection of genetic algorithm parameters and includes the proportions of the population to be produced as a result of reproduction, crossover and mutation, the selection procedure, the population, size the number of generations and a number of other decisions concerning variants of the basic algorithm.

For other details, Goldberg[5] and Davis[1] can be referred.

2.5.2 Genetic Algorithms in Operational Research

Of late, genetic algorithms are in wide use to solve traditional operational research problems like Travelling Salesman problem, Quadratic Assignment problem, Cutting Stock problem and Job Shop Scheduling quite successfully. Many scheduling problems are natural permutation problems, which can be tackled using a genetic algorithm based on one of the permutation crossovers. Permutation-based genetic algorithms have also been used in conjunction with simpler heuristic for the solution of more complex scheduling tasks.

For more details on the use of genetic algorithms in operations researche and other areas, Downland[2] can be referred.

As genetic algorithms appear to be working well with natural permutation problems, an attempt has been made here in this direction of applying genetic algorithms to the dynamic deterministic lot-sizing problem with backordering by modelling the problem as a permutation problem compatible with genetic algorithms. The main advantage felt in the application of genetic algorithms to the lot-sizing problem is the elimination of encoding and decoding procedures as the model deals directly with the permutations of basic code of digits, three in this case, representing set-ups, inventory carrying and stockouts.

3. LOT SIZING USING GENETIC ALGORITHMS

Here, we present the problem formulation with shortage costs after listing the basic assumptions behind the model. The main motivation behind the application of genetic algorithms to single-level uncapacitated lot-sizing problem with stockouts is the convenience and ease with which the main parameters can be represented.

3.1 Assumptions in Lot Sizing with Stockouts

1. The demand is known and occurs at the beginning of each period but changes from one period to another.
2. The planning horizon is finite and composed of several time periods of equal length.
3. The entire requirements for each period must be available at the beginning of each period. All replenishments are constrained to arrive at the beginning of periods. No replenishments arrive part way through a period.
4. There are no quantity discounts.
5. All items are treated independently of other items, with no benefits from joint review or replenishment.
6. The entire order quantity is delivered at the same time.
7. Items required in a period are withdrawn from inventory at the beginning of each period. Thus, the holding cost is applied to the end-of-period inventory and is only applied to inventory held from one period to the next. Items consumed during a period incur no holding cost.
8. Shortage costs apply to the end-of-period shortages and are applied to shortages held from one period to the next
9. All the costs and lead times are known with certainty and are time invariant.
10. We assume zero lead time. It means that orders placed at the beginning of a period are assumed to meet the requirements of that period. This assumption is not a serious limitation, since the lot sizes for a non-zero lead time can be offset (set back) by the lead time.
11. No provisions are made for holding inventory beyond the last period in the planning horizon. It means that the demand beyond the planning horizon is assumed zero.
12. The initial inventory level is zero. If the initial inventory is not zero, it must be subtracted from the demand requirements in the first period to obtain an adjusted requirement for that period. If the initial inventory exceeds the first period demand, the adjustment process is continued until all the inventory is consumed.
13. The demand will be met in entire lots and neither a partial inventory carrying nor a partial shortage incursion is allowed.

3.2 Formulation

The basic uncapacitated lot-size problem with shortages can be formulated as follows:

subject to

$$\text{Minimise } Z = \sum_{t=1}^{T}\left[f_t\delta(X_t) + b_tI_t + c_tS_t\right] \qquad (3.1)$$

$$X_t + I_{t-1} + S_t = I_t + d_t + S_{t-1} \qquad t = 1, \ldots\ldots, T \qquad (3,2)$$

$$X_t \leq M\delta(X_t) \qquad t = 1, \ldots\ldots, T \qquad (3,3)$$

$$X_t \geq 0 \qquad t = 1, \ldots\ldots, T \qquad (3,4)$$

$$I_t \geq 0 \qquad t = 1, \ldots\ldots, T \qquad (3.5)$$

$$S_t \geq 0 \qquad t = 1, \ldots\ldots, T \qquad (3.6)$$

$$S_T \geq 0 \qquad (3.7)$$

$$I_0 = 0, I_T = 0 \qquad (3.8)$$

where:

$X_t \geq 0$ if $\delta(X_t) = 1$
$X_t = 0$ if $\delta(X_t) = 0$
T = number of periods
X_t = Amount to be produced in period t
I_t = Ending inventory in period t
f_t = Set-up cost in period t
b_t = Inventory holding cost per unit held in period t
d_t = Demand during period t
c_t = Shortage cost per unit in period t
S_t = Shortage at the end of period t
M = A large number.

The objective function (3.1) minimises the sum of set-up, inventory carrying and shortage costs over the total number of periods T.

Constraint (3.2) makes sure that the sum of production in a period t, X_t, the inventory carried from the previous period, I_{t-1} and the shortages in a period t, S_t meet the sum of demand in a period t, d_t and the shortages of the previous period t-1, S_{t-1}.

Constraint (3.3) enforces the relation between set-ups and production. A set-up leads to a limited amount of production quantity and whenever there is no set-up, the production quantity X_t equals to zero.

Inequalities (3.4), (3.5) and (3.6) are non-negativity constraints for the production quantity, X_t the quantity of inventory carried to the next period, I_t and the quantity of shortages at the end of a period, S_t. At the most, they can be equal to zero. Constraint (3.7) enforces no stockouts in the last period of planning, T.

Constraint (3.8) follows the assumption that starting and ending inventories are zero.

The above formulation can be further simplified by excluding the redundant variable X_t in this case by combining (3.2) and (3.3). The modified constraint is given below:

$$M\delta_t - I_t + I_{t-1} + S_t - S_{t-1} \geq d_t \qquad t = 1,\ldots, T \qquad (3.9)$$

Constraint (3.9) replaces constraints (3.2) and (3.3) in the final formulation.

3.3 Genetic Algorithms

During the last decade, there has been a great deal of interest in the use of genetic algorithms to solve discrete optimisation problems arising in the area of operational research and was done quite successfully. So, we have decided to use genetic algorithms to solve the lot-sizing problem with shortages and our experience indicates that, the problem is compatible with genetic algorithms and can be successfully solved by using them.

Genetic algorithms are general purpose optimisation methods that have gained wide popularity in recent years. They are an algorithmic formalisation of the twin notions of 'Survival of the fittest' and 'Fit parents are likely to produce even fitter offspring'. This combination has lead to a randomised algorithm with unique features.

The inquiry for robust search has made genetic algorithms become fundamentally different from classical algorithms. The differences are based on the following four principles:

1. Genetic algorithms use a coded representation of the parameters, not the parameters themselves.
2. Genetic algorithms search from a population of solution vectors, not a single solution vector.
3. Genetic algorithms exclusively use values of the function under study and do not consider auxiliary information, such as the derivative.
4. Genetic algorithms use probabilistic transition rules, not deterministic rules.

Genetic algorithms were invented to mimic some of the processes observed in natural evolution. Many people, biologists included, are astonished that life at the level of complexity that we observe could have evolved in the relatively short time suggested by the fossil record. The idea with genetic algorithm is to use this power of evolution to solve optimisation problems. The father of the original genetic algorithm was John Holland who invented it in the early 1970's at University of Michigan.

The continuing price-cum-performance improvements of computational systems had made them attractive for some types of optimisation. In particular, genetic algorithms work very well on mix of continuous and discrete combinatorial problems. Genetic algorithms have been used widely for combinatorial optimisation problems like the travelling salesman problem, the quadratic assignment problem and job shop scheduling. They are less susceptible to stuck at local optima than gradient search methods, but they tend to be computationally-expensive.

Evolution-based optimisation techniques, such as genetic algorithms, have proven to be flexible and problem-independent optimising tools. Because of the simultaneous use of a whole set of solutions, known as population, the ability to recognise good parts of the solutions and an efficient interaction of information between different solutions by crossover and mutation, Genetic algorithms are able to optimise entry parameters without detailed knowledge of the complete problem space.

Genetic algorithms encode a potential solution to a specific problem on a simple chromosome like data structure and apply recombination operators to these structures so as to preserve critical information. Genetic algorithms are often viewed as function optimisers, although the range of problems to which genetic algorithms have been applied is quite broad. An implementation of genetic algorithm begins with a population of typically random chromosomes. One then evaluates these structures and allocates reproductive opportunities in such a way that those chromosomes which represent a better solution to the target problem are given more chances to reproduce than those chromosomes which are poorer solutions. The goodness of a solution is typically defined with respect to the current population.

3.3.1 Basic terms

1. **Individual** A single member of a population. Each individual contains a chromosome which represents a possible solution to the task being tackled, i.e., a single point in the search space. Other information is usually also stored in each individual like fitness.
2. **Offspring** An individual generated by process of reproduction.
3. **Search Space** If the solution to a task can be represented by a set of N real valued parameters, then the job of finding this solution can be

thought of as a search in N dimensional space. This is referred to simply as the search space.

4. **Selection** The process by which some individuals in a population are chosen for reproduction, typically on the basics of favouring individuals with higher fitness.
5. **Fitness** A value assigned to an individual which reflects how well the individual solves the task in hand. A fitness function is used to map a chromosome to a fitness value.
6. **Schema** A pattern of gene values in a chromosome, which may include 'don't care' states. Thus, in a binary chromosome, each schema can be specified by a string of the same length as the chromosome, with each character one of 0, 1, #. A particular chromosome is said to contain a particular schema if it matches the schema. Chromosome 01101 matches schema #110#.
7. **Schema Theorem** It is devised by Holland to explain the behaviour of genetic algorithms. In essence, it says that a genetic algorithm gives exponentially increasing reproductive trials to above average schemata. Since each chromosome contains a great many schemata, the rate of schema processing in the population is very high, leading to a phenomenon known as implicit parallelism. This gives a genetic algorithm with a population of size N, a speed up by a factor of N^3 compared to a random search.
8. **Chromosome length** It is the number of genes present in the chromosome. Each gene generally takes two values either '0' or '1', though we used three values '0', '1' and '2' in this work. Longer chromosomes allow better conversion from the binary chromosome to the real number variable at the cost of longer computational time to reach optimality.
9. **Population size** It is the number of chromosomes in the population. Larger population sizes increase the amount of variation present in the population at the expense of requiring more fitness function evaluations. Researchers found that the best population size is dependent upon both the application and the length of the chromosome.
10. **Crossover** This is the prime distinguishing factor of the genetic algorithms from other optimisation algorithms. The role of crossover is to allow advantageous traits to spread throughout the population so that the population as a whole may benefit from this chance discovery. This models sexual reproduction in nature. Crossover is applied when a new offspring chromosome, based on two parent chromosomes, is created. The algorithm selects one part from the first parent chromosome and another part from the other parent and combines them, resulting in the new offspring chromosome. In this way, valuable genetic sequences are

copied and combined with each other to produce new, may be better solutions. The chromosome part selection and recombination differs between crossover algorithms.

11. **Crossover Rate** It is the probability of crossover reproduction being performed and is frequently termed as crossover probability in literature. A high crossover is used to encourage good mixing of the chromosomes. For most applications a crossover rate of 0.75 to 0.95 is employed.
12. **Mutation** It is the random flipping of the bits or genes, i.e., change a '0' to '1' and vice-versa. Mutation is employed to give new information and reintroduce divergence into a converging population. This is a tool in avoiding local maxima, which is a common problem in stochastic algorithms. It also prevents the population from becoming saturated with chromosomes that all look alike. The mutation can be thought of as an error in the reproduction process. But, this error is helpful and very important since it is the only possible way to create truly new chromosomes, as crossover uses old gene material only.
13. **Mutation Rate** It is the probability of mutation occurring and is frequently termed as mutation probability. Large mutation rates increase the probability of destroying a good chromosome, but prevents premature convergence. The best mutation rate is application dependent and related to both the length of the chromosome and the size of the population. For most applications, a mutation rate of 0.1 to 0.01 is employed.
14. **Roulette Wheel Selection** Also termed as 'proportionate selection', this is the commonly used selection procedure though other types like 'tournament selection' are also in use. Here, a chromosome is selected with probability proportionate to its fitness value. This procedure can be explained by comparing with a roulette wheel having slots on its circumference, sized according to chromosome fitness.
15. **Population Deletion** Suppose there are N parents (or N initial solutions). Two of them are marked at a time to produce N_{C_2} children (or solutions). Out of these N + N_{C_2} solutions we retain best N solutions (by computing the fitness function). These N solutions act as parents for the next generation.

3.3.2 The Basic Genetic Algorithm

1. Initialise a population of chromosomes.
2. Evaluate each chromosome in the population.

3. Create new chromosomes by mating current chromosomes; apply mutation and crossover as the parent chromosomes mate.
4. Delete population members, making room for new chromosomes.
5. Evaluate new chromosomes, insert them into the population.
6. If the predefined number of generations are complete, stop and return the best chromosome, if not, go to 3.

During this process of simulated evolution, an initial population of unexceptional chromosomes will improve as parents are replaced by better and better children. The best individual in the final population can be a highly evolved solution to the problem.

4. SPECIALISE GENETIC ALGORITHM FOR SINGLE-STAGE LOT-SIZING PROBLEM WITH STOCKOUTS

Here, the representation of the lot-sizing problem with stockouts is described and the implementation is given with a flow chart.

4.1 Problem Representation

Genetic algorithms, in general recognise binary code only. As we have three decision variables set-ups, holding inventory and shortages, one more digit needs to be added to the binary code making it a trinary code.

The representation is:

1– Set-ups in the period,
0– No set-up, inventory carried from previous period,
2– No set-up, shortages are incurred and backordered, demand met by the immediate next set-up.

4.2 Genetic Algorithm Implementation

The implementation is just section 3.3.2 explained in detail.

1. Read input parameters; number of periods, set-up costs per unit, inventory costs and shortage costs per unit of each period along with the genetic algorithm parameters like population size, chromosome length, maximum number of generations, crossover probability and mutation probability. The genetic algorithm parameters can be fixed for a particular problem through DoE (Design of Experiments), as the

interaction of genetic algorithms parameters is well documented in literature. However, in this work, genetic algorithm parameters are not fixed by DoE (or in other words, they are not optimised).

2. Initialise population so that it covers a good solution space. This is done by random generation of 0, 1 and 2's in initial population. The random generation will be done using the system in built uniform random generator Irand48, and will be carried out as follows.
   - Generate a uniform random generator between '0' and '1'.
   - Multiply this number by the difference of highest digit, '2' in this case and the lowest one, '0'. Add '1' to this value making it a real value higher than '1'. Now, the above real value is returned as integer.

     For example,

     0.567 will be returned as '0'
     2.876 will be returned as '2'
     1.234 will be returned as '1'
3. After initial population generation, it is adjusted for any discrepancies. These discrepancies may be like a period of inventory carrying following a period of shortage. This problem can be eliminated by modifying the problem characteristics to confirm the assumptions. Hence, it is necessary to, incorporate problem characteristics in the initial population. The following adjustments will be carried out on the entire population.
   - If a period of inventory carrying follows the period of short ages, the inventory carrying period will be adjusted as the one with a setup. It means that periods with shortages are always followed by periods with a setup, which is quite logical. Adjusted of all '0's following a '2' or a sequence of '2's to '1' satisfies this condition.
   - The last period should not incur shortages as that shortage can not be backordered. It can be either a period carrying inventory or a period with a setup. This is accounted for by changing the last bit to either a '0' or a '1', if we come across a '2' at the last position of a chromosome.
4. Now, the objective function values of the initial population will be computed. Facing '1' in a chromosome prompts the programme to add set-up cost to the total value of objective cost function. A '0' takes the control inside the zero loop, in which a counter will be initial to count the number of consecutive '0's thus counting the number of consecutive periods carrying inventory from a set-up. After getting the count which can be a single also, the cost of inventory carrying is added to the objective function by multiplying the cost per unit for carrying inventory from previous period to the present period by the number of

units carried over. The programme takes care of cumulative cost addition. This is explained with an example. If the sequence of a particular solution to a 5-period lot-sizing problem is 10001, then the demands in periods 3 and 4 will be met by the inventory carried from period 1 and this gives a cumulative cost addition as the 4th period demand is met by carrying inventory over periods 2 and 3 and the 3rd period demand by carrying inventory through period 2. The cost of carrying inventory of 5th period is the sum of costs obtained by multiplying the demand of period 5 with costs of carrying p u of periods 2, 3 and 4 periods 1, 2 and 3. The same procedure will be adopted for periods 3 and 2. During this type of situation, the respective inventory carrying cost per unit of a period will be considered in the cumulative cost addition.

A '2' in the sequence meaning shortages, takes the control inside the shortages loop. Here also the number of consecutive '2's if present, will be counted. Then, the shortage cost value is calculated by multiplying the cost of shortages per unit with the number of units in shortage. The cumulative cost addition will be done with the shortages too, if a situation of consecutive periods incurring shortages is encountered. But this will be done in the opposite direction compared to the inventory carrying situation. This is explained with an example.

Assume, the sequence is 10221 in a 5-period lot-sizing situation. Then 3rd and 4th periods are facing shortage of supply. The shortages in 3rd and 4th periods are met by the setup in the 5th period. Hence, the total cost of meeting the shortages in period 3 is the shortage cost of period 3 multiplied by the demand of period 3 in addition to the shortage cost of period 4 multiplied by the demand of period 3. Similar procedure will be repeated for period 4. By this method, the total cost for each chromosome or sequence will be calculated and will be repeated for the entire population.

5. Now, the fitness function value will be calculated. As the intention of lot sizing is minimisation of cost, the inverse of the objective function is taken as fitness function in this particular method.
6. Next, the sum fitness, minimum, maximum and average fitness values of the population will be computed.
7. After that, counter for number of generations will be initiated.
8. Next, the control will be passed on to the generation function, which is the heart of the programme. The main intention of generation function is to generate good individuals from the existing population, i.e., select those parent chromosomes returning minimum cost in the objective function or those with higher fitness, make them reproduce through

crossover and mutate the offsprings.

Every pair selected cannot crossover and the number of times the chromosomes selected will crossover is proportional to the crossover probability. This condition is satisfied by comparing the crossover probability with a uniform random number generated between '0' and '1' before implementing crossover.

Two chromosomes will be selected each time by 'proportionate selection' and the crossover will be performed. Two-point crossover is used in this implementation as it is found giving sub-period results compared to one-point crossover. However, as number of periods increase, 4–,8–,.. point crossover can be tried as they are mentioned to be giving good results in genetic algorithm literature for a population with longer string lengths. The two-point crossover will be carried out as follows:

$parent_1$ 1102102 101
$parent_2$ 1001210 221

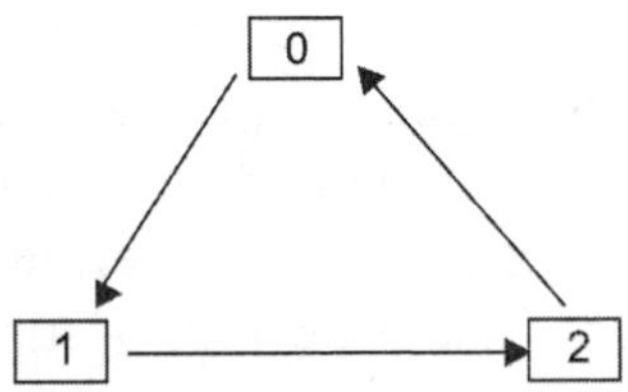

Fig 8.1: First method of mutation

Let the random selection of crossover sites be 2 and 7.
Then after two point crossover, which swaps the bits between the two sites, the children are:

$child_1$ 11 01210 101
$child_2$ 10 02102 221

Before assigning the bits to children, the embedded mutation will be performed. In this work, a cyclical mutation is adopted as we cannot use the traditional flipping of bits due to the presence of three bits in the genetic algorithm coding. Number of times a child undergoes mutation in a population is proportional to mutation probability, which will be very low usually. The cyclical mutation is shown figure 8.1.

Another possible form of mutation is shown figure 8.2. But, as the above form gave better results while dealing with various problems, it is adopted in this particular work figure 8.2.

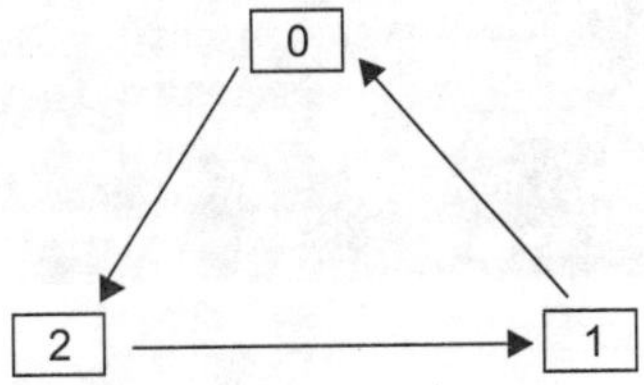

Fig 8.2: Second method of mutation

After the completion of crossover and mutation, the population is adjusted to satisfy the problem specifications. These are explained above while dealing the initial population.

Next, the objective and fitness function values will be determined similar in line to the initial population and is repeated for the entire population in each generation. Finally, the optimal chromosome of the generation will be selected by comparing the objective function values. The one with the lowest numerical value will be the optimal chromosome for that particular generation.

9. Now the population is carried over to the next generation by replacing the old population with the new population.
10. This procedure is repeated for maximum number of generations.

5. RESULTS AND CONCLUSIONS

We used the specialised genetic algorithm to solve the single level lot-sizing problem with shortage costs. We solved 123 problems in total, details of those appear in Tables 8.1 and 8.2. As problem size grows, genetic algorithm searches a large number of solution but that is insignificant compared to total number of solutions existing as is evident from Table 8.1. Also, as problem size grows genetic algorithm has finds better solutions than the by CPLEX package. (CPLEX package was terminated after 10 hours of correct time on HP system). It is to be noted that CPU time taken by genetic algorithm was much less compared to CPV time taken by CPLEX package. Also, as problem size increased, the solutions given by genetic algorithm were better.

With this, successful application of genetic algorithm to single-level lot-sizing system with shortage costs, we hope similar applications might be developed for multi-level lot-sizing problem which by encountered frequently in MRP context.

Table 8.1 Details of problems attempted

Problem Size: No. of Periods	Number of Problems Attempted	Avg Generation No. in which best solution was obtained	No. of solutions searched by GA	No. of solutions possible No. of Periods	Average % closeness reached by GA solution to best-known solution obtained by CPLEX package
10	50	6.24	25,000	59049	100
20	50	47.7	50,000	3.486E9	99.988
30	10	100	100,000	2.05E14	99.992
40	5	181.6	1,25,000	1.22E19	101.192
50	5	198.2	1,50,000	7.17E23	100.37
60	5	213.6	1,75,000	4.24E28	101.4825
70	8	195.6	2,00,000	2.5E33	102.368

Table 8.2 Time taken by genetic algorithm and CPLEX package.

Problem Size: No. of Periods	Avg CPU time taken by CPLEX package on HP 9000 (sec.)	Avg CPU time taken by GA algorithm on HP 9000 (sec.)
10	0.03	0.10
20	1.8	0.10
30	209.8	0.18
40	440	1.3
50	473.7	0.24
60	594.1	0.42
70	647.2	0.47

REFERENCES

1. Davis L, ed. Handbook of Genetic Algorithms, Van Nostrand Reinhold, New York, 1991.
2. Downland KA, Genetic Algorithms-A Tool For OR, J of Operational Research Society, 47(4), 1996, 550-561.
3. Elmaghraby SE and VY Bawl, Optimisation of Batch Ordering Under A Deterministic Variable Demand, Management Science, 18(9), 1972, 508-517.
4. Evans JR, DR Anderson, DJ Sweeney and TA Williams, Applied Productions and Operations Management, 3rd ed, West Publishing Company, New York, 1990.
5. Goldberg, DE, Genetic Algorithms in Search Optimisation and Machine Learning, Addison-Wesley, 1982.
6. Manne AS, Programming of Economic Lot Sizes, Management Science, 4(1), 1958, 115-135.

7. Silver EA and HC Meal, A Heuristic For Selecting Lot Size Quantities For The Case of A Deterministic Time Varying Demand Rate and Discrete Opportunities For Replenishment, Production and Inventory Management, 14, 1973, 64-74.
8. Swoveland C, A Deterministic Multi-period Production Planning Model With Piecewise Concave Production and Holding-Backorder Costs, Management Science, 21, (9), 1975, 1007-1013.
9. Tersine RJ, Production and Material Management, Elsevier North Holland Inc, New York, 1980.
10. Wagner HM and TM Whitin, Dynamic Version of the Economic Lot Size Model, Management Science, 5(1), 1059, 89-96.
11. Zangwill WI, A Backlogging Model and A Multi-echelon Model of a Dynamic Economic Lot Size Production System-A Network Approach, Management Science 15(9), 1969, 506-521.

9 Multi-pass Heuristic for Improved Performance in MRP Systems with Large Variation in Capacity Utilisation of Machine Centres

R R K Sharma, Vikas Wadhwani

1. INTRODUCTION

In MRP systems important decisions are lot sizing, scheduling, planning lead times, and capacity planning. Decisions Material Requirement Planning in (MRP) systems are interdependent. However, a few operating procedures are available which consider these interactions. For computational convenience, practising managers often use simple rules for each of the decision areas, such as, lot sizing, sequencing and planned lead times. For example, Wagner-Whitin[15] algorithm may be used for lot sizing, SPT (Shortest Processing Time) scheduling rule may be used for sequencing and fixed planned lead times may be used for introducing assemblies in the shop. Once this is done, we incur specific set-up cost, inventory-carrying cost and we have specific due date performance. If no attempt is made to revise any of the decisions, such as lot sizing and sequencing, then heuristic used is called 'Single-pass Heuristic'. A brief literature review on 'Single-pass Heuristics' is provided in this chapter. If we choose to suitably revise some of the decisions, then these are called 'Multi-pass Heuristics'. Multi-pass Heuristics revise some decisions in successive iterations and attempt to improve the performance on some criteria. MRP systems are evaluated on a variety of criteria such as set-up cost, inventory-carrying cost, units lateness and aggregate lateness.

Here, we introduce the parameter of machine utilisation in MRP systems in the context of 'Multi-pass Heuristics'. We show that some of these multi-pass heuristics (that are available in literature) work well only when there is little variation in the machine capacity utilisation and fails to improve performance when there is large variation in machine capacity utilisation. Later, we develop a multi-pass heuristic that improves performance when there is a large variation in machine capacity utilisation in MRP context.

2. LITERATURE REVIEW

Biggs[1] showed that main effects of lot sizing and sequencing rules and the interaction between these are significant at the level of 0.01 significance and argued that it is possible that a particular sequencing rule may work in 'opposite direction' to a particular lot-sizing rule and vice versa. Biggs,[1] studied the interaction of priority rules with the capacity levels and reported that these are significant. He found that the Critical Ratio Rule (CRR) performed consistently well over different levels of capacity. Later, Goodwin and Weeks,[7] reported that CRR for scheduling gives consistently better results over a variety of criteria and with a variety of lot-sizing rules. Collier[3] and Billington et al[2] pointed out that certain lot-sizing rules may hurt the capacity utilisation. Grasso and Taylor[8] studied main effects and interaction effects among four factors, namely, lead time, buffering alternative, lot-size rule and cost value on total cost and reported that main effects of each factor and the interaction between lead time distribution and lot-size rule and that between buffering alternative and cost value on total cost are significant. Now, we briefly review the works where initial decisions in an area is modified later.

South and Stewart[13] report their experience at Hix Corporation wherein 50 per cent increase in lot sizes and planned manufacturing lead time resulted in low system tardiness without increase in Work-in-Process (WIP) inventory costs. An intuitive explanation could be that the increase in lot sizes reduces the number of set-ups while releasing the shop capacity. This leads to reduction in queue length before the processing centres which further leads to low tardiness. In the case of Hix Corporation, the effects are balanced in such a manner that no increase in WIP inventory takes place. Billington et al[2] formulated capacity/lot size/lead time problem as mixed integer linear programming problem and suggested product structure compression to reduce problem size. Models with lot sizing and sequencing together become large and are intractable to the conventional integer programming techniques. Single-stage optimisation procedures, such as Wagner-Whitin[15] is used due to its simplicity, is likely to yield sub-optimal solutions as stagewise interactions are ignored.

In literature, very few multi-pass heuristics have been reported. This Heuristic modifies the variable production cost in each iteration and considers interactions between multi-level lot sizing, It is shown to perform better than the single-pass heuristic due to McLaren[9] which modifies the set-up costs but tends to become more complex to implement as the number of stages increases and is computationally more expensive as lot-sizing decision at one level affects the decision at every other level. Fry et al[4] give heuristics for pure assembly systems, whereas Fry et al[5] give a procedure for scheduling when machine capacities are unbalanced. Below, we give three multi-pass heuristics developed by earlier researchers in detail.

3. PREVIOUS MULTI-PASS HEURISTICS

In view of Biggs[1] and Goodwin and Weeks[7] findings, a single-pass heuristic for MRP system would give better results if CRR is used for scheduling. For comparison of results, we used a single-pass heuristic which used CRR for scheduling and Wagner-Whitin[15] rule for lot sizing.

After solving the lot-sizing problem, we simulate the MRP system by using the CRR for scheduling and using the fixed times for introducing lots into the shop (that is, all lots are introduced into the shop with the same lead times) to obtain the solution for the single-pass Heuristic. In this solution, it is natural that the actual inventory-carrying cost is higher than the theoretical inventory-carrying cost. This is due to delays involved in set-up, processing and waiting times at machines. If for some assembly or component, there is a large difference in theoretical and actual inventory-carrying costs, then it may be possible to revise lot sizes by using an artificially inflated holding cost figure to obtain a improved solution with respect to due dates. This is because when holding cost is high, it reduces lot size. This strategy for improvement was deployed by Sharma[11] and is given as Heuristic H2.

At an assembly machine, if some assemblies come early and some much later, then it delays the assembly process and can result in poor due date performance and higher inventory-carrying costs. If in a succeeding simulation (or iteration), one expedites the delayed assemblies at relevant machines and delays the assemblies that have come early then it could lead to lesser variation in arrival times at an assembly machine and henceforth, lead to improvement in due date performance and improve the inventory-carrying costs. This approach was followed by Sharma and Sinha[10] and is given here as Heuristics H1.

3.1 Heuristic H1

This heuristic is due to Sharma and Sinha[10] and details of the same are given below. The coordination index for assembly 'j' at an assembly machine 'i' is denoted by c(i, j). BestSol is the best solution obtained so far with respect to total units lateness.

Step 1: Initialisation. Set c (i,j) =1, for all lots and assembly machines. Using Wagner-Whitin algorithm for lot sizing and Critical Ratio Rule for sequencing simulate the Material Requirement Planning system. Set BestSol to the solution obtained.

Step 2: Compute coordination index for assembly "j" as equal to [1+(a-b)/b], where a = Reaching time for lot at an assembly machine 'i', and b = Mean time of reaching an assembly machine 'i'. We modify the priority index of the lot for subsequent runs at processing centres before this assembly machine 'i' as a product of (–1), co-ordination index and critical ratio and is used for sequencing in the subsequent simulation run. This is done for all assemblies "j" before an assembly machine "i" and is repeated for all assembly machines.

Step 3: Use the priority indices calculated in step 2 and again simulate the Material Requirement Planning system. Update BestSol if a better solution is obtained.

Step 4: Perform steps 2 and 3 twenty times.

3.2 Heuristic H2

Sharma[11] has attempted to improve the stockout performance of the system by selectively reducing the lot sizes. The criteria for selecting the components for lot-size modifications was based on the difference in actual and the oretical inventory-carrying costs. The components for which the difference exceeded 10 per cent (this limit is set arbitrarily) were chosen for lot-size modification. The lot sizes were modified by increasing the holding costs of the relevant components. This approach was reported to have better stockout performance over the original result (the one without the lot-size modification), for case when variation in machine capacity utilisation was low.

Let R be the set of parts with difference in actual and theoretical holding costs exceeding 10 per cent and S be the set of parts already considered twice in the iterative procedure. Let K(j) denote the number of times the part 'j' has been considered in the iterative procedure and BestSol denote the best solution arrived at with respect to aggregate lateness. The steps of the heuristic are described below

Step 1: Initialisation. Set K(j) to zero for all j. Using Wagner-Whitin algorithm for the lot sizing and the CRR (lead-time remaining-work remaining/work remaining) for sequencing, simulate the MRP system to prepare the set R and initialise the following.

$S \leftarrow 0$, $K(j) \leftarrow 0$ for all j, BestSol $\leftarrow \infty$

Step 2: Select part 'j' from set R, which has the highest percentage difference in theoretical and actual holding costs. Increase the holding cost of part 'j' in steps of 0.2 until the lot size changes.
[**Explanation**: If we increase holding cost by 0.2, then lot size is expected to go down. However, it does not go down at first instance, there is an increase in holding cost, then we increase the holding cost of 'j' by 0.2 again and keep doing it until the lot size shows a reduction, after the application of Wagner-Whitin algorithm].
Set $[K(j) = K(j) + 1]$ and if $[K(j) = 2]$, then update $S = S + (j)$. If the current solution is better than the BestSol with respect to aggregate lateness, then update BestSol $\leftarrow$Current solution.

Step 3: Simulate and prepare the set R afresh and let
$R \leftarrow R — S$

Step 4: If R = { }, then stop, else go to step 2.

An increase in holding costs is likely to reduce lot sizes and improve the due date performance but an excessive decrease in lot sizes may increase number of set-ups and adversely affect the due date performance (as more capacity may be lost in set-ups now), hence number of times a part or sub-assembly may be considered for holding cost modification is limited to two. These two heuristics are computationally attractive as they take constant time to run (20 iterations).

Table 9.1 Performance details of Heuristics H1 and H2 when there is large variation in machine capacity utilisation

	H1			H2		
Problem No	TAL	TUL	TC	TAL	TUL	TC
1	-13%	-3%	2%	0%	0%	0%
2	28%	-0%	5%	1%	1%	50%
3	0%	0%	-8%	-3%	-3%	-20%
4	5%	0%	-19%	8%	3%	-178%
5	0%	-3%	-2%	13%	1%	-12%
6	11%	4%	1%	0%	0%	0%
7	-1%	-0%	-4%	-3%	3%	-142%
8	-1%	1%	10%	-3%	6%	3%
9	11%	6%	2%	14%	13%	-5%

Contd...

Performance details of Heuristics H1 and H2 when there is large variation in machine capacity utilisation

	H1			H2		
Problem No	TAL	TUL	TC	TAL	TUL	TC
10	0%	6%	−3%	7%	16%	−3%
11	7%	7%	0%	21%	35%	4%
12	10%	5%	9%	10%	10%	−26%
13	14%	2%	23%	0%	0%	−3%
14	0%	10%	−19%	−24%	−10%	23%
15	34%	0%	14%	0%	0%	−1%

Table 9.2 Performance details of Heuristics H1 and H2 when there is little variation in machine capacity utilisation

	H1			H2		
Problem No	TAL	TUL	TC	TAL	TUL	TC
1	12%	−13%	3%	3%	0%	-7%
2	25%	28%	−3%	23%	1%	−20%
3	4%	0%	4%	0%	-3%	0%
4	9%	5%	7%	12%	8%	−13%
5	19%	0%	−33%	12%	13%	−40%
6	11%	11%	2%	0%	0%	0%
7	6%	−1%	−8%	17%	−3%	−6%
8	22%	−1%	29%	5%	-3%	8%
9	16%	11%	-9%	18%	14%	-3%
10	17%	0%	−1%	6%	7%	−1%
11	10%	7%	4%	25%	21%	−1%
12	17%	10%	3%	29%	10%	20%
13	11%	14%	25%	0%	0%	0%
14	7%	90%	−3%	52%	−24%	0%
15	17%	34%	-7%	0%	0%	−39%

Abbreviations:

TAL – Total Aggregate Lateness

TUL – Total Units Lateness

TC– Total Cost (Sum of set-up and inventory-carrying costs)

Table 9.3 Summary of t-tests for performance of H1 and H2 for both cases

Total Units Lateness		
	For large variation in machine capacities	For little variation in machine capacities
	t-value (calculated)	t-value (calculated)
Original Vs H1	2.38	8.581 (*)
Original Vs H2	1.846	6.598 (*)

Contd...

Total Aggregate Lateness		
	For large variation in machine capacities	For little variation in machine capacities
	t-value (calculated)	t-value (calculated)
Original Vs H1	2.080	7.426 (*)
Original Vs H2	1.006	6.11 (*)
Total Cost		
	For large variation in machine capacities	For little variation in machine capacities
	t-value (calculated)	t-value (calculated)
Original Vs H1	0.236	0.214
Original Vs H2	1.814	1.624

(*) Significant at ∝ = 0.005 and degrees of freedom = 12 as table t-value is 2.974.

4. RESULTS OF PREVIOUS HEURISTICS

We constructed 30 MRP problems with as diverse product structures as possible (that is, we chose product structures that were tall, broad and combination of the two). Out of these, 15 MRP problems had machine utilisation (with the application of Wagner-Whitin algorithm for lot sizing and CRR for scheduling in a single-pass heuristic) varying uniformly between 20 and 85 per cent (henceforth referred to as with large variation in machine utilisation) and other 15 MRP problems had machine utilisation varying uniformly between 70 and 75 per cent (henceforth referred to as with low variation in machine utilisation). For preparing each problem, we took on an average around five days. Problem details are too voluminous to be given here and are given in Wadhwani.[14] Corresponding to a product structure, we created one problem with large variation in machine utilisation and one problem with low variation in machine utilisation. The shop had 15 general purpose machines and 10 assembly machines. Maximum number of assemblies/components in a product structure was 26 and routing sequence was randomly generated and an assembly/component requiring processing visited on an average three machines. The data of processing times, set-up times, cost of products, due date requirements of demands and demand figures are too voluminous and are not given here. Each simulation was a run for a period of two years.

Both these problem sets were solved by Heuristics H1 and H2 described above and the detailed performance is given by Sharma and Wadhwani.[6] They, provides evidence to show that previous heuristics do not work when there is large variation in machine capacity utilisation in MRP system. Sharma and Wadhwani[6] offer intuitive explanation for non performance of H1 and H2 in conditions of large variation in capacity utilisation of machines. Moreover, when there are bottlenecks, improvements are possible if the schedule of bottleneck machines drive the system, see Goldratt[6] and this does not happen with both the Heuristics, H1 and H2.

5. NEW HEURISTIC

Earlier, we offered some explanation for poor performance of Heuristics H1 and H2 when there is large variation in machine capacity utilisation in a MRP system. We feel that when there is a bottleneck facility that holds up shop performance, then we could bring about improvement by selectively tinkering with the lead times.

The basic concept is this, when there are some bottleneck machines (machines with high machine utilisation) in the system, then due to these machines the processing of assemblies gets delayed and the lateness (both units and aggregate) increases, because the queue at the front of these machines become lengthy. If some component has to be processed through this then it will take a lot of time due to this queue and its parent cannot be produced before it gets processed on the bottleneck machine and this way finished assembly gets delayed.

Consider product structure shown in Figure 9.1 and suppose that assembly number 6 and 10 have to be processed on a bottleneck machine. Since the assembly 10 has to pass the bottleneck machine, so it get delayed and because of this, assembly 6 is delayed.

Example

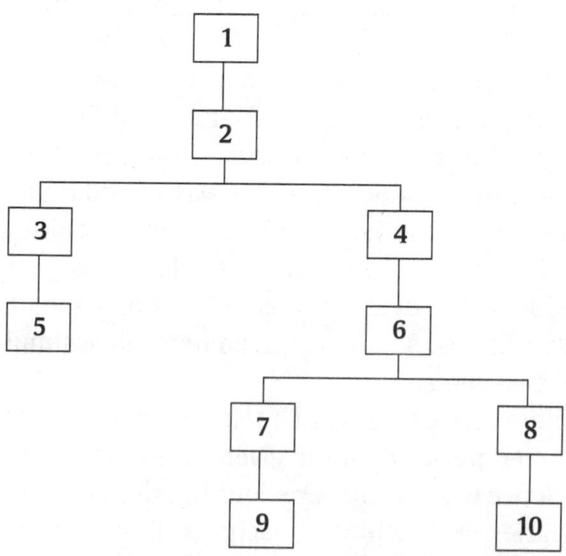

Figure 9.1 Product Structure

One way of improving the performance is to increase the lead time of assembly number 10 as well as the lead time of all the assemblies that are children of assembly number 6. This will lead to the earlier production of assembly number 6 and it could be expected that total aggregate and units lateness will be reduced. This is the idea behind the heuristic developed.

5.1 Heuristic Developed (H3)

Let M be set of machines with capacity utilisation more than 85 per cent (arbitrary value) of capacity utilisation of highest utilised machine. Let R_I be the set of assemblies which have to be processed at I^{th} machine of set M, and the bestSol denote the best solution with respect to total units lateness.

Step 1: Initialisation, using Wagner-Whitin (1958) for lot sizing and CRR for scheduling, simulate the MRP system to prepare set M and R_I.

Step 2: Select machine I from set M which has highest capacity utilisation, increase the lead times of all the assemblies belonging to set R_I correspond to I^{th} machine, and all children by a suitable time unit (chosen as 50 minutes in this study). We also increase the lead times of all children of assemblies belonging to set R_I by this unit of time.

Step 3: $M \leftarrow M - I$

Step 4: If M ={ } then, continue, else go to step 2

Step 5: Simulate using Wagner-Whitin for lot sizing and CRR with increased lead times of assemblies and stop.

If the quantum of increase in lead time was small then repeated application of H3 brought improvements. If it was large then we tended to miss the region of improvement (improvement in TAL and TUL with insignificant increase in total costs). For the problems considered by us, we found that when quantum of lead time increase was kept at 50 min, it lead to maximum improvement was realised and further application of H3 led to no further improvement.

6. PERFORMANCE OF NEW HEURISTIC

We created 27 MRP problems with machine capacity utilisation uniformly varying from 20 to 85 per cent and tested the performance Heuristic H3. Problem details are given in Wadhwani.[6] Detailed performance data are also available in Sharma and Wadhwani.[12] Here, we briefly give the salient results.

6.1 Results

On the basis of the results generated by performing the t-test on percentage improvement figures on various performance criteria, following can be inferred:

1. **Total units lateness** For this criterion, the Heuristic H3 gives better result than the best-known single-pass heuristic, when variance in machine utilisation is high and statistically significant at 0.5 per cent significant level.
2. **Total aggregate lateness** For this criterion, the Heuristic H3 gives better result than the best-known single-pass heuristic, when variance in machine utilisation is high and is statistically significant at 0.5 percent significant level.
3. **Total inventory-carrying cost** For this criterion, the Heuristic H3 gives no significant increase in inventory-carrying cost than the best-known single-pass heuristic, when variance in machine utilisation is high.

We see that the new heuristic developed is able to improve performance significantly on the criterion of aggregate and units lateness with insignificant increase of inventory-carrying cost, when there is large variation in machine capacity utilisation in the shop for MRP system.

7. DISCUSSION

Biggs[1] has suggested that best 'single-pass' heuristic that practicing managers can use is the one which uses CRR rule for scheduling along with any suitable rule for lot sizing. This was verified by Biggs[1] for various levels of capacity. However, when 'multi-pass' heuristics are considered, our preliminary work seems to suggest that when there is large variation in machine capacity utilisation in the shop in MRP system, the heuristic that changes lot sizes (Sharma[11]) and the heuristic that changes schedules (Sharma and Sinha[10]), fail to improve performance on the criteria of total aggregate lateness and total units lateness and the 'multi-pass' heuristic that changes the lead times seems to improve performance. Sharma and Sinha reported that their heuristics improved performance when there is little variation in machine capacity utilisation in the shop in MRP system.

When there is large variation in machine capacity utilisation in the shop in MRP system, there are obvious bottlenecks in the production system and literature suggests that one should identify and eliminate the bottlenecks to improve performance, see Goldratt.[6] He also suggested that the schedules of bottleneck machines should drive the system. Based on these ideas, the 'multi-pass' Heuristic H3 is developed that improves performance over the best known 'single-pass' Heuristic. Due to limited sample size, the results may not be universally applicable, due to the fact that problem preparation takes huge effort and further research is required in this direction.

8. CONCLUSIONS

It was observed that when there is large variation in machine capacity utilisation in the shop in MRP system, then the 'multi-pass' Heuristics due to Sharma and Sinha[10] and Sharma[11] are ineffective in improving the performance. The heuristic developed here that selectively changes lead times gives significantly better performance for this case on the criterion of total units lateness and total aggregate lateness with insignificant increase in total inventory-carrying cost.

Managers using MRP systems need to be aware of two situations: (1) there is low variation in machine capacity utilisation and (2) there is large variation in machine capacity utilisation. They need to use appropriate 'multi-pass' heuristic to improve performance of the production system as outlined. This is a useful contribution of this study.

Table 9.4 Percentage improvement in the performance criteria due to Heuristic H3 over the best-known single-pass euristic

Problem No	Total units lateness	Total aggregate lateness	Total cost
PROBLEM 1	4%	13%	5%
PROBLEM 2	10%	16%	1%
PROBLEM 3	47%	68%	–1%
PROBLEM 4	2%	6%	–6%
PROBLEM 5	18%	48%	–2%
PROBLEM 6	13%	80%	1%
PROBLEM 7	11%	20%	5%
PROBLEM 8	13%	25%	1%
PROBLEM 9	30%	69%	5%
PROBLEM 10	13%	66%	–17%
PROBLEM 11	18%	25%	–4%
PROBLEM 12	0%	2%	0%
PROBLEM 13	10%	44%	7%
PROBLEM 14	0%	6%	–3%
PROBLEM 15	38%	46%	2%
PROBLEM 16	24.5%	14.8%	0.0%
PROBLEM 17	12.3%	5.83%	11.3%
PROBLEM 18	4.75%	14.6%	4.00%
PROBLEM 19	10.1%	47.4%	–3.29%
PROBLEM 20	4.84%	19.5%	8.33%
PROBLEM 21	8.64%	22.8%	9.09%
PROBLEM 22	34.8%	21.6%	8.83%
PROBLEM 23	9.43%	18.8%	–3.79%
PROBLEM 24	14.7%	20.4%	5.17%
PROBLEM 25	12.3%	31.0%	–6.19%
PROBLEM 26	1.4%	18.8%	–1.6%
PROBLEM 27	24.5%	22.8%	–3.78%

Table 9.5 Summary of t-test for performance of Heuristic H3

Performance criteria	t-value for difference in H3 and original
Total aggregate lateness	6.302 (*)
Total units lateness	6.858 (*)
Total cost	1.438

(*) significant at $\alpha = 0.005$ and df = 26 as table t-value is 2.771.

REFERENCES

1. Biggs JR. Priority Rules for Shop Floor Control in A Material Requirement Planning under Various Levels of Capacity, *International Journal of Production Research,* 23(1), 33-36, 1985.
2. Billington P, McClain J and Thomos LJ, The Interaction of Lead Time Determination, Lot Sizing decisions and Capacity Planning in MRP Systems, Proceedings, American Institute of Decision Sciences, Eleventh Annual Meeting, 1979.
3. Collier DA A Comparison of MRP Lot Sizing Methods Considering Capacity Change Cost, *Journal of Operations Management,* August. 1980.
4. Fry TD, Oliff MD, Minor ED, Leong GK. The Effects of Product Structure and Sequencing Rule on Assembly Shop Performance, *International Journal of Production Research,* Vol. 27, 671-686, 1989.
5. Fry TD, Philipoom PR, Markland RE. Dispatching in a Multi-stage Job Shop Where Machine Capacities are Unbalanced, *International Journal of Production Research,* Vol. 26, No. 7, 1193-1223, 1988.
6. Goldratt EM. Computerised Shop Floor Scheduling, *International Journal of Production Research,* Vol. 26, No. 3, 443-455, 1988.
7. Goodwin JS and Weeks JK. Evaluating Scheduling Policies in A Multi-level Assembly System, *International Journal of Production Research,* 24, 247-257, 1986.
8. Grasso ET and Taylor BW. A Simulation Based Experimental Investigation of Supply Timing Uncertainty in MRP Systems, *International Journal of Production Research,* 22(3), 485-497, 1984.
9. McLaren BJ. A Study of Multi-level Lot Sizing Procedures for Material Requirements Planning System, unpublished PhD dissertation, Purdue University,1976.
10. Sharma RRK and Sinha S. A Sequencing Based Multi-pass Heuristic for Improved Performance in MRP Context, in Ding-Zhu DU, Zhang XS and Wang, W (eds), *Lecture Notes in Operations Research,* World Publishing Corporation, Beijing, 659-668, 1996.
11. Sharma RRK. Heuristic to Modify Lot Sizes to Improve Performance in MRP Context, *Industrial Engineering Encyclopaedia, International Journal of Industrial Engineering,* ISBN 0-9654599-X, 1999.
12. Sharma RRK and Wadhwani V, Multi-pass Heuristic for Improved Performance in MRP Systems with Large Variation in Capacity Utilisation of Machine Centres, Asian Journal of Technology, *Operations and Management,* V1, 2006, (accepted to appear).

13. South JB and Stewart RJ. A 50% Increase in Lot Size and Planned Manufacturing Lead Time with No Increase in Work-in-Process Inventory, *Production and Inventory Management,* First Quarter, 27(1), 19-25, 1986.
14. Wadhwani V Heuristic for Improved Performance in MRP System When Variance in Machine Utilisation is High, Unpublished M Tech. dissertation, Department of Industrial and Management Engineering, IIT Kanpur, India, 2000.
15. Wagner HM and Whitin TM. Dynamic Version of Economic Lot Size Model, *Management Science,* October, 89-96, 1958.

10 Comparative Ranking of Different Multi-pass Heuristics in the Context of Large and Small Variation in Capacity Utilisation of Machine Centres

R R K Sharma, Sameer Agarwal

1. INTRODUCTION

Several heuristics have been given in previous chapters. In this chapter, we present a study that compares their performance in the context of large and small variation in capacity utilisation of machine centres.

2. LITERATURE REVIEW

Biggs[2] in his work 'Priority rules for shop floor control in a Material Requirement Planning (MRP) system under various levels of capacity' has studied the effects of using priority scheduling rules for capacity management and shop floor control in an MRP production system. The results of the study show that the application of different priority rules does cause such a system to perform differently. The indications are that a practitioner could cause his MRP system to perform in a more desirable fashion by his choice of priority scheduling rules for shop floor control under various capacity levels. See Orlicky[10] and Vollman[15] for a brief review on MRP systems.

Russell and Taylor[12] studied the impact of product structure on the performance of priority dispatching rules. Two types of BoM were studied. It was found that as BoM gets taller with more levels, the probability that the job will finish after its due date increases. It was also reported that performance of Shortest Processing Time (SPT) sequencing rule improves as product structures get taller.

The effects of product structure and sequencing rule on assembly shop performance was studied by Fry, Oliff, Minor and Keong.[5] In this paper, an effort was made to study the effect of product structure on the performance of 14 selected priority rules in a simulated multi-stage Stage job shop, results from this study suggests that Shortest Processing Time (SPT) is not appropriate for a shop that performs assembly operations. This study indicates that Branch Critical Ratio Rule (BCR) performs well on the criterion of Mean Absolute Lateness (MAL).

Scheduling policies in a multi-level assembly system was studied by, Goodwin and Weeks.[8] This paper orders in preference various scheduling policies comprised of dispatching and regeneration rules in a multi-level assembly production system. Traditional expected-value statistical and second-degree stochastic dominance preference ordering rules are used to identify the most efficient scheduling policies for risk-averse managers using various measures of performance. The results indicate that selection of an efficient regeneration rule is contingent upon the selection of a dispatching rule and these rules must be selected jointly to develop efficient scheduling policies. For this study, simple intuitively appealing scheduling policies were found to be efficient.

Dispatching in a multi-stage job shop where machine capacities are studied by Fry, Philipoom and Markland.[6] In this paper, the performance of selected dispatching rules in an unbalanced multi-stage job shop was evaluated to determine whether the performance was consistent for jobs which were routed through the bottleneck and which bypass the bottleneck. The results indicated that sequencing rules, which were based on due date, tend to be the overall better performers for both types of jobs. No rule was found to be superior in all cases for all measures. Another reason was that the results for the job that pass through the bottleneck were not the same for the jobs which bypass the bottleneck. Also, the degree of capacity imbalance or due date allowance did cause a significant change in the ranking of sequencing rule performance.

Potty[11] developed multi-pass heuristic for improved stockout performance. In this work, two heuristics were used to improve the stockout performance. In those heuristics, lot sizes were selectively reduced in steps to get the desired improvement. The criterion for choosing the part for revising the lot size was based on the difference in its actual and theoretical inventory-carrying cost. After choosing the part its holding cost was changed to revise the lot size. The results indicated that increase in the holding cost reduces the lot size which may increase the number of set-ups and adversely affect the due date performance (as more capacity may be lost in set-ups now). To take care of this the modification in the lot size was limited to two times. Potty[11] has reported that his heuristic did not work in MRP system with large variation in machine capacity utilisation. Potty's[11] study was limited in value due to small computational experience provided by him. Later, Sharma[13] gave a large computational experience of

36 problems, which found that Potty's[11] heuristic worked in case of MRP system with low variation in capacity utilisation.

Yoganandan[18] attempted to obtain better performance using multipass heuristic by modifying the scheduling rule in successive iterations. In this approach after the scheduling was done, the assemblies arriving later/earlier than 50 per cent (this 50 per cent is arbitrary) of the subassemblies arriving at an assembly centre were identified and for the subsequent rescheduling of their critically at the previous processing centre was increased/decreased. The rescheduling was attempted for maximum of 20 times. Yoganandan reported that his heuristic performed well in case of low variation in machine utilisation.

Sinha[14] has attempted to study the effect of coordination between various components reaching to assembly centre in MRP context. In it, it has been attempted to reduce the time lag between components so that the time of waiting at a centre by the components can be saved and by doing it the performance of the MRP system can be improved. In order to do this, a coordination index along with a standard scheduling rule is used to decide the priority of components at levels earlier than the level at which it gets assembled. On application of this approach, it was observed that it gave significantly better results on important parameters like total aggregate lateness and total unit lateness in case of low variation in machine utilisation.

Gupta[9] searched for those assemblies (having child assemblies) that show lateness due their child assemblies reaching late at the corresponding assembly centre. After that a list of component assemblies of these critical assemblies till the last level of product structure, which these critical assemblies consist of, is prepared. Basically, the list consists of component assemblies with repetition. Now, they are counted for the number of repetition for every unique component assembly and assign it to 'Criticality Index' of this unique assembly. After that, they searched for non-bottleneck machines. For it, machines having their capacity utilisation less than 75 per cent are regarded as non-bottleneck (the limit is set arbitrarily). Every component in the list was given priority on these machines with a modified CRR value. The factor of modification was kept between 0.4 and 0.5.

Modified CRR value

= CRR value - (factor of modification) * Criticality Index

Gupta reported that his heuristic performed well in case of high variation of machine utilisation.

Vikas[17] developed heuristic that selectively increases the lead times of assemblies, which are going through the bottleneck machines. When there are some bottleneck machines in the system then due to these machines, the processing of assemblies gets delayed and the lateness increases, since the queue at the front of these machines becomes lengthy and if some component has to be processed through this, then it will take a lot of time due to this queue and its parent can not be produced before it gets processed on the bottleneck machines and in this way, finished assembly gets delayed. The approach used in the heuristic, increases the lead time of assembly which has to pass through the bottleneck machine as well as lead time of all the assembly that are children of this assembly. This will lead to manufacture of the assembly before time. It has been reported that heuristic developed is able to improve significantly on the criterion of aggregate and unit lateness with insignificant increase of inventory-carrying cost. Vikas's Heuristic is written for the case of high variation of machine utilisation.

In this work, we plan to generate comparative experience for all these heuristics listed above, which was not available before.

3. MULTI-PASS HEURISTICS

In view of Biggs[1,2,3] and Goodwin and Weeks[7,8] findings, a single-pass heuristic for MRP system would give better results if CRR is used for scheduling. Thus, for comparing performance of multi-pass heuristics, we used the result of single-pass heuristic which used CRR for scheduling and Wagner-Whitin[16] rule for lot sizing.

After solving the lot-sizing problem, we simulate the MRP system by using the CRR for scheduling and using the fixed times for introducing lots into the shop (that is, all lots are introduced into the shop with the same lead times) to obtain the solution for the single-pass heuristic. Here, it is natural that actual inventory-carrying cost is higher than the theoretical inventory-carrying cost, due to delays involved in set-up, processing and waiting times at machining centres. If for some assembly or component, there is large difference in theoretical and actual inventory-carrying costs, then it may be possible to revise lot sizes by using an artificially inflated holding cost figure to obtain an improved solution with respect to due dates. This is because when holding cost is high, it reduces lot sizes. This strategy for improvement was deployed by Potty[11] and Sharma[13] and is given as Heuristic H3. Sharma[13] has essentially presented the heuristic due to Potty[11] with sufficient computational experience.

At an assembly centre, if some assemblies come early and some much later, then it delays the assembly process and can result in poor due date performance and higher inventory-carrying costs. If in a succeeding simulation (iteration), one expedites the delayed assemblies at relevant machining centres and delays the assemblies that have come early at relevant machining centres, then it could lead to lesser variation in arrival times at an assembly centre. This leads to improvement in due date performance and improves the inventory-carrying costs. This approach was followed by Yoganandan,[18] Sinha[14] and is given as Heuristics H1 and H2 respectively.

Gupta,[9] searched for those assemblies (having child assemblies) that show lateness due to their child assemblies reaching late at the corresponding assembly centre and also searched for non-bottleneck machines. A list of component is prepared and every component in the list was given priority on these machines with a modified CRR value. The factor of modification was kept between 0.4 and 0.5. Heuristic developed by Gupta[9] is given as Heuristic H4.

Vikas[17] developed heuristic that selectively increased the lead times of assemblies, which are going through the bottleneck machines. Heuristic developed is able to improve performance significantly on the criterion of aggregate lateness with insignificant increase of inventory-carrying cost. This heuristic is given as Heuristic H5.

3.1 Heuristic H1

This heuristic is due to Sharma and Sinha (1996) and details of the same are given below:
The coordination index for assembly 'j' at assembly centre 'i' is denoted by c(i,j). BestSol is the best solution obtained so far with respect to total units lateness.

Step 1: Initialisation. Set c (i,j) equal to one for all lots and assembly centres. Using Wagner-Whitin algorithm for lot sizing and Critical Ratio Rule for sequencing simulate the Material Requirement Planning system. Set BestSol to the solution obtained.

Step 2: Compute coordination index for assembly 'j' as equal to [1 + (a – b)/b], where a = Reaching time for lot at an assembly centre 'i', and b = Mean time of reaching an assembly centre 'i'. We modify the priority index of the lot for subsequent runs at processing centres before this assembly centre 'i' as a product of (–1), coordination index and critical ratio and is used for sequencing in the subsequent simulation run. This is done for all assemblies 'j' before an assembly centre 'i' and is repeated for all assembly centres.

Step 3: Use the priority indices calculated in step 2, simulate the MRP system. Update BestSol if a better solution is obtained.
Step 4: Perform steps 2 and 3 twenty times.

3.2 Heuristic H2

Yoganandan[18] attempted to obtain better performance by modifying the scheduling rule in successive iterations. In this approach, after the scheduling was done, the assemblies arriving later/earlier than 50 percent (arbitrary value) of the sub-assemblies arriving at an assembly centre were identified, and for the subsequent rescheduling their critically at the previous processing centre was increased/decreased. The rescheduling was attempted for maximum of 20 times.

Let L_j be the set of sub-assemblies/components that arrived later than at least 50 per cent of the sub-assemblies arriving at the assembly centre 'i' and let E_j be the set of sub-assemblies/components that come earlier than at least 50 per cent of the sub-assemblies arriving at the assembly centre 'i'. Let BestSol denote the best solution arrived at with respect to aggregate lateness. The steps of the heuristic are given below.

Step 1: Set BestSol $\leftarrow$ infinity
Step 2: Using Wagner-Whitin algorithm for the lot sizing, the critical ratio rule (lead time remaining-work remaining/work remaining) for sequencing, simulate the material requirement planning system. Set BestSol $\leftarrow$ current solution.
Step 3: Prepare sets L_j and E_j for each of the assembly centres in the shop. Add 0.1 to the critical ratio of the lot belonging to set L_j of the assembly centre 'i' and subtract 0.1 from the critical ratio of the lot belonging to set E_j of the assembly centre 'i' and reschedule the lots by simulation using the revised critical ratios, obtain the current value of aggregate lateness. If the current solution is better than BestSol with respect to aggregate lateness, then set BestSol $\leftarrow$ current solution.
Step 4: Repeat step 3 for 20 times.
An increase in the value of critical ratio for a component results in it getting a higher priority and arrives early at an assembly centre. The opposite happens when the critical ratio is decreased. So it is expected that aggregate lateness is reduced and a better coordinated arrival before an assembly centre results and hence, inventory-carrying cost also reduces.

3.3 Heuristic H3

Potty[11] have attempted to improve the stockout performance of the system by selectively reducing the lot sizes. The criteria for selecting the components for lot size modifications were based on the difference in actual and theoretical inventory-carrying costs. The components for which the difference exceeded 10 per cent (this limit is set arbitrarily) were chosen for lot size modification, the lot sizes were modified by increasing the holding costs of the relevant components. This approach was reported to have better stockout performance over the original result (the one without the lot size modification) for case when variation in machine capacity utilisation was low. Let R be the set of parts with difference in actual and theoretical holding costs exceeding 10 per cent and S be the set of parts already considered twice in the iterative procedure. Let K(j) denote the number of times the part 'j' has been considered in the iterative procedure and BestSol denote the best solution arrived at with respect to aggregate lateness. The steps of the heuristic are described below:

Step 1: Initialisation. Set K(j) to zero for all j. Using Wagner- Whitin algorithm for the lot sizing and the critical ratio rule (lead-time remaining-work remaining/work remaining) for sequencing, simulate the material recruitment planning system to prepare the set R and initialise the following.

$S \leftarrow O$, K (j) ? $\leftarrow$ for all j, BestSol $\leftarrow \infty$

Step 2: Select part 'j' from set R, which has the highest percentage difference in theoretical and actual holding costs. Increase the holding cost of part 'j' in steps of 0.2 until the lot size changes. Set [K (j) = K (j) + 1] and if [K (j) = 2], then update S = S + (j). If the current ɔlution is better than the BestSol with respect to aggregate lateness, then update BestSol $\leftarrow$ Current solution.

Step 3: Simulate and prepare the set R afresh and let R$\leftarrow$ R – S

Step 4: If R = { } then, stop, else go to step 2.

An increase in holding costs is likely to reduce lot sizes and improve the due date performance, but an excessive decrease in lot sizes may increase number of set-ups and adversely affect the due date performance (as more capacity may be lost in set-ups), so number of times a part or sub-assembly may be considered for holding cost modification is limited to two.

3.4 Heuristic H4

In this approach, Gupta,[9] searched for those assemblies (having child assemblies) that show lateness due to their child assemblies reaching late at the corresponding assembly centre. After that a list of component assemblies of these critical assemblies tills the last level of product structure, which these critical assemblies consist of. Basically, the list consists of components assemblies with repetition. Now, they counted the number of repetition for every unique component assembly and assign it to 'Criticality Index' of this unique assembly. After that, they searched for non-bottleneck machines. For it, machines with capacity utilisation less than 75 per cent (arbitrary value) are regarded as non-bottleneck. Every component in the list was given priority on these machines with a modified CRR value. The factor of modification was kept between 0.4 and 0.5. Modified CRR value = CRR value - (factor of modification) * Criticality Index. Let R be the set of critical assemblies with lateness and M is the set of non-bottleneck machines. BestSol denotes the best solution arrived at with respect to total unit lateness. The steps of heuristic are described below:

Step 1: Initialisation. Using Wagner-Whitin algorithm for the lot sizing the critical ratio rule (lead time remaining-work remaining/work remaining) for sequencing, simulate the material requirement planning system to prepare the set R and M. Let S be the set of components already considered in the iterative procedure. Initialise the following.

BestSol +- - infinity and S $\leftarrow$ 0.

Step 2: Select part j from set R and find the modified CRR value.
Update S $\leftarrow$ S + {j}.

Step 3: If j has to be routed through non-bottleneck, give it priority with modified CRR value, else, let factor of modification = 0.

Step 4: Let R $\leftarrow$ R – S.
If R = 0, then go to step 5, else go to step 2.

Step 5: If the current solution is better than the BestSol with respect to total unit lateness then update, BestSol $\leftarrow$ Current solution.

Step 6: Simulate it for 20 times and search the best solution.

3.5 Heuristic H5

This heuristic is due to Vikas[17] and details of the same are given below.

Let M be set of machines with capacity utilisation more than 85 per cent (arbitrary value) of capacity utilisation of the highest utilised machine. Let R_J be the set of assemblies which has to be processed at I^{th} machine of set M, and the BestSol denote the best solution with respect to total unit lateness.

Step 1: Initialisation, using Wagner-Whitin (1958) for lot sizing and CRR for Scheduling simulate the material requirement planning system to prepare set M and R_I.

Step 2: Select machine I from set M which has the highest capacity utilisation, increase the lead times of all the assemblies belonging to set R_I, correspond to I^{th} machine and all their children assemblies by a suitable time unit (chosen as 50 time units in this study). Also increase the lead times of all children of assemblies belonging to set R_1 by this unit of time.

Step 3: $M \leftarrow M - I$

Step 4: If M = { }, then continue, else go to step 2.

Step 5: Simulate using Wagner-Whitin algorithm for lot sizing and CRR with increased lead times of assemblies, stop.

4. RESULTS AND DISCUSSION

On the simulation model developed, 20 test problem were tried. While designing the problems, it was tried to keep a variety of product structures, as it has been reported by Fry et al.[5] that different product structures behave differently with different scheduling rules. By doing this, it was to be seen if the heuristics were consistent. The various time figures (such as, processing times, set-up times) and cost figures (such as, holding cost, processing cost, set-up costs) were randomly generated. The details of test problems and the results obtained (including "t" test results) appear in Tables 10.1 (A–T) and 10.2 (A–F) respectively.

4.1 Comparison of results

For comparing the results of the five heuristics, test of significance ("t" test) was performed over the data of percentage improvement given by each heuristic over the combination of Wagner-Within[16] rule and CRR rule whose results appear under the head 'Original'. The five heuristics for which test was performed are HI, H2, H3, H4 and H5.

The results obtained on 20 problems which have been tried are given in Tables 10.1.A to table 10.1.T. The analysis of the results of the five heuristics are as follows.

4.2 Discussion

On the basis of results generated by performing the "t"-test (see Table 10.2.A to 10.2.F) on percentage improvement figures on various performance criteria the following can be inferred (Freund and Miller[4]).

4.2.1 Total Unit Lateness

1. **When variance in machine utilisation is low** For this criterion all heuristics give better results except Heuristic H4 and are statistically significant at 5 per cent significance level. Among all the Heuristics H5 has shown the best result. Heuristic H1 is performing better than Heuristic H2, but results are not significant at 5 per cent significance level. Heuristic, H3 is performing better than Heuristic H2, but in this case also, results are not significant at 5 per cent significance level. If we rank above heuristic on this criterion, Heuristic H5 performed best, followed by Heuristics H1, H2 and H3 respectively. In case of Heuristic H4, solution has worsened even than original.
2. **When variance in machine utilisation is high** For this criterion, all heuristics are statistically significant at 5 per cent significance level. Heuristic H5 works better than original at 5 per cent significance level. By comparing Heuristics H1, H2, H3 and H4 we find that Heuristics H3 and H4 are better than Heuristics H1 and H2.

4.2.2 Total Aggregate Lateness

1. **When variance in machine utilisation is low** The results obtained by Heuristics H1, H2, H3 and H5 are better than original and statistically significant than 5 per cent significance level. In case of Heuristic H4, solution has even worsened than the original. Heuristic H2 is performing better than Heuristic H5 but its result is not significant at 5 per cent level. Heuristics H1, H2 and H5 are performing better than Heuristic H3.
2. **When variance in machine utilisation is high** All heuristics are performing better than original at 5 per cent significance level. Heuristic H4 is performing better than Heuristics H1, H2 and H3. Heuristic H5 is performing better than Heuristic H4. Heuristic H3 is performing better than Heuristics H1 and H2, but results are not significant at 5 per cent significance level.

4.2.3 Total Inventory-Carrying Cost

1. **When variance in machine utilisation is low** Heuristics H1 and H5 give better results than all other heuristics but the results are not statistically significant at 5 per cent significance level. Heuristics H2 and H4 are also performing at same level. Heuristic H3 is least in performance when compared to all other heuristics.
2. **When variance in machine utilisation is high** We find that for this criterion the inventory cost is almost the same for all heuristics except Heuristic H3 with 5 per cent significance level.

5. CONCLUSION

One of the primary aims of this research is to test the performance of different multi-pass heuristic available in literature. Bigg[3] had earlier shown that Critical Ratio Rule performed better on a variety of performance criteria which was later confirmed by the studies of Goodwin and Weeks.[8]

Multi-pass heuristics developed by researchers (Potty, Yoga, Nandan, Sharat Sinha, Gupta and Vikas) performed well on average. Heuristic H5 performed well in case of high and low variance in machine utilisation. Heuristics H1, H2 and H3 performed well in case of low variance in machine utilisation. Heuristic H4 performed well in case of high variance in machine utilisation. Also, Heuristics H1, H2 and H3 gave good results in high variance of machine utilisation on some criteria. Heuristic H4 did not perform well in case of low variance in machine utilisation.

Scope for Future Work

Some related areas where work can be done are as follows:

1. In many cases the variability in improvement is high, which implies that these rules do not perform well on all the product structures. Hence, one needs to develop a framework which suggests a matching rule to a given product structure. This research has gathered sufficient evidence to show such a framework is possible.
2. In actual practice, the lead time of different assemblies is different.A study can be done on all these heuristics when the lead time of all the child assemblies is not same.
3. The Heuristics H1, H2, H3, H4 and H5 can be combined one by one and the comparative study can be done among all heuristics.

Table 10.1.A Result of Problem 1

High Variance in Machine Utilisation						
	Original	H1	H2	H3	H4	H5
Total unit lateness	2.58891E+10	2.46395E+10	2.57808E+10	2.56179E+10	2.58891E+10	2.57672E+10
Total aggregate lateness	5.21038E+12	4.73452E+12	5.83796E+12	5.32545E+12	5.01198E+12	5.30730E+12
Total set-up cost	3.59490E+05	3.59490E+05	3.59490E+05	4.69707E+06	3.59490E+05	3.59490E+05
Total inventory cost	1.51766E+08	1.27577E+09	2.95917E+08	1.34530E+09	2.50259E+08	1.51767E+08
Theoretical inventory cost	5.38247E+07	5.38247E+07	5.38247E+07	5.38247E+07	5.38247E+07	5.38247E+07
Machine utilisation	4.20000E-01	4.40000E-01	4.20000E-01	4.20000E-01	4.20000E-01	4.20000E-01
Co-ordination range	6.70000E+07	4.30000E+07	7.40000E+07	6.70000E+07	4.80000E+07	6.70000E+07

Low Variance in Machine Utilisation						
	Original	H1	H2	H3	H4	H5
Total unit lateness	8.10759E+09	8.06728E+09	7.40089E+09	8.10759E+09	8.03374E+09	7.93157E+09
Total aggregate lateness	1.69367E+12	1.52023E+12	1.53398E+12	1.69031E+12	1.68002E+12	1.52932E+12
Total set-up cost	3.59490E+05	3.59490E+05	3.59490E+05	4.69707E+06	3.59490E+05	3.59490E+05
Total inventory cost	2.00391E+08	1.84267E+08	1.10924E+08	2.00387E+09	1.43442E+08	1.99463E+08
Theoretical inventory cost	5.38247E+07	5.38247E+07	5.38247E+07	5.38247E+07	5.38247E+07	5.38247E+07
Machine utilisation	5.90000E-01	5.90000E-01	6.40000E-01	5.90000E-01	5.90000E-01	6.00000E-01
Co-ordination range	1.70000E+07	2.20000E+07	1.70000E+07	1.70000E+07	1.70000E+07	1.70000E+07

Table 10.1.B Result of Problem 2

High Variance in Machine Utilisation						
	Original	H1	H2	H3	H4	H5
Total unit lateness	1.19417E+10	1.19417E+10	1.23873E+10	1.09588E+10	1.17029E+10	1.18198E+10
Total aggregate lateness	2.73120E+12	2.73120E+12	2.58650E+12	2.38516E+12	2.65875E+12	2.63440E+12
Total set-up cost	2.96225E+05	2.96225E+05	2.96225E+05	4.38962E+06	2.96225E+05	2.96225E+05
Total inventory cost	2.69819E+08	2.69819E+08	1.40932E+08	1.54588E+09	7.48968E+07	2.69381E+08
Theoretical inventory cost	2.62328E+07	2.62328E+07	2.62328E+07	2.63553E+07	2.62328E+07	2.62328E+07
Machine utilisation	5.70000E-01	5.70000E-01	5.50000E-01	5.90000E-01	5.80000E-01	5.80000E-01
Co-ordination range	3.30000E+07	3.30000E+07	3.90000E+07	3.20000E+07	3.30000E+07	3.30000E+07

Low Variance in Machine Utilisation						
	Original	H1	H2	H3	H 4	H5
Total unit lateness	8.89559E+09	8.43292E+09	7.79019E+09	8.74994E+09	8.61166E+09	8.35043E+09
Total aggregate lateness	1.71959E+12	1.48392E+12	1.43417E+12	1.67824E+12	1.69366E+12	1.50427E+12
Total set-up cost	2.96225E+05	2.96225E+05	2.96225E+05	4.38962E+06	2.96225E+05	2.96225E+05
Total inventory cost	4.95036E+08	3.05018E+08	1.59414E+08	4.93212E+09	4.19860E+08	4.29398E+08
Theoretical inventory cost	2.62328E+07	2.62328E+07	2.62328E+07	2.63553E+07	2.62328E+07	2.62328E+07
Machine utilisation	6.40000E-01	6.80000E-01	7.30000E-01	6.50000E-01	6.60000E-01	6.80000E-01
Co-ordination range	2.00000E+07	2.20000E+07	2.10000E+07	2.00000E+07	2.00000E+07	1.90000E+07

Table 10.1.C Result of Problem 3

High Variance in Machine Utilisation						
	Original	H1	H2	H3	H4	H5
Total unit lateness	7.54419E+09	7.35463E+09	7.52386E+09	7.54419E+09	7.25979E+09	7.21923E+09
Total aggregate lateness	8.25355E+11	7.83247E+11	7.75896E+11	8.25355E+11	7.90070E+11	7.72699E+11
Total set-up cost	2.28367E+05	2.28367E+05	2.28367E+05	1.23585E+06	2.28367E+05	2.28367E+05
Total inventory cost	1.43875E+08	1.75249E+08	5.65182E+07	1.43875E+09	6.88406E+07	1.46102E+08
Theoretical inventory cost	6.91525E+06	6.91525E+06	6.91525E+06	6.91525E+06	6.91525E+06	6.91525E+06
Machine utilisation	4.50000E-01	4.60000E-01	4.50000E-01	4.50000E-01	4.60000E-01	4.70000E-01
Co-ordination range	2.40000E+07	2.30000E+07	2.40000E+07	2.40000E+07	2.00000E+07	2.20000E+07

Low Variance in Machine Utilisation						
	Original	H1	H2	H3	H4	H5
Total Unit Lateness	5.40448E+09	5.27587E+09	4.47018E+09	5.40448E+09	5.57754E+09	4.71358E+09
Total aggregate lateness	5.40633E+11	4.73482E+11	4.13782E+11	5.40633E+11	5.46559E+11	4.19150E+11
Total set-up cost	2.38602E+05	2.38602E+05	2.38602E+05	1.23325E+06	2.38602E+05	2.38602E+05
Total inventory cost	1.66497E+06	1.24822E+06	9.77092E+06	1.66497E+07	1.44217E+06	2.07428E+06
Theoretical inventory cost	7.71275E+06	7.71275E+06	7.71275E+06	7.71275E+06	7.71275E+06	7.71275E+06
Machine utilisation	5.10000E-01	5.30000E-01	6.20000E-01	5.10000E-01	5.00000E-01	5.90000E-01
Co-ordination range	1.40000E+07	1.20000E+07	1.20000E+07	1.40000E+07	1.30000E+07	1.20000E+07

Table 10.1.D Result of Problem 4

High Variance in Machine Utilisation						
	Original	H1	H2	H3	H4	H5
Total Unit Lateness	5.79715E+09	5.79715E+09	5.79715E+09	5.97305E+09	5.79715E+09	5.64821E+09
Total aggregate lateness	8.56052E+11	8.56052E+11	7.62498E+11	8.35429E+11	7.94904E+11	8.17676E+11
Total set-up cost	3.38537E+05	3.38537E+05	3.38537E+05	6.63216E+06	3.38537E+05	3.38537E+05
Total inventory cost	7.85585E+05	7.85585E+05	5.41771E+06	1.97709E+06	5.93305E+05	2.46950E+06
Theoretical inventory cost	7.14800E+06	7.14800E+06	7.14800E+06	7.58900E+06	7.14800E+06	7.14800E+06
Machine utilisation	6.80000E-01	6.80000E-01	6.80000E-01	6.60000E-01	6.80000E-01	6.90000E-01
Co-ordination range	1.40000E+07	1.40000E+07	1.60000E+07	1.60000E+07	1.40000E+07	1.40000E+07

Low Variance in Machine Utilisation						
	Original	H1	H2	H3	H4	H5
Total Unit Lateness	4.98468E+09	4.98468E+09	4.74701E+09	4.88991E+09	5.18868E+09	4.43661E+09
Total aggregate lateness	7.36088E+11	7.36088E+11	6.62107E+11	7.13152E+11	7.20450E+11	6.05872E+11
Total set-up cost	3.38537E+05	3.38537E+05	3.38537E+05	4.16964E+06	3.38537E+05	3.38537E+05
Total inventory cost	2.97860E+07	2.97860E+07	1.50095E+07	2.38083E+08	3.31427E+07	1.84218E+07
Theoretical inventory cost	7.14800E+06	7.14800E+06	7.14800E+06	7.23375E+06	7.14800E+06	7.14800E+06
Machine utilisation	7.40000E-01	7.40000E-01	7.80000E-01	7.50000E-01	7.20000E-01	8.40000E-01
Co-ordination range	1.40000E+07	1.40000E+07	1.30000E+07	1.40000E+07	1.30000E+07	1.30000E+07

Table 10.1.E Result of Problem 5

High Variance in Machine Utilisation						
	Original	H1	H2	H3	H4	H5
Total Unit Lateness	7.16534E+09	7.10426E+09	7.04344E+09	5.85101E+09	7.16531E+09	6.93514E+09
Total aggregate lateness	9.68978E+11	9.18476E+11	9.15736E+11	7.45031E+11	9.26182E+11	8.99410E+11
Total set-up cost	2.96700E+05	2.96700E+05	2.96700E+05	4.23957E+06	2.96700E+05	2.96700E+05
Total inventory cost	2.97342E+06	1.52739E+08	3.61332E+07	2.37739E+07	2.87380E+06	2.97342E+06
Theoretical inventory cost	6.28315E+06	6.28315E+06	6.28315E+06	6.64330E+06	6.28315E+06	6.28315E+06
Machine Utilisation	5.60000E-01	5.60000E-01	5.60000E-01	5.90000E-01	5.60000E-01	5.70000E-01
Co-ordination range	1.70000E+07	2.10000E+07	1.90000E+07	1.40000E+07	1.60000E+07	1.60000E+07

Low Variance in Machine Utilisation						
	Original	H1	H2	H3	H4	H5
Total Unit Lateness	3.72568E+09	3.72568E+09	3.39355E+09	3.27125E+09	3.73905E+09	3.34640E+09
Total aggregate lateness	6.05749E+11	6.05749E+11	4.98458E+11	5.23969E+11	5.84126E+11	4.82547E+11
Total set-up cost	2.96700E+05	2.96700E+05	2.96700E+05	4.23957E+06	2.96700E+05	2.96700E+05
Total inventory cost	1.21366E+07	1.21366E+07	5.30378E+06	4.85435E+07	2.97049E+06	5.10666E+06
Theoretical inventory cost	6.28315E+06	6.28315E+06	6.28315E+06	6.64330E+06	6.28315E+06	6.28315E+06
Machine utilisation	7.60000E-01	7.60000E-01	8.30000E-01	7.90000E-01	7.60000E-01	8.50000E-01
Co-ordination range	1.00000E+07	1.00000E+07	9.80000E+06	9.20000E+06	1.00000E+07	8.90000E+06

Table 10.1.F Result of Problem 6

High Variance in Machine Utilisation						
	Original	H1	H2	H3	H4	H5
Total Unit Lateness	3.86745E+09	3.77252E+09	3.68439E+09	3.40658E+09	3.88106E+09	3.70494E+09
Total aggregate lateness	6.09373E+11	5.31657E+11	5.38481E+11	5.11693E+11	6.10859E+11	5.03204E+11
Total set-up cost	3.81320E+05	3.81320E+05	3.81320E+05	6.55884E+06	3.81320E+05	3.81320E+05
Total inventory cost	2.67365E+06	8.81092E+06	6.53831E+06	1.48186E+07	2.47450E+06	1.88123E+06
Theoretical inventory cost	7.93690E+06	7.93690E+06	7.93690E+06	8.35830E+06	7.93690E+06	7.93690E+06
Machine utilisation	6.30000E-01	6.50000E-01	6.70000E-01	6.60000E-01	6.30000E-01	6.40000E-01
Co-ordination range	1.00000E+07	1.10000E+07	9.60000E+06	8.50000E+06	1.00000E+07	9.50000E+06

Low Variance in Machine Utilisation						
	Original	H1	H2	H3	H4	H5
Total Unit Lateness	3.43470E+09	3.36627E+09	3.40703E+09	3.31870E+09	3.60422E+09	2.76355E+09
Total aggregate lateness	5.26323E+11	4.76824E+11	4.75970E+11	4.80751E+11	5.44626E+11	3.56490E+11
Total set-up cost	3.81320E+05	3.81320E+05	3.81320E+05	6.55884E+06	3.81320E+05	3.81320E+05
Total inventory cost	7.71847E+06	3.17726E+07	2.93486E+07	1.43493E+08	5.43891E+06	1.03835E+07
Theoretical inventory cost	7.93690E+06	7.93690E+06	7.93690E+06	8.35830E+06	7.93690E+06	7.93690E+06
Machine utilisation	6.80000E-01	6.90000E-01	6.90000E-01	6.40000E-01	6.50000E-01	8.20000E-01
Co-ordination range	9.10000E+06	9.70000E+06	8.50000E+06	7.60000E+06	9.60000E+06	6.60000E+06

Table 10.1.G Result of Problem 7

High Variance in Machine Utilisation						
	Original	H1	H2	H3	H4	H5
Total Unit Lateness	8.62654E+08	8.38318E+08	8.53846E+08	8.62654E+08	9.68850E+08	5.85026E+08
Total aggregate lateness	1.11383E+11	9.56178E+10	9.57989E+10	1.11383E+11	1.17611E+11	4.78185E+10
Total set-up cost	1.00855E+05	1.00855E+05	1.00855E+05	1.44667E+06	1.00855E+05	1.00855E+05
Total inventory cost	1.40837E+07	8.75878E+06	2.94823E+06	1.40800E+08	1.40099E+07	6.70732E+06
Theoretical inventory cost	1.40755E+07	1.40755E+07	1.40755E+07	1.40755E+07	1.40755E+07	1.40755E+07
Machine Utilisation	5.60000E-01	5.80000E-01	5.70000E-01	5.60000E-01	5.00000E-01	8.30000E-01
Co-ordination range	2.10000E+06	2.10000E+06	1.90000E+06	2.10000E+06	2.30000E+06	1.60000E+06

Low Variance in Machine Utilisation						
	Original	H1	H2	H3	H4	H5
Total Unit Lateness	7.26563E+08	6.86393E+08	7.02884E+08	7.26563E+08	7.53687E+08	5.08625E+08
Total aggregate lateness	1.06323E+11	8.67462E+10	9.03574E+10	1.06323E+11	1.08269E+11	2.84801E+10
Total set-up cost	1.00855E+05	1.00855E+05	1.00855E+05	1.44667E+06	1.00855E+05	1.00855E+05
Total inventory cost	1.23147E+07	2.83547E+06	1.14834E+07	1.23200E+08	1.30219E+07	1.09691E+07
Theoretical inventory cost	1.40755E+07	1.40755E+07	1.40755E+07	1.40755E+07	1.40755E+07	1.40755E+07
Machine Utilisation	6.30000E-01	6.70000E-01	6.50000E-01	6.30000E-01	6.10000E-01	9.00000E-01
Co-ordination range	1.90000E+06	1.90000E+06	1.80000E+06	1.90000E+06	1.90000E+06	1.30000E+06

Table 10.1.H Result of Problem 8

High Variance in Machine Utilisation						
	Original	**H1**	**H2**	**H3**	**H4**	**H5**
Total Unit Lateness	7.88644E+08	7.88644E+08	7.29254E+08	7.88644E+08	7.37340E+08	5.93866E+08
Total aggregate lateness	1.15193E+11	1.15193E+11	9.99647E+10	1.15317E+11	1.05089E+11	5.96918E+10
Total set-up cost	1.18450E+05	1.18450E+05	1.18450E+05	3.74047E+06	1.18450E+05	1.18450E+05
Total inventory cost	2.01301E+06	2.01301E+06	6.19776E+05	1.73624E+07	4.38761E+05	1.63748E+06
Theoretical inventory cost	1.54818E+07	1.54818E+07	1.54818E+07	1.54818E+07	1.54818E+07	1.54818E+07
Machine utilisation	5.80000E-01	5.80000E-01	6.30000E-01	5.80000E-01	6.20000E-01	7.70000E-01
Co-ordination range	2.00000E+06	2.00000E+06	1.90000E+06	2.00000E+06	1.90000E+06	1.50000E+06

Low Variance in Machine Utilisation						
	Original	**H1**	**H2**	**H3**	**H4**	**H5**
Total Unit Lateness	8.35412E+08	8.35412E+08	7.23196E+08	8.35412E+08	7.26946E+08	5.88607E+08
Total aggregate lateness	1.17579E+11	1.17579E+11	9.77502E+10	1.17708E+11	1.05325E+11	6.02049E+10
Total set-up cost	1.18450E+05	1.18450E+05	1.18450E+05	3.74047E+06	1.18450E+05	1.18450E+05
Total inventory cost	1.16605E+06	1.16605E+06	2.21738E+06	8.09163E+06	2.98068E+06	4.18317E+05
Theoretical inventory cost	1.54818E+07	1.54818E+07	1.54818E+07	1.54818E+07	1.54818E+07	1.54818E+07
Machine utilisation	5.90000E-01	5.90000E-01	6.90000E-01	5.90000E-01	6.80000E-01	8.40000E-01
Co-ordination range	2.00000E+06	2.00000E+06	1.90000E+06	2.00000E+06	1.80000E+06	1.50000E+06

Table 10.1.I Result of Problem 9

High Variance in Machine Utilisation						
	Original	H1	H2	H3	H4	H5
Total Unit Lateness	4.71563E+09	4.71563E+09	4.71563E+09	4.57903E+09	4.71563E+09	4.56668E+09
Total aggregate lateness	6.89071E+11	6.89071E+11	6.25254E+11	5.65968E+11	6.91260E+11	5.98053E+11
Total set-up cost	3.27750E+05	3.27750E+05	3.27750E+05	8.02866E+06	3.27750E+05	3.27750E+05
Total inventory cost	4.66543E+06	4.66543E+06	3.21490E+05	5.10285E+07	3.49987E+06	4.66543E+06
Theoretical inventory cost	9.77575E+06	9.77575E+06	9.77575E+06	1.08660E+07	9.77575E+06	9.77575E+06
Machine utilisation	4.30000E-01	4.30000E-01	4.30000E-01	3.90000E-01	4.30000E-01	4.40000E-01
Co-ordination range	1.10000E+07	1.10000E+07	1.00000E+07	1.00000E+07	1.10000E+07	1.10000E+07

Low Variance in Machine Utilisation						
	Original	H1	H2	H3	H4	H5
Total Unit Lateness	1.57224E+09	1.50238E+09	1.55733E+09	1.43143E+09	1.55120E+09	1.35626E+09
Total aggregate lateness	2.67698E+11	2.27707E+11	2.38711E+11	2.24068E+11	2.69809E+11	1.80819E+11
Total set-up cost	3.27750E+05	3.27750E+05	3.27750E+05	8.02866E+06	3.27750E+05	3.27750E+05
Total inventory cost	5.71025E+06	6.84165E+06	6.67319E+06	6.82672E+07	1.04603E+07	1.31258E+07
Theoretical inventory cost	9.77575E+06	9.77575E+06	9.77575E+06	1.08660E+07	9.77575E+06	9.77575E+06
Machine utilisation	7.60000E-01	8.00000E-01	7.70000E-01	7.10000E-01	7.70000E-01	8.80000E-01
Co-ordination range	3.40000E+06	3.80000E+06	4.10000E+06	3.20000E+06	3.60000E+06	3.30000E+06

Table 10.1.J Result of Problem 10

High Variance in Machine Utilisation						
	Original	H1	H2	H3	H4	H5
Total Unit Lateness	1.53034E+10	1.21207E+10	1.32988E+10	1.47887E+10	1.28926E+10	1.45586E+10
Total aggregate lateness	1.92847E+12	1.62224E+12	1.73170E+12	1.84912E+12	1.71044E+12	1.84774E+12
Total set-up cost	4.79780E+05	4.79780E+05	4.79780E+05	8.59808E+06	4.79780E+05	4.79780E+05
Total inventory cost	9.36022E+08	9.29845E+07	3.17126E+08	7.73637E+09	2.54197E+08	6.27004E+08
Theoretical inventory cost	2.22710E+07	2.22710E+07	2.22710E+07	2.23813E+07	2.22710E+07	2.22710E+07
Machine utilisation	4.50000E-01	5.70000E-01	5.20000E-01	4.50000E-01	5.40000E-01	4.70000E-01
Co-ordination range	3.20000E+07	3.20000E+07	3.30000E+07	3.20000E+07	2.70000E+07	3.20000E+07

Low Variance in Machine Utilisation						
	Original	H1	H2	H3	H4	H5
Total Unit Lateness	7.13786E+09	7.13786E+09	7.98550E+09	7.63896E+09	7.22578E+09	6.85356E+09
Total aggregate lateness	1.22740E+12	1.22740E+12	1.13615E+12	1.24036E+12	1.20010E+12	1.14002E+12
Total set-up cost	4.79780E+05	4.79780E+05	4.79780E+05	8.59808E+06	4.79780E+05	4.79780E+05
Total inventory cost	1.37279E+08	1.37279E+08	1.86037E+08	1.35644E+09	1.79165E+08	1.59250E+08
Theoretical inventory cost	2.22710E+07	2.22710E+07	2.22710E+07	2.23813E+07	2.22710E+07	2.22710E+07
Machine utilisation	7.60000E-01	7.60000E-01	6.80000E-01	7.10000E-01	7.50000E-01	7.90000E-01
Co-ordination range	1.80000E+07	1.80000E+07	2.00000E+07	2.00000E+07	1.90000E+07	1.80000E+07

Table 10.1.K Result of Problem 11

High Variance in Machine Utilisation						
	Original	H1	H2	H3	H4	H5
Total Unit Lateness	7.15753E+09	7.15753E+09	6.57513E+09	7.15742E+09	7.15753E+09	7.06275E+09
Total aggregate lateness	9.80881E+11	9.80881E+11	8.46691E+11	9.55862E+11	9.88187E+11	9.32990E+11
Total set-up cost	3.61100E+05	3.61100E+05	3.61100E+05	5.21157E+06	3.61100E+05	3.61100E+05
Total inventory cost	8.00584E+07	8.00584E+07	3.67466E+07	1.04755E+09	7.69935E+07	8.00584E+07
Theoretical inventory cost	2.64115E+07	2.64115E+07	2.64115E+07	2.64115E+07	2.64115E+07	2.64115E+07
Machine utilisation	5.00000E-01	5.00000E-01	5.40000E-01	5.00000E-01	5.00000E-01	5.10000E-01
Co-ordination range	2.40000E+07	2.40000E+07	1.50000E+07	2.40000E+07	2.40000E+07	2.30000E+07

Low Variance in Machine Utilisation						
	Original	H1	H2	H3	H4	H5
Total Unit Lateness	4.98099E+09	4.66930E+09	4.92123E+09	4.98097E+09	4.96386E+09	4.27331E+09
Total aggregate lateness	6.99124E+11	6.22782E+11	6.27815E+11	6.98555E+11	7.09603E+11	6.45992E+11
Total set-up cost	3.61100E+05	3.61100E+05	3.61100E+05	5.21157E+06	3.61100E+05	3.61100E+05
Total inventory cost	1.29773E+07	2.00790E+07	1.22577E+07	1.29776E+08	3.20687E+07	2.38480E+07
Theoretical inventory cost	2.64115E+07	2.64115E+07	2.64115E+07	2.64115E+07	2.64115E+07	2.64115E+07
Machine utilisation	6.80000E-01	7.30000E-01	6.90000E-01	6.80000E-01	6.80000E-01	8.00000E-01
Co-ordination range	1.50000E+07	1.50000E+07	1.50000E+07	1.50000E+07	1.50000E+07	1.20000E+07

Table 10.1.L Result of Problem 12

High Variance in Machine Utilisation						
	Original	H1	H2	H3	H4	H5
Total Unit Lateness	4.71025E+09	4.71025E+09	4.41581E+09	4.71025E+09	4.41581E+09	4.36756E+09
Total aggregate lateness	5.71859E+11	5.71859E+11	4.91378E+11	5.71859E+11	5.49150E+11	5.13850E+11
Total set-up cost	1.08905E+05	1.08905E+05	1.08905E+05	1.95704E+06	1.08905E+05	1.08905E+05
Total inventory cost	5.20590E+07	5.20590E+07	2.27800E+08	5.20590E+08	2.23604E+08	4.29979E+07
Theoretical inventory cost	2.19035E+07	2.19035E+07	2.19035E+07	2.19035E+07	2.19035E+07	2.19035E+07
Machine utilisation	4.90000E-01	4.90000E-01	5.20000E-01	4.90000E-01	5.20000E-01	5.30000E-01
Co-ordination range	1.30000E+07	1.30000E+07	8.60000E+06	1.30000E+07	9.60000E+06	1.20000E+07

Low Variance in Machine Utilisation						
	Original	H1	H2	H3	H4	H5
Total Unit Lateness	2.75723E+09	2.75723E+09	2.80803E+09	2.75723E+09	3.02184E+09	2.39333E+09
Total aggregate lateness	4.18483E+11	4.18483E+11	3.88295E+11	4.18483E+11	4.47490E+11	3.32466E+11
Total set-up cost	1.08905E+05	1.08905E+05	1.08905E+05	1.95704E+06	1.08905E+05	1.08905E+05
Total inventory cost	1.37128E+07	1.37128E+07	1.01199E+07	1.37128E+08	2.44510E+07	7.50128E+06
Theoretical inventory cost	2.19035E+07	2.19035E+07	2.19035E+07	2.19035E+07	2.19035E+07	2.19035E+07
Machine utilisation	6.60000E-01	6.60000E-01	6.40000E-01	6.60000E-01	6.00000E-01	7.50000E-01
Co-ordination range	7.40000E+06	7.40000E+06	7.60000E+06	7.40000E+06	7.20000E+06	6.80000E+06

Table 10.1.M Result of Problem 13

High Variance in Machine Utilisation						
	Original	H1	H2	H3	H4	H5
Total Unit Lateness	5.24412E+09	4.25486E+09	4.35040E+09	5.24412E+09	4.31012E+09	4.59502E+09
Total aggregate lateness	6.65957E+11	5.07479E+11	5.14633E+11	6.65957E+11	5.49441E+11	5.54592E+11
Total set-up cost	1.36160E+05	1.36160E+05	1.36160E+05	1.48996E+06	1.36160E+05	1.36160E+05
Total inventory cost	8.69322E+07	1.88085E+07	4.95838E+07	8.69322E+08	4.06641E+07	1.15392E+08
Theoretical inventory cost	1.18215E+07	1.18215E+07	1.18215E+07	1.18215E+07	1.18215E+07	1.18215E+07
Machine utilisation	5.00000E-01	7.20000E-01	7.10000E-01	5.00000E-01	7.10000E-01	6.70000E-01
Co-ordination range	1.40000E+07	1.30000E+07	1.20000E+07	1.40000E+07	1.00000E+07	1.10000E+07

Low Variance in Machine Utilisation						
	Original	H1	H2	H3	H4	H5
Total Unit Lateness	5.94493E+09	5.80346E+09	4.91720E+09	5.94493E+09	6.13529E+09	5.18494E+09
Total aggregate lateness	7.76028E+11	6.91288E+11	7.77028E+11	7.75396E+11	7.27040E+11	7.17051E+11
Total set-up cost	4.79780E+05	4.79780E+05	4.79780E+05	8.59808E+06	4.79780E+05	4.79780E+05
Total inventory cost	1.33503E+07	1.33503E+07	9.83416E+06	5.33979E+07	1.16754E+07	8.61733E+06
Theoretical inventory cost	7.71275E+06	7.71275E+06	7.71275E+06	7.71275E+06	7.71275E+06	7.71275E+06
Machine utilisation	5.20000E-01	5.20000E-01	5.30000E-01	5.00000E-01	5.30000E-01	5.30000E-01
Co-ordination range	1.70000E+07	1.70000E+07	1.40000E+07	1.30000E+07	1.20000E+07	1.30000E+07

Table 10.1.N Result of Problem 14

High Variance in Machine Utilisation						
	Original	**H1**	**H2**	**H3**	**H4**	**H5**
Total Unit Lateness	2.74046E+09	1.62113E+09	1.70207E+09	2.46239E+09	2.74448E+09	2.27664E+09
Total aggregate lateness	3.89137E+11	2.21316E+11	2.28763E+11	3.27885E+11	3.89626E+11	2.72667E+11
Total set-up cost	2.37545E+05	2.37545E+05	2.37545E+05	5.88518E+06	2.37545E+05	2.37545E+05
Total inventory cost	2.77558E+07	3.08900E+07	2.56025E+06	1.22369E+08	5.91609E+07	1.30802E+07
Theoretical inventory cost	1.12360E+07	1.12360E+07	1.12360E+07	1.23581E+07	1.12360E+07	1.12360E+07
Machine utilisation	6.10000E-01	7.80000E-01	7.50000E-01	6.00000E-01	6.00000E-01	6.90000E-01
Co-ordination range	5.80000E+06	2.60000E+06	4.30000E+06	5.50000E+06	5.50000E+06	4.80000E+06

Low Variance in Machine Utilisation						
	Original	**H1**	**H2**	**H3**	**H4**	**H5**
Total Unit Lateness	3.12302E+09	2.35243E+09	2.45195E+09	2.81447E+09	3.06955E+09	2.82173E+09
Total aggregate lateness	4.58519E+11	2.84172E+11	3.58951E+11	3.90676E+11	4.54896E+11	3.52696E+11
Total set-up cost	2.37545E+05	2.37545E+05	2.37545E+05	5.88518E+06	2.37545E+05	2.37545E+05
Total inventory cost	2.41762E+07	3.19000E+07	7.68721E+06	9.57240E+07	3.57885E+07	2.41762E+07
Theoretical inventory cost	1.12360E+07	1.12360E+07	1.12360E+07	1.23581E+07	1.12360E+07	1.12360E+07
Machine utilisation	6.40000E-01	6.70000E-01	7.30000E-01	6.50000E-01	6.50000E-01	6.90000E-01
Co-ordination range	6.70000E+06	2.90000E+06	6.90000E+06	6.00000E+06	6.10000E+06	6.10000E+06

Table 10.1. O Result of Problem 15

High Variance in Machine Utilisation						
	Original	H1	H2	H3	H4	H5
Total Unit Lateness	5.98567E+09	5.91807E+09	6.29729E+09	6.01257E+09	5.91807E+09	6.13348E+09
Total aggregate lateness	8.50749E+11	7.94999E+11	8.26446E+11	8.50594E+11	8.39467E+11	7.98799E+11
Total set-up cost	2.19880E+05	2.19880E+05	2.19880E+05	3.57725E+06	2.19880E+05	2.19880E+05
Total inventory cost	8.49197E+06	2.16386E+08	7.73390E+07	8.38564E+07	1.64369E+08	9.59948E+06
Theoretical inventory cost	1.21155E+07	1.21155E+07	1.21155E+07	1.23605E+07	1.21155E+07	1.21155E+07
Machine utilisation	6.10000E-01	6.20000E-01	5.80000E-01	6.10000E-01	6.20000E-01	6.00000E-01
Co-ordination range	1.70000E+07	1.70000E+07	2.00000E+07	1.70000E+07	1.50000E+07	1.70000E+07

Low Variance in Machine Utilisation						
	Original	H1	H2	H3	H4	H5
Total Unit Lateness	4.22440E+09	4.22440E+09	4.45422E+09	4.22423E+09	4.11615E+09	4.15659E+09
Total aggregate lateness	7.06510E+11	7.06510E+11	6.45823E+11	7.02922E+11	6.96421E+11	6.38611E+11
Total set-up cost	2.19880E+05	2.19880E+05	2.19880E+05	3.57725E+06	2.19880E+05	2.19880E+05
Total inventory cost	6.17192E+06	6.17192E+06	3.14371E+07	2.14955E+07	1.25285E+07	5.63464E+05
Theoretical inventory cost	1.21155E+07	1.21155E+07	1.21155E+07	1.23605E+07	1.21155E+07	1.21155E+07
Machine utilisation	8.60000E-01	8.60000E-01	8.20000E-01	8.60000E-01	8.80000E-01	8.80000E-01
Co-ordination range	1.20000E+07	1.20000E+07	1.40000E+07	1.20000E+07	1.20000E+07	1.10000E+07

Table 10.1.P Result of Problem 16

High Variance in Machine Utilisation						
	Original	H1	H2	H3	H4	H5
Total Unit Lateness	7.74694E+09	7.74694E+09	7.55736E+09	6.08109E+09	7.63858E+09	7.40841E+09
Total aggregate lateness	1.40272E+12	1.40272E+12	1.27632E+12	9.53397E+11	1.41987E+12	1.25403E+12
Total set-up cost	3.71212E+05	3.71212E+05	3.71212E+05	8.30139E+06	3.71212E+05	3.71212E+05
Total inventory cost	3.86627E+06	3.86627E+06	2.61743E+06	2.48595E+07	2.54536E+07	4.26740E+06
Theoretical inventory cost	7.73355E+06	7.73355E+06	7.73355E+06	8.55920E+06	7.73355E+06	7.73355E+06
Machine utilisation	6.30000E-01	6.30000E-01	6.40000E-01	6.20000E-01	6.40000E-01	6.60000E-01
Co-ordination range	1.90000E+07	1.90000E+07	2.00000E+07	1.60000E+07	1.90000E+07	1.80000E+07

Low Variance in Machine Utilisation						
	Original	H1	H2	H3	H4	H5
Total Unit Lateness	6.08193E+09	6.08193E+09	5.98749E+09	4.91639E+09	6.14992E+09	5.64816E+09
Total aggregate lateness	1.10201E+12	1.10201E+12	1.00184E+12	7.27770E+11	1.12694E+12	9.57579E+11
Total set-up cost	3.71212E+05	3.71212E+05	3.71212E+05	8.30139E+06	3.71212E+05	3.71212E+05
Total inventory cost	2.31714E+07	2.31714E+07	1.14363E+07	1.04953E+08	2.49590E+07	4.78146E+07
Theoretical inventory cost	7.73355E+06	7.73355E+06	7.73355E+06	8.55920E+06	7.73355E+06	7.73355E+06
Machine utilisation	7.60000E-01	7.60000E-01	7.70000E-01	6.90000E-01	7.50000E-01	8.20000E-01
Co-ordination range	1.60000E+07	1.60000E+07	1.60000E+07	1.30000E+07	1.60000E+07	1.50000E+07

Table 10.1.Q Result of Problem 17

High Variance in Machine Utilisation						
	Original	H1	H2	H3	H4	H5
Total Unit Lateness	6.40113E+09	6.32654E+09	6.38756E+09	6.40113E+09	6.41469E+09	6.61801E+09
Total aggregate lateness	9.86121E+11	8.72365E+11	9.44346E+11	9.86121E+11	1.01220E+12	9.46147E+11
Total set-up cost	1.40530E+05	1.40530E+05	1.40530E+05	2.38270E+06	1.40530E+05	1.40530E+05
Total inventory cost	6.27050E+06	7.58220E+06	4.84319E+06	6.27046E+07	7.78839E+06	8.27668E+06
Theoretical inventory cost	1.31004E+07	1.31004E+07	1.31004E+07	1.31004E+07	1.31004E+07	1.31004E+07
Machine utilisation	5.10000E-01	5.10000E-01	5.10000E-01	5.10000E-01	5.10000E-01	4.90000E-01
Co-ordination range	2.00000E+07	2.10000E+07	2.00000E+07	2.00000E+07	2.00000E+07	2.10000E+07

Low Variance in Machine Utilisation						
	Original	H1	H2	H3	H4	H5
Total Unit Lateness	3.63780E+09	3.63780E+09	3.90877E+09	3.63780E+09	3.85557E+09	3.67280E+09
Total aggregate lateness	5.63989E+11	5.63989E+11	5.42493E+11	5.63989E+11	5.86763E+11	5.15174E+11
Total set-up cost	1.52260E+05	1.52260E+05	1.52260E+05	2.70457E+06	1.52260E+05	1.52260E+05
Total inventory cost	2.37807E+07	2.37807E+07	2.65814E+07	2.37807E+08	8.24853E+07	1.26064E+07
Theoretical inventory cost	1.31004E+07	1.31004E+07	1.31004E+07	1.31004E+07	1.31004E+07	1.31004E+07
Machine utilisation	7.00000E-01	7.00000E-01	6.50000E-01	7.00000E-01	6.60000E-01	6.90000E-01
Co-ordination range	9.10000E+06	9.10000E+06	1.10000E+07	9.10000E+06	1.00000E+07	1.10000E+07

Table 10.1.R Result of Problem 18

High Variance in Machine Utilisation						
	Original	H1	H2	H3	H4	H5
Total Unit Lateness	4.03411E+09	3.80048E+09	3.55984E+09	3.69532E+09	3.63776E+09	3.66850E+09
Total aggregate lateness	4.79571E+11	4.38603E+11	4.07725E+11	4.49819E+11	4.44678E+11	4.26794E+11
Total set-up cost	9.23450E+04	9.23450E+04	9.23450E+04	1.04253E+06	9.23450E+04	9.23450E+04
Total inventory cost	4.70603E+06	2.65817E+06	3.93026E+06	4.48903E+07	1.99458E+07	4.10961E+06
Theoretical inventory cost	1.13438E+07	1.13438E+07	1.13438E+07	1.13438E+07	1.13438E+07	1.13438E+07
Machine Utilisation	4.60000E-01	4.90000E-01	5.20000E-01	5.00000E-01	5.10000E-01	5.10000E-01
Co-ordination range	1.10000E+07	1.20000E+07	1.00000E+07	1.00000E+07	1.00000E+07	1.00000E+07

Low Variance in Machine Utilisation						
	Original	H1	H2	H3	H4	H5
Total Unit Lateness	3.78700E+09	3.30920E+09	3.48911E+09	3.81397E+09	3.75653E+09	3.50264E+09
Total aggregate lateness	4.71524E+11	4.14956E+11	4.05387E+11	4.76048E+11	4.70930E+11	4.01497E+11
Total set-up cost	9.23450E+04	9.23450E+04	9.23450E+04	1.04253E+06	9.23450E+04	9.23450E+04
Total inventory cost	2.08098E+07	8.34043E+06	1.10909E+07	2.08098E+08	3.64687E+07	2.08098E+07
Theoretical inventory cost	1.13438E+07	1.13438E+07	1.13438E+07	1.13438E+07	1.13438E+07	1.13438E+07
Machine Utilisation	5.40000E-01	6.20000E-01	5.90000E-01	5.40000E-01	5.50000E-01	5.90000E-01
Co-ordination range	1.00000E+07	9.80000E+06	9.70000E+06	9.90000E+06	9.90000E+06	9.30000E+06

Table 10.1.S Result of Problem 19

High Variance in Machine Utilisation						
	Original	H1	H2	H3	H4	H5
Total unit lateness	4.74E+09	4.74E+09	4.74E+09	4.29597E-09	4.74E+09	4.59E+09
Total aggregate lateness	7.36E+11	7.36E+11	6.64E+11	6.37291E-11	7.25E+11	6.78E+11
Total set-up cost	1.62E+05	1.62E+05	1.62E+05	4.30584E-06	1.62E+05	1.62E+05
Total inventory cost	0.00E+00	0.00E+00	9.36E+05	0.00000E-00	0.00E+00	0.00E+00
Theoretical inventory cost	1.13E+07	1.13E+07	1.13E+07	1.15128E-07	1.13E+07	1.13E+07
Machine utilisation	6.30E-01	6.30E-01	6.30E-01	6.60000E-01	6.30E-01	6.50E-01
Co-ordination range	1.30E+07	1.30E+07	1.30E+07	1.10000E+07	1.20E+07	1.20E+07

Low Variance in Machine Utilisation						
	Original	H1	H2	H3	H4	H5
Total Unit Lateness	3.76E+09	3.76E+09	3.60E+09	3.50913E+09	3.90E+09	3.65E+09
Total aggregate lateness	6.08E+11	6.08E+11	5.15E+11	5.49168E+11	5.90E+11	5.15E+11
Total set-up cost	1.62E+05	1.62E+05	1.62E+05	2.99663E+06	1.62E+05	1.62E+05
Total inventory cost	5.53E+06	5.53E+06	8.45E+06	0.00000E+00	0.00E+00	0.00E+00
Theoretical inventory cost	1.13E+07	1.13E+07	1.13E+07	1.15128E+07	1.13E+07	1.13E+07
Machine utilisation	7.10E-01	7.10E-01	7.40E-01	7.30000E-01	6.80E-01	7.30E-01
Co-ordination range	1.20E+07	1.20E+07	1.10E+07	9.70000E+06	1.10E+07	1.00E+07

Table 10.1.T Result of Problem 20

High Variance in Machine Utilisation						
	Original	H1	H2	H3	H4	H5
Total Unit Lateness	4.66819E+09	4.64119E+09	4.75325E+09	4.66819E+09	4.89565E+09	4.55516E+09
Total aggregate lateness	6.38144E+11	6.20746E+11	6.25017E+11	6.38023E+11	6.58454E+11	5.90898E+11
Total Set-up cost	1.63047E+05	1.63047E+05	1.63047E+05	3.74558E+06	1.63047E+05	1.63047E+05
Total inventory cost	1.52985E+06	6.03943E+06	5.90003E+06	2.64909E+07	1.19962E+06	6.48671E+06
Theoretical inventory cost	1.35243E+07	1.35243E+07	1.35243E+07	1.35243E+07	1.35243E+07	1.35243E+07
Machine utilisation	6.80000E-01	6.80000E-01	6.60000E-01	6.80000E-01	6.50000E-01	6.90000E-01
Co-ordination range	1.50000E+07	1.50000E+07	1.40000E+07	1.50000E+07	1.30000E+07	1.40000E+07

Low Variance in Machine Utilisation						
	Original	H1	H2	H3	H4	H5
Total Unit Lateness	3.45960E+09	3.45960E+09	3.72447E+09	3.45960E+09	3.95149E+09	3.31065E+09
Total aggregate lateness	5.16077E+11	5.16077E+11	5.05414E+11	5.16077E+11	5.67143E+11	4.55903E+11
Total set-up cost	1.58677E+05	1.58677E+05	1.58677E+05	2.07569E+06	1.58677E+05	1.58677E+05
Total inventory cost	4.96739E+07	4.96739E+07	2.67563E+07	4.96738E+08	2.59022E+06	6.03339E+07
Theoretical inventory cost	1.35243E+07	1.35243E+07	1.35243E+07	1.35243E+07	1.35243E+07	1.35243E+07
Machine utilisation	8.40000E-01	8.40000E-01	7.80000E-01	8.40000E-01	7.40000E-01	8.80000E-01
Co-ordination range	1.10000E+07	1.10000E+07	1.10000E+07	1.10000E+07	1.10000E+07	1.00000E+07

Table 10.2.A Data of "t" test for Total Units Lateness (Case When Variance in M/C Capacity Utilisation is Low)

Original Vs H1			
α	Degrees of freedom	Calculated value	Value from table(t)
0.05	19	2.284	1.729

$H_0 : \mu = 0, H_1 : \mu > 0; (t > t_{calc})$ H_o rejected

Original Vs H2			
α	Degrees of freedom	Calculated value	Value from table(t)
0.05	19	2.168	1.729

$H_0 : \mu = 0, H_1 : \mu > 0; (t > t_{calc})$ H_o rejected

Original Vs H3			
α	Degrees of freedom	Calculated value	Value from table(t)
0.05	19	2.089	1.729

$H_0 : \mu = 0, H_1 : \mu > 0; (t > t_{calc})$ H_o rejected

Original Vs H4			
α	Degrees of freedom	Calculated value	Value from table(t)
0.05	19	1.264	1.729

$H_0 : \mu = 0, H_1 : \mu > 0; (t < t_{calc})$ H_o accepted

Original Vs H5			
α	Degrees of freedom	Calculated value	Value from table(t)
0.05	19	5.506	1.729

$H_0 : \mu = 0, H_1 : \mu > 0; (t > t_{calc})$ H_o rejected

H1 Vs H2			
α	Degrees of freedom	Calculated value	Value from table(t)
0.05	19	0.555	1.729

$H_0 : \mu_1 - \mu_2 = 0; H_1 : \mu_1 - \mu_2 > 0; (t < t_{calc})$ H_o accepted

H1 Vs H3			
α	Degrees of freedom	Calculated value	Value from table(t)
0.05	19	0.458	1.729

$H_0 : \mu_1 - \mu_2 = 0; H_1 : \mu_1 - \mu_2 > 0; (t < t_{calc})$ H_o accepted

H1 Vs H4			
α	Degrees of freedom	Calculated value	Value from table(t)
0.05	19	2.701	1.729

$H_0 : \mu = 0, H_1 : \mu > 0; (t > t_{calc})$ H_o rejected

H1 Vs H5			
α	Degrees of freedom	Calculated value	Value from table(t)
0.05	19	2.891	1.729

$H_0 : \mu_1 - \mu_2 = 0; H_1 : \mu_1 - \mu_2 > 0; (t > t_{calc})$ H_o rejected

H2 Vs H3			
α	Degrees of freedom	Calculated value	Value from table(t)
0.05	19	1.052	1.729

$H_0 : \mu_1 - \mu_2 = 0; H_1 : \mu_1 - \mu_2 > 0; (t < t_{calc})$ H_o accepted

H2 Vs H4			
α	Degrees of freedom	Calculated value	Value from table(t)
0.05	19	3.25	1.729

$H_0 : \mu_1 - \mu_2 = 0; H_1 : \mu_1 - \mu_2 > 0$; $(t > t_{calc})$ H_o rejected

H2 Vs H5			
α	Degrees of freedom	Calculated value	Value from table(t)
0.05	19	2.316	1.729

$H_0 : \mu_1 - \mu_2 = 0; H_1 : \mu_1 - \mu_2 > 0$; $(t > t_{calc})$ H_o rejected

H3 Vs H4			
α	Degrees of freedom	Calculated value	Value from table(t)
0.05	19	2.542	1.729

$H_0 : \mu_1 - \mu_2 = 0; H_1 : \mu_1 - \mu_2 > 0$; $(t > t_{calc})$ H_o rejected

H3 Vs H5			
α	Degrees of freedom	Calculated value	Value from table(t)
0.05	19	3.104	1.729

$H_0 : \mu_1 - \mu_2 = 0; H_1 : \mu_1 - \mu_2 > 0$; $(t > t_{calc})$ H_o rejected

H4 Vs H5			
α	Degrees of freedom	Calculated value	Value from table(t)
0.05	19	6.277	1.729

$H_0 : \mu_1 - \mu_2 = 0; H_1 : \mu_1 - \mu_2 > 0$; $(t > t_{calc})$ H_o rejected

Table 10.2.B Data of "t" test for Total Units Lateness
(Case When Variance in M/C utilisation is High)

Original Vs H1

α	Degrees of freedom	Calculated value	Value from table(t)
0.05	19	1.812	1.729

$H_0 : \mu = 0, H_1 : \mu > 0; (t > t_{calc}) H_o$ rejected

Original Vs H2

α	Degrees of freedom	Calculated value	Value from table(t)
0.05	19	1.959	1.729

$H_0 : \mu = 0, H_1 : \mu > 0; (t > t_{calc}) H_o$ rejected

Original Vs H3

α	Degrees of freedom	Calculated value	Value from table(t)
0.05	19	2.835	1.729

$H_0 : \mu = 0, H_1 : \mu > 0; (t > t_{calc}) H_o$ rejected

Original Vs H4

α	Degrees of freedom	Calculated value	Value from table(t)
0.05	19	2.472	1.729

$H_0 : \mu = 0, H_1 : \mu > 0; (t > t_{calc}) H_o$ rejected

Original Vs H5

α	Degrees of freedom	Calculated value	Value from table(t)
0.05	19	3.061	

$H_0 : \mu = 0, H_1 : \mu > 0; (t > t_{calc}) H_o$ rejected

H1 Vs H2

α	Degrees of freedom	Calculated value	Value from table(t)
0.05	19	0.064	1.729

$H_0 : \mu_1 - \mu_2 = 0; H_1 : \mu_1 - \mu_2 > 0 ; (t < t_{calc}) H_o$ accepted

H1 Vs H3

α	Degrees of freedom	Calculated value	Value from table(t)
0.05	19	0.070	1.729

$H_0 : \mu_1 - \mu_2 = 0; H_1 : \mu_1 - \mu_2 > 0 ; (t < t_{calc}) H_o$ accepted

H1 Vs H4

α	Degrees of freedom	Calculated value	Value from table(t)
0.05	19	0.964	1.729

$H_0 : \mu_1 - \mu_2 = 0; H_1 : \mu_1 - \mu_2 > 0 ; (t < t_{calc}) H_o$ accepted

H1 Vs H5

α	Degrees of freedom	Calculated value	Value from table(t)
0.05	19	0.561	1.729

$H_0 : \mu_1 - \mu_2 = 0; H_1 : \mu_1 - \mu_2 > 0 ; (t < t_{calc}) H_o$ accepted

H2 Vs H3

α	Degrees of freedom	Calculated value	Value from table(t)
0.05	19	0.474	1.729

$H_0 : \mu_1 - \mu_2 = 0; H_1 : \mu_1 - \mu_2 > 0 ; (t < t_{calc}) H_o$ accepted

H2 Vs H4			
α	Degrees of freedom	Calculated value	Value from table(t)
0.05	19	1.003	1.729

$H_0 : \mu_1 - \mu_2 = 0; H_1 : \mu_1 - \mu_2 > 0 ; (t < t_{calc})$ H_o accepted

H2 Vs H5			
α	Degrees of freedom	Calculated value	Value from table(t)
0.05	19	0.402	1.729

$H_0 : \mu_1 - \mu_2 = 0; H_1 : \mu_1 - \mu_2 > 0 ; (t < t_{calc})$ H_o accepted

H3 Vs H4			
α	Degrees of freedom	Calculated value	Value from table(t)
0.05	19	0.848	1.729

$H_0 : \mu_1 - \mu_2 = 0; H_1 : \mu_1 - \mu_2 > 0 ; (t < t_{calc})$ H_o accepted

H3 Vs H5			
α	Degrees of freedom	Calculated value	Value from table(t)
0.05	19	0.563	0.563

$H_0 : \mu_1 - \mu_2 = 0; H_1 : \mu_1 - \mu_2 > 0 ; (t < t_{calc})$ H_o accepted

H4 Vs H5			
α	Degrees of freedom	Calculated value	Value from table(t)
0.05	19	1.799	1.729

$H_0 : \mu_1 - \mu_2 = 0; H_1 : \mu_1 - \mu_2 > 0 ; (t > t_{calc})$ H_o rejected

Table 10.2.C Data of "t" test for Total Aggregate Lateness (Case When Variance in M/C Capacity Utilisation is Low)

Original Vs H1			
α	Degrees of freedom	Calculated value	Value from table(t)
0.05	19	3.644	1.729

$H_0 : \mu = 0, H_1 : \mu > 0; (t > t_{calc}) H_o$ rejected

Original Vs H2			
α	Degrees of freedom	Calculated value	Value from table(t)
0.05	19	8.109	1.729

$H_o : \mu = 0, H_1 : \mu > 0; (t > t_{calc}) H_o$ rejected

Original Vs H3			
α	Degrees of freedom	Calculated value	Value from table(t)
0.05	19	2.486	1.729

$H_o : \mu = 0, H_1 : \mu > 0; (t > t_{calc}) H_o$ rejected

Original Vs H4			
α	Degrees of freedom	Calculated value	Value from table(t)
0.05	19	0.019	1.729

$H_0 : \mu = 0, H_1 : \mu > 0; (t < t_{calc}) H_o$ accepted

Original Vs H5			
α	Degrees of freedom	Calculated value	Value from table(t)
0.05	19	5.087	1.729

$H_0 : \mu = 0, H_1 : \mu > 0; (t > t_{calc}) H_o$ rejected

H1 Vs H2			
α	Degrees of freedom	Calculated value	Value from table(t)
0.05	19	0.429	1.729

$H_0 : \mu_1 - \mu_2 = 0; H_1 : \mu_1 - \mu_2 > 0 ; (t < t_{calc}) H_o$ accepted

H1 Vs H3			
α	Degrees of freedom	Calculated value	Value from table(t)
0.05	19	1.627	1.729

$H_0 : \mu_1 - \mu_2 = 0; H_1 : \mu_1 - \mu_2 > 0 ; (t < t_{calc}) H_o$ accepted

H1 Vs H4			
α	Degrees of freedom	Calculated value	Value from table(t)
0.05	19	2.198	1.729

$H_0 : \mu_1 - \mu_2 = 0; H_1 : \mu_1 - \mu_2 > 0 ; (t > t_{calc}) H_o$ rejected

H1 Vs H5			
α	Degrees of freedom	Calculated value	Value from table(t)
0.05	19	1.916	1.729

$H_0 : \mu_1 - \mu_2 = 0; H_1 : \mu_1 - \mu_2 > 0 ; (t > t_{calc}) H_o$ rejected

H2 Vs H3			
α	Degrees of freedom	Calculated value	Value from table(t)
0.05	19	3.098	1.729

$H_0 : \mu_1 - \mu_2 = 0; H_1 : \mu_1 - \mu_2 > 0; (t > t_{calc}) H_o$ rejected

H2 Vs H4			
α	Degrees of freedom	Calculated value	Value from table(t)
0.05	19	3.896	1.729

$H_0 : \mu_1\text{-}\mu_2 = 0; H_1 : \mu_1\text{-}\mu_2 > 0; (t > t_{calc})$ H_o rejected

H2 Vs H5			
α	Degrees of freedom	Calculated value	Value from table(t)
0.05	19	1.666	1.729

$H_0 : \mu_1\text{-}\mu_2 = 0; H_1 : \mu_1\text{-}\mu 2 > 0; (t < t_{calc})$ H_o accepted

H3 Vs H4			
α	Degrees of freedom	Calculated value	Value from table(t)
0.05	19	1.189	1.729

$H_0 : \mu_1\text{-}\mu_2 = 0; H_1 : \mu_1\text{-}\mu_2 > 0; (t < t_{calc})$ H_o accepted

H3 Vs H5			
α	Degrees of freedom	Calculated value	Value from table(t)
0.05	19	3.061	1.729

$H_0 : \mu_1\text{-}\mu_2 = 0; H_1 : \mu_1\text{-}\mu_2 > 0; (t > t_{calc})$ H_o rejected

H4 Vs H5			
α	Degrees of freedom	Calculated value	Value from table(t)
0.05	19	2.024	1.729

$H_0 : \mu_1\text{-}\mu_2 = 0; H_1 : \mu_1\text{-}\mu_2 > 0; (t > t_{calc})$ H_o rejected.

Table 10.2.D Data of "t" test for Total Aggregate Lateness Case When Variance in M/C utilisation is High)

Original Vs H1			
α	Degrees of freedom	Calculated value	Value from table(t)
0.05	19	2.936	1.729

$H_0 : \mu = 0, H_1 : \mu > 0; (t > t_{calc}) H_o$ rejected

Original Vs H2			
α	Degrees of freedom	Calculated value	Value from table(t)
0.05	19	2.139	1.729

$H_0 : \mu = 0, H_1 : \mu > 0; (t > t_{calc}) H_o$ rejected

Original Vs H3			
α	Degrees of freedom	Calculated value	Value from table(t)
0.05	19	2.514	1.729

$H_0 : \mu = 0, H_1 : \mu > 0; (t > t_{calc}) H_o$ rejected

Original Vs H4			
α	Degrees of freedom	Calculated value	Value from table(t)
0.05	19	3.050	1.729

$H_0 : \mu = 0, H_1 : \mu > 0; (t > t_{calc}) H_o$ rejected

Original Vs H5			
α	Degrees of freedom	Calculated value	Value from table(t)
0.05	19	4.842	1.729

$H_0 : \mu = 0, H_1 : \mu > 0; (t > t_{calc}) H_o$ rejected

H1 Vs H2			
α	Degrees of freedom	Calculated value	Value from table(t)
0.05	19	1.051	1.729

$H_0 : \mu_1 - \mu_2 = 0; H_1 : \mu_1 - \mu_2 > 0; (t < t_{calc}) H_o$ accepted

H1 Vs H3			
α	Degrees of freedom	Calculated value	Value from table(t)
0.05	19	0.296	1.729

$H_0 : \mu_1 - \mu_2 = 0; H_1 : \mu_1 - \mu_2 > 0; (t < t_{calc}) H_o$ accepted

H1 Vs H4			
α	Degrees of freedom	Calculated value	Value from table(t)
0.05	19	0.1.228	1.729

$H_0 : \mu_1 - \mu_2 = 0; H_1 : \mu_1 - \mu_2 > 0; (t < t_{calc}) H_o$ accepted

H1 Vs H5			
α	Degrees of freedom	Calculated value	Value from table(t)
0.05	19	0.390	1.729

$H_0 : \mu_1 - \mu_2 = 0; H_1 : \mu_1 - \mu_2 > 0; (t < t_{calc}) H_o$ accepted

H2 Vs H3			
α	Degrees of freedom	Calculated value	Value from table(t)
0.05	19	0.984	1.729

$H_0 : \mu_1 - \mu_2 = 0; H_1 : \mu_1 - \mu_2 > 0; (t < t_{calc}) H_o$ accepted

H2 Vs H4			
α	Degrees of freedom	Calculated value	Value from table(t)
0.05	19	2.023	1.729

$H_0 : \mu_1 - \mu_2 = 0; H_1 : \mu_1 - \mu_2 > 0; (t > t_{calc})$ H_o rejected

H2 Vs H5			
α	Degrees of freedom	Calculated value	Value from table(t)
0.05	19	0.735	1.729

$H_0 : \mu_1 - \mu_2 = 0; H_1 : \mu_1 - \mu_2 > 0; (t < t_{calc})$ H_o accepted

H3 Vs H4			
α	Degrees of freedom	Calculated value	Value from table(t)
0.05	19	1.318	1.729

$H_0 : \mu_1 - \mu_2 = 0; H_1 : \mu_1 - \mu_2 > 0; (t < t_{calc})$ H_o accepted

H3 Vs H5			
α	Degrees of freedom	Calculated value	Value from table(t)
0.05	19	0.229	1.729

$H_0 : \mu_1 - \mu_2 = 0; H_1 : \mu_1 - \mu_2 > 0; (t < t_{calc})$ H_o accepted

H4 Vs H5			
α	Degrees of freedom	Calculated value	Value from table(t)
0.05	19	2.261	1.729

$H_0 : \mu_1 - \mu_2 = 0; H_1 : \mu_1 - \mu_2 > 0; (t > t_{calc})$ H_o rejected

Table 10.2.E Data of "t" test for Total Inventory Cost
(Case when Variance in M/C Capacity Utilisation is Low)

Original Vs H1			
α	Degrees of freedom	Calculated value	Value from table(t)
0.05	19	0.289	1.729

$H_0 : \mu = 0, H_1 : \mu > 0; (t < t_{calc}) H_o$ accepted

Original Vs H2			
α	Degrees of freedom	Calculated value	Value from table(t)
0.05	19	1.170	1.729

$H_0 : \mu = 0, H_1 : \mu > 0; (t < t_{calc}) H_o$ accepted

Original Vs H3			
α	Degrees of freedom	Calculated value	Value from table(t)
0.05	19	8.357	1.729

$H_0 : \mu = 0, H_1 : \mu > 0; (t > t_{calc}) H_o$ rejected

Original Vs H4			
α	Degrees of freedom	Calculated value	Value from table(t)
0.05	19	1.704	1.729

$H_0 : \mu = 0, H_1 : \mu > 0; (t < t_{calc}) H_o$ accepted

Original Vs H5			
a	Degrees of freedom	Calculated value	Value from table(t)
0.05	19	0.036	1.729

$H_0 : \mu = 0, H_1 : \mu > 0; (t < t_{calc}) H_o$ accepted

H1 Vs H2			
α	Degrees of freedom	Calculated value	Value from table(t)
0.05	19	1.642	1.729

$H_0 : \mu_1 - \mu_2 = 0; H_1 : \mu_1 - \mu_2 > 0; (t < t_{calc}) H_o$ accepted

H1 Vs H3			
α	Degrees of freedom	Calculated value	Value from table(t)
0.05	19	1.933	1.729

$H_0 : \mu_1 - \mu_2 = 0; H_1 : \mu_1 - \mu_2 > 0; (t > t_{calc}) H_o$ rejected

H1 Vs H4			
α	Degrees of freedom	Calculated value	Value from table(t)
0.05	19	1.414	1.729

$H_0 : \mu_1 - \mu_2 = 0; H_1 : \mu_1 - \mu_2 > 0; (t < t_{calc}) H_o$ accepted

H1 Vs H5			
α	Degrees of freedom	Calculated value	Value from table(t)
0.05	19	1.199	1.729

$H_0 : \mu_1 - \mu_2 = 0; H_1 : \mu_1 - \mu_2 > 0; (t < t_{calc}) H_o$ accepted

H2 Vs H3			
α	Degrees of freedom	Calculated value	Value from table(t)
0.05	19	5.876	1.729

$H_0 : \mu_1 - \mu_2 = 0; H_1 : \mu_1 - \mu_2 > 0; (t > t_{calc}) H_o$ rejected

H2 Vs H4			
α	Degrees of freedom	Calculated value	Value from table(t)
0.05	19	2.113	1.729

$H_0 : \mu_1 - \mu_2 = 0; H_1 : \mu_1 - \mu_2 > 0; (t > t_{calc})$ H_o rejected

H2 Vs H5			
α	Degrees of freedom	Calculated value	Value from table(t)
0.05	19	1.486	1.729

$H_0 : \mu_1 - \mu_2 = 0; H_1 : \mu_1 - \mu_2 > 0; (t < t_{calc})$ H_o accepted

H3 Vs H4			
α	Degrees of freedom	Calculated value	Value from table(t)
0.05	19	8.608	1.729

$H_0 : \mu_1 - \mu_2 = 0; H_1 : \mu_1 - \mu_2 > 0; (t > t_{calc})$ H_o rejected

H3 Vs H5			
α	Degrees of freedom	Calculated value	Value from table(t)
0.05	19	9.563	1.729

$H_0 : \mu_1 - \mu_2 = 0; H_1 : \mu_1 - \mu_2 > 0; (t > t_{calc})$ H_o rejected

H4 Vs H5			
α	Degrees of freedom	Calculated value	Value from table(t)
0.05	19	0.300	1.729

$H_0 : \mu_1 - \mu_2 = 0; H_1 : \mu_1 - \mu_2 > 0; (t < t_{calc})$ H_o accepted

Table 10.2.F Data of "t" test for Total Inventory Cost (Case When Variance in M/C Utilisation is High)

Original Vs H1

α	Degrees of freedom	Calculated value	Value from table(t)
0.05	19	1.858	1.729

$H_0 : \mu = 0, H_1 : \mu > 0; (t > t_{calc})$ H_o rejected

Original Vs H2

α	Degrees of freedom	Calculated value	Value from table(t)
0.05	19	2.083	1.729

$H_0 : \mu = 0, H_1 : \mu > 0; (t > t_{calc})$ H_o rejected

Original Vs H3

α	Degrees of freedom	Calculated value	Value from table(t)
0.05	19	10.819	1.729

$H_0 : \mu = 0, H_1 : \mu > 0; (t > t_{calc})$ H_o rejected

Original Vs H4

α	Degrees of freedom	Calculated value	Value from table(t)
0.05	19	1.430	1.729

$H_0 : \mu = 0, H_1 : \mu > 0; (t < t_{calc})$ H_o accepted

Original Vs H5

α	Degrees of freedom	Calculated value	Value from table(t)
0.05	19	0.997	1.729

$H_0 : \mu = 0, H_1 : \mu > 0; (t < t_{calc})$ H_o accepted

H1 Vs H2

α	Degrees of freedom	Calculated value	Value from table(t)
0.05	19	0.615	1.729

$H_0 : \mu = 0, H_1 : \mu > 0; (t < t_{calc})$ H_o accepted

H1 Vs H3

α	Degrees of freedom	Calculated value	Value from table(t)
0.05	19	2.548	1.729

$H_0 : \mu_1 - \mu_2 = 0; H_1 : \mu_1 - \mu_2 > 0; (t > t_{calc})$ H_o rejected

H1 Vs H4

α	Degrees of freedom	Calculated value	Value from table(t)
0.05	19	1.30	1.729

$H_0 : \mu_1 - \mu_2 = 0; H_1 : \mu_1 - \mu_2 > 0; (t > t_{calc})$ H_o rejected

H1 Vs H5

α	Degrees of freedom	Calculated value	Value from table(t)
0.05	19	0.930	1.729

$H_0 : \mu_1 - \mu_2 = 0; H_1 : \mu_1 - \mu_2 > 0; (t < t_{calc})$ H_o accepted

H2 Vs H3

α	Degrees of freedom	Calculated value	Value from table(t)
0.05	19	2.582	1.729

$H_0 : \mu_1 - \mu_2 = 0; H_1 : \mu_1 - \mu_2 > 0; (t > t_{calc})$ H_o rejected

H2 Vs H4			
α	Degrees of freedom	Calculated value	Value from table(t)
0.05	19	1.799	1.729

$H_0: \mu_1 - \mu_2 = 0; H_1: \mu_1 - \mu_2 > 0; (t > t_{calc})$ H_o rejected

H2 Vs H5			
α	Degrees of freedom	Calculated value	Value from table(t)
0.05	19	1.564	1.729

$H_0: \mu_1 - \mu_2 = 0; H_1: \mu_1 - \mu_2 > 0; (t < t_{calc})$ H_o accepted

H3 Vs H4			
α	Degrees of freedom	Calculated value	Value from table(t)
0.05	19	6.702	1.729

$H_0: \mu_1 - \mu_2 = 0; H_1: \mu_1 - \mu_2 > 0; (t > t_{calc})$ H_o rejected

H3 Vs H5			
α	Degrees of freedom	Calculated value	Value from table(t)
0.05	19	14.031	1.729

$H_0: \mu_1 - \mu_2 = 0; H_1: \mu_1 - \mu_2 > 0; (t > t_{calc})$ H_o rejected

H4 Vs H5			
α	Degrees of freedom	Calculated value	Value from table(t)
0.05	19	1.741	1.729

$H_0: \mu_1 - \mu_2 = 0; H_1: \mu_1 - \mu_2 > 0; (t > t_{calc})$ H_o rejected

REFERENCES

1. Baker KR, Introduction to Sequencing and Scheduling, John Willey and Sons, 1974.
2. Biggs JR, Heuristic Lot Sizing and Sequencing Rules in A Multi-stage, Production Inventory System, *Decision Sciences,* 10, 96-115, 1979.
3. Biggs JR, Priority Rules for Shop Floor Control in A Material Requirements Planning System under Various Levels of Capacity, *International Journal of Production Research,* 23(1), 33-46, 1985.
4. Freund and Miller, Probability and Statistics for Engineer, Prentice Hall of India Pvt, Ltd 1997
5. Fry TP, Timothy D, Oliff Michael D, Minor Elliot D, Leong G Keong, The Effects of Product Structure and Sequencing Rule on Assembly Shop Performance, International Journal of Production Research, 1989, 27 No. 27, 671-686.
6. Fry TP, Philipoom PR and Markland RE, Dispatching in Multi-stage Job Shop Where Machine Capacities are Unbalanced. *International Journal of Production Research,* 27, 671-686, 1989.
7. Goodwin JS and Weeks JK. Operating Policies for Scheduling Assembled Products. *Decision Sciences,* 13, 585-603, 1982.
8. Goodwin JS and Weeks JK. Evaluating Scheduling Policies in A Multi-level Assembly System. *International Journal of Production Research,* 24, 247-257, 1986.
9. Gupta SK, Multipass Heuristic for Improved performance with Imbalance in Capacity utilisation in MRP context, M Tech Dissertion, liT, Kanpur, 1997
10. Orlicky Joseph, Material Requirement Planning, McGraw Hill Book Company, 1975.
11. Potty VS Simulation of Heuristics, Lot Sizing and Sequencing procedures in MRP, M Tech dissertion, IIT, Kanpur, 1990.
12. Russell RS and Taylor BW, An evaluation of Sequencing rules for an assembly shop, *Decision Sciences,* 16, 196-212, 1985.
13. Sharma RRK, Heuristic to modify lot sizes to improve performance in MRP context, in *Industrial Engineering Encyclopaedia,* published by International Journal of Industrial Engineering, USA, ISBN 0-9654599-X, 1999.
14. Sinha Sharat, Development of improved sequencing based heuristic and comparison of its performance with other lot sizing and sequencing based heuristic in MRP context, Unpublished M. Tech. dissertation, Department of Industrial and Management Engineering, IIT Kanpur-1994.

15. Vollman, Thomas E, Production Planning and Control System, Galgotia Publication Pvt Ltd, 1989.
16. Wagner HM and Whitin TM, Dynamic Version of Economic Lot Size Model, *Management Science,* October, 1958, 89-96.
17. Wadhwani V, Heuristic for Improved Performance in MRP when Variance in Machine Utilisation is High, M Tech Dissertion, IIT, Kanpur, 2000
18. Yoganandan, SR *Heuristic for Coordinated Scheduling in Material Requirement Planning* System, Unpublished M. Tech. dissertation, Indian Institute of Technology, Kanpur-1992.

11 A Summary on Few Works on MRP Systems

R R K Sharma, S Shahi

1. PARAMETERS AFFECTING THE EFFECTIVENESS OF MRP SYSTEMS

Yeung et al[1] identify the important parameters which affect the effectiveness of MRP systems. It starts with a framework of MRP systems which constitutes production and resource planning, demand management, MPS, capacity planning and shop floor systems. Then, it focusses on MPS, where the factors affecting MPS directly also affect the performance of MRP systems. Literature review is classified into several groups:

1. **Impact of MPS frozen interval on MRP performance** If demand is deterministic, freezing MPS has little effect on set-up cost and inventory cost. But, if demand is uncertain, the impact more complex.
2. **Impact of MPS replanning frequency on MRP performance** Keeping in mind the total cost, frequent replanning is not desirable.
3. **Impact of product structure on MRP performance** For simple product structures, the impact is easy to study but for complex structures with commonality, it is not known how total cost reacts.
4. **Impact of forecast error on MRP performance** Forecast error increases the total cost of MRP system but sometimes higher forecast error might create excess inventory. Thus, reducing shortage cost will provide protection against unexpected demand.
5. **Impact of safety stock on MRP performance** Safety stocks can reduce cost but care should be taken in selecting the right quantity of safety stock since too much safety stock may result in higher rescheduling and inventory cost.

After this literature survey, comments have been made on the limitations of previous research and these limitations can indicate direction for future research.

2. INTEGRATING GROUP TECHNOLOGY AND MRP SYSTEM

Darrow and Gupta[2] present an approach to integrate Group Technology (GT) concepts with traditional MRP concepts. In MRP systems, component parts are scheduled independently with the timing and quantity determined by MRP. GT can be applied to component parts with the aim of standardisation of parts by focussing on part design and realising economies in production by batching sets of similar parts. These economies are achieved by processing parts with similarities in GT machine cells. The cells are laid out in a manner so as to reduce WIP inventory across the line. Thus, the basic group scheduling problem is how to take advantage of part similarities to lower the set-up and inventory cost. This problem is like a multi-dimensional lot-sizing problem using which scheduling sequence for the batch is determined. A heuristic was developed to model this and results were compared with a benchmark, typically Wagner-Whitin algorithm. It is seen that the heuristic performed very well when compared to optimal Wagner-Whitin solution. Thus, it is possible to realise substantial savings by integrating MRP with GT as mentioned above.

3. EFFECT OF BATCH SIZE SELECTION ON MRP PERFORMANCE

For an MRP system to perform well, it is necessary to have planned lead times and optimum batch size parameters see Enns.[3] They take a look at the effect batch sizes have on MRP performance. If batch sizes are small, set-ups will be incurred more frequently leading to longer waiting times, whereas large batch sizes can lead to co-ordination problems and high inventories. Enns[3] designed and conducted an experiment, wherein, the production environment was assumed to be producing two products and each of these products had three levels of operations. The quantity of each raw material required for its corresponding parent, production rate, planned lead time, demand pattern and set-up time were available. Excel spreadsheet was used to determine the product release requirements. Simulation was run for different batch sizes and corresponding utilisation, WIP inventory, mean lateness and tardiness were determined. It was found that particular batch sizes led to better degree of tardiness and lower WIP inventories.

4. CYCLE TIME REDUCTION BY IMPROVED MRP BASED PRODUCTION PLANNING

One of the major drawbacks of MRP is the use of lead times which is determined by approximate considerations. Estimation of accurate lead times and lead time offsets are important for a successful MRP schedule. These lead times, if underestimated, cause excessive resource workloads and if overestimated, cause long cycle times and high WIP cost. An approach is presented to improve MRP based production planning by reducing product cycle times. Lead Time Evaluation and Scheduling Algorithm (LETSA), developed by Agrawal et al,[4] is used to obtain these values. LETSA exploits the critical path of the network of operations to create an optimal schedule. This network obtained from the BoM structure, represents the precedence relationships among operations. LETSA algorithm proceeds in a backward scheduling manner, wherein, the last operation is scheduled first and the remaining operations are scheduled subsequently. It generates a feasible schedule with a near optimal cycle time and lead time offsets are also considered while schedule is created. Now, to calculate the optimal batch size, LETSA is run iteratively varying the batch size thus identifying the batch size for which WIP cost are minimal. Based on LETSA schedule generated for the optimal batch size, lead time for each part is determined. Since there can be other product in the system, a capacity scaling method is required to provide realisable lead times. For this purpose, either Exact Capacity Scaling (ECS) or Bottleneck Capacity Scaling (BCS) is used.

ECS is the ratio of the total workload requirement of each work centre to a product's workload on that work centre. The lead time is then inflated by taking a weighted sum of the scaling factor and the original lead time. For BCS, the workload of the bottleneck is used and the lead time is inflated as in ECS method. BCS is found to be superior to ECS since BCS results in shorter lead times. Using this algorithm, not only cycle time but also schedule cost gets minimised.

5. DUE DATE SETTING WITH SUPPLY CONSTRAINTS IN SYSTEMS USING MRP

The basic decision faced by a supplier is whether to commit to a requested due date for a customer order or not. Quoting due dates greater than the requested date can result in loss of goodwill, whereas fulfilling the order very early can increase finished goods' inventory cost. Hegedus and Hopp[5] propose a new model for quoting due dates in a make-to-order environment. This method simultaneously considers service level, inventory and order-acceptance cost. Assuming that orders cannot be delivered before they are requested, Hegedus and Hopp[5] suggest a cost minimisation formulation for a single demand order and later on extend it to multiple order problems. The cost function includes holding cost, tardy cost and delay cost. Here, tardy cost is the cost of holding the finished good inventory and delay cost represents the delay between quoted due date and requested due date. Results show that to minimise cost, the expected tardiness cost should equal the sum of expected inventory-holding cost and the delay cost rate i.e., as tardiness cost approaches the sum of delay and holding cost. The solution quotes due dates closer to the requested due date and if it exceeds, requested due date is quoted. It is demonstrated that the optimal policy is to always quote the requested due date, i.e., use a 'Yes' policy.

6. CAPACITY CONSTRAINT MRP SYSTEMS

MRP in its basic form assumes that there are no capacity constraints. Billington et al[6] introduce capacity constrained and multi-stage production scheduling problems. This chapter addresses how to simultaneously determine lot-size, lead time and capacity utilisation plan. For a general product structure which depicts issues of commonality, the capacity/lot-size/lead time problem is formulated as a mixed-integer linear programme called MRP-ILP. The objective function is a cost minimisation function which includes holding cost, set-up cost, over-time and under-time cost. Constraints regarding inventory, time and production capacity have been included in the ILP. Since the model complexity is very high, product structure compression is suggested as a means to simplify the objective function. Few guidelines have been suggested as to how to compress the product structure. For the product structure, given in this work, an 81 per cent reduction is achieved which simplifies the ILP significantly and can be used simultaneously to determine lot size, lead time and capacity utilisation plan.

7. CAPACITY SENSiTIVE REQUIREMENTS PLANNING

In a multi-stage environment, in which there are many parent-component relationships, the capacity constraints are not addressed by a typical MRP system. Harl and Ritzman[7] explore a way to make MRP systems more sensitive to capacity requirements. According to this research, lot-sizing and capacity decisions should be made sequentially rather than simultaneously. Harl and Ritzman explore a way to systematically change selected parts of MRP to suite the capacity requirements. The algorithm modifies the lot sizes suggested by the MRP system so that the workload inputs to each work centre conform better to available processing capacity. After performing the weekly MRP and CRP computer runs, a mature Planned Order Release (POR) is obtained. The algorithm then evaluates the POR with respect to the CRP capacity profiles. To identify which PORs are to be changed, a ratio of targets to workloads is calculated and its deviation from 1 is noted. POR with highest ratio is a potential candidate for lot size increase and vice versa. After identifying the candidates, it is ensured that the deviation of this ratio from 1 is within a threshold so as not to significantly alter the average lot sizes released by the system. In case lot size decreases, it should be ensured that the reduced size will cover net requirements. If these conditions are satisfied, POR is changed and the entire process is to be continued for multiple iterations. Action notices denoting these changes are finally printed out along with the suggested deviations to smoothen capacity requirements.

8. CAPACITY CONTROL POLICIES FOR MRP SYSTEMS

Historically, MRP assumes sufficient productive capacity to meet the requirements. Therefore, MRP results have to be coupled with some means of controlling capacity. Gutzmann and Wysk[8] evaluate the performances of two heuristic capacity control policies and their associated parameters on cost of production. The two policies are:

1. **Simple production-switching (PS) control policy** As per this policy, there are two levels of production, low (one shift per week) and high (two shifts or more per week). A Control Limit (CL) is specified for the number of standard hours in the work centre queue. If the work centre queue at the beginning of the week exceeds CL, high production level is implemented for that week and vice versa.
2. **Backlog reduction (BR) policy** In this policy, a Control Limit (CL), a Reduction Factor (RF) greater than zero, nominal and maximum work-week length is specified. If the number of standard hours in queue at the beginning of the week exceeds CL, an extended work-week is calculated using reduction factor and if it is less than CL, nominal work-week length is implemented.

Sensitivity of labour and inventory-holding cost are evaluated for the above two policies for different product could be flat, tall or tall/flat mix. The results infer that PS policies were preferred for tall/flat product structure mix and BR policies were not preferred for tall/flat product mix. Moreover, CL had a direct impact on WIP inventory, whereas RF had more impact on labour. From these observations, some generic recommendations have been suggested:

- Labour-intensive policies to be used when ratio of holding to labour cost is high.
- Labour-conservative policies to be used when ratio of holding to labour cost is low.
- Product structures have a great impact on production cost and control policy alternatives.

9. FINITE CAPACITY MRP SYSTEM

Pandey et al[9] present a Finite Capacity MRP (FCMRP) which help in obtaining capacity based production plans. The FCMRP is executed in two stages. First, capacity based production schedule is generated from the input data like part details, BoM, inventory status and existing schedule. Based on these, part requirements are classified into purchased and manufactured parts. Schedule for purchased parts are obtained from purchase lead times while for manufactured parts, processing and set-up times are used for scheduling. Secondly, an algorithm is used to produce appropriate material requirements plan to satisfy schedules obtained from stage 1. The algorithm consists of two parts. The first part of algorithm carries out batch explosion and scheduling. Batch with highest priority is the starting point and its due date is set as the latest finish time. From here, backward scheduling is employed to compute batch order release dates and net requirements. If the due date for a batch is found to be infeasible, the programme stops and the batch explosion process compute the maximum required quantity from BoM. Now, forward scheduling is done from the lowest level of part hierarchy and is done until the end product is scheduled. Backward scheduling starts from the end product and moves to the lower levels of part hierarchy. The second part of the algorithm is responsible for batch deletion since deletion of some scheduled batches becomes necessary in case of order cancellations or modifications. FCMRP and conventional MRP algorithms are compared and it is found that FCMRP produces precise estimates of production lead time and yields better plans.

10. FINITE CAPACITY SCHEDULING METHOD FOR MRP

One of the main drawbacks of MRP based production scheduling is that capacity constraints are not considered in the scheduling logic. Nagendra and Das[10] address this problem by redesigning the MRP methodology so as to permit finite capacity scheduling with and without lot size restrictions. Nagendra and Das[10] discuss the Progressive Capacity Analyser (PCA) which is capable of generating a production schedule that satisfies lot size restrictions, demand requirements and capacity constraints. The first step in PCA is to define a global linear program (GLP) which functions as a master scheduler and generates a capacity feasible POR. GLP tries to minimise inventory holding and backorder cost keeping in mind the capacity constraints. This POR is inputted into lot-sized MRP (LMRP) which generates a lot-size feasible solution which aims at minimising total units rescheduled backwards. The Level Linear Program (LLP) checks if the POR output from LMRP stage is capacity feasible and if the POR quantity is changed accordingly. It is done only for one BoM level at a time. This capacity feasible solution might violate lot size conditions. The Lot Aggregating Heuristic (LAH) resolves these violations and the output of this stage forms the input into LMRP stage of next level. This iteration continues till the lowest level is reached in the product structure. Thus, the PCA procedure has an advantage of working in conjunction with MRP explosion process, thus, rendering a feasible solution.

11. CAPACITY SENSITIVE SET-UP PARAMETERS FOR MRP LOT-SIZING

Raturi and Hill[11] present simple procedures for determining capacity sensitive set-up parameters for MRP lot-sizing. They present an approach to estimate set-up parameters using shadow prices of capacity at each work centre. To estimate the shadow prices, creation of a manufacturing schedule is considered as a mathematical programming problem which minimises cost like inventory and set-up, subject to capacity constraints. The inventory-carrying cost are subdivided into WIP inventory and storeroom inventory. At the time of MRP generation, shadow price of capacity for each work centre is calculated from current or future demand for all end items. It is then used to calculate set-up parameters for an operation at a work centre. Order set-up parameters for an item is the product of set-up time for that item in a work centre and the shadow price at that work centre. Since the materials flow for an item is restricted by the capacity of the most tightly constrained work centre, lower bound on the lot size should be specified by the most constrained work centre. Since set-up parameters depend on future demand and capacity data, variations in order set-up parameters can be expected and this has to be reduced by exponentially smoothing the parameters. These smoothed parameters are used in calculating lot sizes using standard MRP lot-sizing procedures. The simulation experiment conducted in these lines demonstrates significant enhancing of MRP system performance by reducing average inventory cost and average lateness on customer orders. Capacity sensitive procedures for determining set-up parameters tend to plan small lot sizes for orders that require non-bottleneck work centres and large lot sizes for orders that require bottleneck work centres, thus improving the performance of MRP systems.

12. DEVELOPMENT AND IMPLEMENTATION OF A GENERIC ORDER RELEASE SCHEME

Koh et al[12] introduce the development and implementation of a Generic Order Release Scheme (GORS) to model finite-capacitated MRP environments. This method can be used to accurately simulate effects of production fluctuations in this environment. The planning platform models the MRP system and control platform models the finite-capacitated system. The planning platform makes use of customer demand which is derived from the MPS sub-module. The relationships between parts are obtained from BoM, which gives the quantity per unit required to manufacture each sub-assembly or finished product. The lead times for these parts are retrieved and used for backward scheduling. Using this information along with inventory details, explosion is done and a POR is obtained. In the control platform, POR schedule is the input and capacities are assigned based on the resources and sequence of visits for parts to each work station. To model this, knowledge of set-up times and operation times are a must. Using these inputs, queues are modelled at the entrance of each resource. The main problem with this modelled is that there is a relationship between parts and this dependency between parts affects the resource allocation from PORs. This cannot be effectively modeled by this model. To solve this problem, an Order Release Scheme (ORS) is developed. This employs a concept of parent-child relationship between parts and this is given due consideration along with POR schedule while assigning capacities to different resources.

13. CAPACITY REQUIREMENTS PLANNING SYSTEMS

Harl[13] mentioned several procedures to balance capacity requirements and to adjust POR. The heuristics presented in this paper provide a way to integrate capacity requirements plan and material requirements plan into a more effective total system by modifying planned orders accordingly, thus overcoming a critical shortcoming of MRP. The heuristic algorithms proposed here, can change some of the PORs on an exception basis, so that the load profiles will be smoother. A statistic Delta (Δ) is used which indicates expected capacity utilisation of work centres which are on the expected routing path of the planned orders. The further Δi deviates from 1.00, the severe the capacity problem. A positive deviation indicates that the present load is lower than the future planned load and the POR can be increased to balance the capacity utilisation and vice versa. Thus, if Δi > 1.00, lot size increase is achieved and vice versa. The paper also describes alternative-load balancing techniques using target utilisation. Thus, once the MRP system determines the POR schedule for each item, the proposed heuristics evaluate these PORs with respect to capacity and selected orders are changed to make the capacity utilisations more balanced. This process is called Requirements Adjustment and the paper describes different alternatives available to do this adjustment. It is seen that some of the heuristics improve MRP performance significantly even for multiple items and multiple work centres.

14. LP-BASED HEURISTICS FOR THE CAPCITATED LOT-SIZING PROBLEM

Alfieri et al[14] present LP-based rounding heuristics for solving Capacitated Lot-sizing Problem (CLSP). Using the CSLP, it is possible to determine the lot sizes for a set of items to meet the demand at minimal cost. The assumptions made are that set-up times are negligible and there are no initial and final inventories. The CSLP model can be formulated using Natural Formulation (NF), Plant Location Formulation (PLF) or Shortest Path Formulation (SPF). The LP-based heuristics rely on the idea of solving the CLSP by rounding the fractional solution to an integer one. The two successive rounding approaches proposed are:

1. **Naïve successive round-up** In this method, if any set-up variable is larger than a threshold value, it will be rounded to the next highest integer and vice versa. If the solution is an integer, stop the process, otherwise, select the largest fractional set-up variable and round it up to 1. This process is done iteratively till the solution takes an integer value.
2. **Curtailed branch and bound** In this method also, if any set-up variable is larger than a threshold value, it will be rounded to the next highest integer and vice versa. If the solution is an integer, stop the process,

otherwise, optimise the variables by a standard branch and bound.

It is observed that the use of shortest path formulation followed by the application of curtailed branch and bound seems to be reasonably robust and the best among all alternatives.

15. INTERACTIVE BETWEEN LOT-SIZEING DECISING AND MPS FRUZING DECISIONS

Selection of lot-sizing rules and MPS freezing parameters significantly influence MRP performance. Zhao and Lam[15] examine the interaction between lot-sizing decisions and MPS freezing decisions under deterministic demand. Different factors considered for simulation experiment are product structure, demand pattern, inventory cost and schedule instability. Different lot-sizing rules like Silver Meal (SM), Cost Modified Silver Meal (MSM), Part Period Balancing (PPB), EOQ and combinations like SM/LFL, PPB/LFL have been considered for simulation. This study, however, does not consider capacity constraints. The results indicate that lot-sizing selection significantly influence total cost and schedule instability. Out of the 14 lot-sizing rules included in this analysis, combinations of Cost Modified Silver-Meal (MSM), lot-for-lot (LFL) and Cost Modified Part Period Balancing (MPPB) like MSM/LFL, SM/LFL and MPPB/LFL are the best rules. It is also found that freezing parameters under deterministic demand are not influenced by lot-sizing rule used.

16. HYBRID GENETIC ALGORITHM

Dellaert and Jeunet[16] use a hybrid genetic algorithm (GA) to solve uncapacitated multi-level lot-sizing (MLLS) problem. Initially, the mathematical formulation of MLLS is done as a mixed integer programme by considering constant cost parameters, lead times for various sub-assemblies, set-up cost, inventory holding cost and production cost. The objective function is the sum of set-up and inventory holding cost. Rather than letting the GA algorithm to explore a large set of possible solutions, specific generic operators are designed which limit the search to a set of feasible solutions. To further increase the search efficiency, the size of the set of possible solutions is reduced by removing orders from periods where there is no net demand. The results are compared with other MLLS heuristics like period order method, STIL algorithm and Wagner-Whitin based algorithms. It is observed that GA promises optimal solution in not only fixed horizon problems but also rolling schedule environment and has lower computational requirements. However, parameter setting is to be carefully examined as it will directly affect the algorithm performance.

17. MANUFACTURING LOT-SIZING UNDER MRP-II ENVIRONMENT

Kim and Hosni[17] presents a multi-level capacitated lot-size optimisation model and an efficient heuristic which can be implemented under MRP-II environment. The traditional methods like Wagner-Whitin algorithms do not solve multi-level lot-sizing problems properly since capacity constraints is a major factor in MRP-II environment. The model considers capacity of work centres, lead time information and inter-relationships between parent and child items to compute lot sizes. The objective function is to minimise sum of ordering cost and inventory cost. However, it does not consider shortage cost. The heuristic used to solve this LP uses a master schedule which does not consider capacity constraints. A backward approach is used to find overloaded work centres and the lot sizes are modified to fit the resource capacities. This process is done iteratively to come to the optimal solution. This procedure used in this model is very simple and it is very easy to develop spreadsheet application for this heuristic.

18. EFFECTIVENES OF USING LOT-SIZING RULES TO COPE WITH THE MRP SYSTEM NERVOUSNESS

Ho et al[18] investigate the effectiveness of using lot-sizing rules to cope with system nervousness in MRP systems. Using various dampening methods like safety stock, safety lead time and safety capacity, system nervousness can be reduced. This, however, needs to be evaluated against cost of carrying extra inventories so that the improvement in performance can be justified. The experiments examine the impact of using lot-sizing in an environment characterised by uncertainties in demand and lead times. Moreover, an evaluation of the ability of different lot-sizing rules like Lot-for-lot (LFL), EOQ, Part Period Balancing (PPB), Least Total Cost (LTC) and Silver Meal (SM) to cope with system nervousness is done. To measure the rescheduling efforts, two measurements are considered:

1. **Total number of Rescheduling Messages (TRM)** TRM provides an indicator of the degree of uncertainty within the production system. More

number of rescheduling messages will lead to changes in due dates and large number of such disruptions cause system nervousness.

2. **Weighted Rescheduling Measure (WR)** It is calculated by multiplying schedule deviation by the lot size. This measure is used in instances when the number of rescheduling messages may not be representative of the efforts involved in rescheduling tasks.

The comprehensive performance measure in this study is the Total Cost (TC) which is the sum of inventory-carrying cost, set-up cost and rescheduling cost. In the simulation experiment, lead time variations and demand uncertainties are simulated and rescheduling messages are generated and implemented to meet the revised due dates. For different lot-sizing rules, TC and WR measures are calculated. The major findings are:

- If lead time uncertainty is low, rescheduling cost are low. Once lead time uncertainty increases, cost of rescheduling becomes significant. Moreover, as demand lumpiness increases, all lot-size rules except EOQ performs well.
- In terms of WR, PPB and LTC are better lot-size rules but in terms of TC, SM is the best rule.
- LFL results in most nervous MRP systems. PPB and LTC turn out to be most effective and in most conditions LTC dominates PPB.
- EOQ should not be considered as a lot-sizing rule to reduce system nervousness.

19. GENETIC ALOGRITHM TO SOLVE THE GENERAL MULTI-LEVEL LOT-SIZING PROBLEM WITH TIME VARYING

Dellaert et al[19] present a Genetic Algorithm (GA) to solve the multi-level Lot-sizing (MLLS) problem with no capacity constraints or restrictive assumptions on product structure. It is considered that cost may vary with time. This assumption of time-varying cost is valid since cost like inventory-carrying cost, storage cost, deterioration, obsolescence and opportunity cost is very likely to fluctuate over time. Specific generic operators have been designed to constrain the search to the set of feasible solutions than relying on penalty schemes. The MLLS problem consists in finding a sequence of lot sizes that minimises the sum of set-up and inventory-carrying cost. The objective function is the sum of time varying purchase or production cost, set-up and inventory holding cost for all items. Searching for an optimal solution to the MLLS problem is equivalent to finding a binary matrix so as to minimise the objective function. After this, to constrain the search operation, different genetic operators like single-bit mutation, cumulative mutation, inversion, period crossover or product crossover are designed. The advantages of this heuristic is the simplicity of formulation and cost-efficiency and this makes it an attractive tool for simulation. For small as well as large problems, GA has shown its ability to improve on initial solutions within reasonable time frame.

20. BRANCH AND BOUND LOGIC

Prentis and Khumawala[20] serve as a review of Branch and Bound (B&B) logic to solve MRP lot-sizing problems and briefly introduces Look Ahead Method (LAM) heuristic procedure. From the BoM, the multi-level, multi-component, multi-parent product structure can be determined. B&B process continually partitions the product structure into reduced subsets which are identified as branches and nodes. Lower bounds are calculated for each node and subsets with lower bound higher than to equal to the feasible solution is removed. These nodes, which represent lot sizes, not leading to optimal solution are pruned or removed. LAM heuristic modifies B&B procedure by using a B&B single-level optimising subroutine to increase the lower bound values faster. In B&B, the information regarding higher numbered nodes are not taken into account while calculating the lower bounds of lower numbered nodes. If the higher numbered item's solution is added to the lower bound values, then pruning can be enhanced. This is the idea behind the development of LAM heuristic. However, the number of nodes when using LAM heuristic grows exponentially with the problem size. To avoid this total average modification (TAM) heuristic is used. In this approach, the item's set-up cost is adjusted by summing the product of Time-between-Orders (TBO) and component part's set-up cost. Moreover, only the parent's immediate components on the next lower level are included and components after the next lower level are ignored when adjusting for set-up cost. This simplifying assumption reduces the number of nodes drastically without compromising on the solution which considers the general product structure and variable production/purchasing cost for each item. The two heuristics LAM and TAM are tested for computational efficiency. For the problems tested, LAM was proved optimal 100 per cent of the time while TAM averaged only 3 per cent above optimal cost. However, for larger problems, performance and cost savings produced by TAM was superior to that of Wagner-Whitin algorithm.

21. JOINT OPTIMISATION OF LOT SIZES, SAFETY STOCKS AND SAFETY LEAD TIME

Uncertainty in production and delivery lead times is a major problem for the control of production systems. MRP uses the estimate of lead times to come up with a planned order release schedule for each component. Therefore, any deviation between the estimated and the actual lead time will affect the operation of the MRP system. Another uncertainty considered is from external demand and buffering technique commonly used is safety stock. The purpose of this study (Molinder[21]) is to examine how the level of uncertainty in lead time and demand affect the optimal levels of safety stocks and safety lead times of different MRP systems. The simulation experiment conducted provides further insight into which of the two buffering techniques–safety stocks or safety lead times will perform best in an MRP environment. The performance measures considered are total production cost which includes inventory carrying cost, backlog cost and set-up cost, and the stock-out level. It is seen from the simulation experiments that high level of lead time and demand variability has a strong effect on the level of optimal safety stock as well as safety lead time. For low stock-out/inventory holding cost ratio, lowest cost are obtained by using safety stock. For higher values of this ratio, the preference for safety lead time alternative increases as the demand variability becomes higher. Thus, for smaller values of demand variability, safety stock is the better option while for higher values of demand variability, safety lead times are the better option.

22. OPTIMAL MULTI-LEVEL LOT-SIZING

Steinberg and Napier,[22] present a model for determining optimal lot sizes for purchases, assembly and manufacturing quantities at each level of a multi-level production-inventory system. This multi-level production inventory system is modelled as a constrained generalised network with fixed charge arcs and side constraints. The network structure captures the complexity of interactions of lot-sizing decisions for all components of the system and yields optimal decisions aimed at minimising the purchasing, inventory, assembly and production cost. Initially, the sales forecasts as well as orders on hand are input into the MPS where lot sizes are determined by balancing it with available capacity. Proceedings from the MPS are used in developing the generalised network model which contains nodes like purchase nodes, component nodes, assembly nodes which represent components at a particular level and arcs like purchase arcs, inventory arcs and manufacturing arcs which indicate flow from one node to another. The objective function is to minimise the sum of cost of single unit flow multiplied by the quantity of flow from one node to another. This network model is solved using traditional methods like Kirchoff's equilibrium method. This method offers several computational advantages for small problems. Larger problems, however, should be decomposed into several smaller ones if commonality of components is present and these separate smaller problems may be solved for each family without affecting the optimality of the procedure.

23. OPTIMAL AND HEURISTIC LOT-SIZING PROBLEMS

Chiu and Lin[23] present a study of optimal and heuristic lot-sizing problems for multi-stage production/inventory systems in an MRP system. The approaches used in solving a multi-stage lot-sizing problem are dynamic programming, integer programming model and Branch and Bound (B&B) model. The dynamic programming system is based on the concept of minimising total production, set-up and holding cost. It is assumed that demand is deterministic, production is instantaneous and there is no backlogging. Using the concept of echelon stock, each stage is regarded as an independent single stage which is then represented by topology structure. The optimal solution is obtained by finding the shortest path which in turn minimises the cost of the system. It is seen that the solution time increases exponentially with the length of the planning horizon but only linearly with the number of stages. It is also seen that the heuristic approach developed in this paper performs better in an MRP environment than dynamic programming model. However, the solution times of both dynamic programming and heuristic approach do not depend on the product structure.

24. BUFFERING AGAINST UNCERTAINTY IN MRP

Uncertainty affects a number of items including cost, lead times, choice of lot-sizing rules and other shop-floor control policies. A number of approaches like safety stocks, safety lead times and hedging and over-planning, safety capacity have been suggested to deal with uncertainty. Guide and Srivastava[24]focus on the work done so far and identifies the gaps in the literature which need to be fully addressed. The focus of this paper will be on common forms of buffering i.e., safety stocks and safety lead times. Literature review have been segmented based on type of uncertainty–demand quantity uncertainty, demand quantity and time uncertainty, supply quantity and timing uncertainty and demand and supply quantity and timing uncertainty. The main gaps in the studies so far are:

- Effect of complexity of product structure in service performance
- Limited amount of realism – None of the works reviewed benchmarks of parameters used in an industrial setting.
- Ignores the interactions between MRP and MPS, forecasting and other functional areas.

25. CHOOSING OPTIMAL BUFFERING STRATEGIES

Etienne[25] proposes a model and procedures for dealing with the buffering problem and choosing optimal buffering strategies in MRP. This paper presents the buffering problem mathematically and develops decision rules for choosing an optimal buffering strategy. The different types of uncertainty faced are timing uncertainty, demand uncertainty or combination of both. It is first essential to first find the cost of safety time strategy and the cost of safety stock strategy. For choosing optimal buffering strategy, the point of indifference between safety stock and safety time is calculated. If the quantity of material required to support normal MPS activity is greater than a threshold as given in the paper, to minimise cost, safety lead time is the better strategy. Moreover, at lower values of service level, safety time is the favourable cost minimisation strategy and higher service levels favour safety stock. However, in case of quantity uncertainty, safety time strategy does not help much and safety stock is the only option left. In such a situation, rather than carrying permanent safety stock, it is better to build the safety stock into the order of the material since it eliminates the existence of safety stock during idle periods. If timing and quantity uncertainty are faced simultaneously, the most logical way to deal with both is to build a safety stock for quantity uncertainty into the order for the material and then apply safety time to the augmented order.

26. EFFECTIVENESS OF DAMPENING PROCEDURES TO COPE UP WITH MRP SYSTEM NERVOUSNESS

Ho et al[26] provide a comprehensive overview of conventional buffering techniques and dampening procedures and analyses their effectiveness in coping with MRP system nervousness. System nervousness is the result of uncertainty existing within or outside the production system. Dampening procedures are a compromise between maintaining valid priorities as a result of rescheduling and minimising the adverse effects of system nervousness. Dampening methods commonly used are related to lot-sizing rules, inventory buffering techniques like safety stock, safety lead time and safety capacity. The article then explains the differing dampening procedures commonly used.

- Static dampening procedure which assumes that each production system has certain degrees of flexibility, like overtime, for absorbing changes without changing the due dates of open orders. A static "no rescheduling fence" is used for this purpose. The most serious weakness of this is that the fence is static and is rarely revised regardless of any important change that may occur.
- In an automatic rescheduling procedure, "feasibility" of rescheduling is determined using the minimum lead time. Rescheduling an order is not feasible if rescheduling message is generated inside the minimum lead time. This, however, overlooks cost of rescheduling and capacity utilisation.
- Cost based dampening procedures uses the cost of rescheduling for making rescheduling decisions. If the cost of rescheduling is less than the cost of not rescheduling, it is termed as 'cost effective' or significant and is implemented. However, estimation of these cost needs to be well defined.

No one method is ideal and a mix of different dampening procedures is used for better system performance.

27. EVALUATING DAMPENING EFFECTS

Ho[27] investigates the effectiveness of using lot-sizing rules to dampen system nervousness in MRP systems under stochastic environment conditions using a simulation study. The different lot-sizing rules considered are Lot-For-Lot (LFL), EOQ, Part Period Balancing (PPB), or Least Total Cost (LTC). To measure the dampening effect, two measurements are considered.

1. **Total Number of Rescheduling Messages (TRM)** TRM provides an indicator of the degree of uncertainty within the production system. Implementation of TRMs lead to changes in due dates and a large number of such disruptions cause system nervousness.
2. **Weighted Rescheduling Measure (WR)** It is calculated by multiplying schedule deviation by the lot size.

In the simulation experiment, lead time variations and demand uncertainties are simulated and rescheduling messages are generated and implemented to meet the revised due dates. For different lot-sizing rules,

TRM and WR measures are calculated. The major findings are:

- Demand lumpiness leads to fewer TRMs but larger WRs for all lot-sizing rules.
- LFL results in most nervous MRP systems. PPB and LTC turn out to be most effective and in most conditions LTC dominates PPB.
- EOQ should not be considered as a lot-sizing rule to reduce system nervousness.

28. MRP SYSTEM NERVOUSNESS

Blackburn et al[28] present alternative methods to deal with nervousness. Comparison of these alternative methods is made under rolling schedule conditions so as to mimic reality as close as possible. The paper starts with discussing the reasons for nervousness mainly uncertainty in demand/supply and variations in lot-sizing decisions. The different strategies for dealing with nervousness are:

1. **No revision of decisions within the planning horizon** According to this method, rescheduling is allowed only after the end set of periods, i.e., the schedules are freezed for a planned number of periods and rescheduling decisions can be made only after the completion of these periods. This approach eliminates nervousness due to variation in lot-sizing decisions but the system is still vulnerable to end item demand variability.
2. **Lot-for-lot policy** This approach requires orders to be placed in the same periods at each stage. This reduces nervousness caused due to change in factors.
3. **Buffer stocks** Using of buffers like safety stocks can reduce nervousness. However, it increases the total inventory-carrying cost.
4. **Forecast beyond planned horizon** This approach uses forecasts of demand beyond the planning horizon to prevent small orders being placed near the end of the horizon.
5. **Change cost procedure** This approach involves changing of setup cost for a period to include the additional cost from the previous schedule. For a particular period, if no set-up was previously scheduled, effective set-up cost will include the additional set-up cost also. This approach will ensure that the production schedule will be changed only when the set-up cost, inventory cost and schedule change cost get optimised simultaneously.

A set of simulation experiments were conducted to compare the effectiveness of the above strategies. The results show that Strategy 1 may lead to shortage of items thus reducing the service levels. So under conditions of demand uncertainty, this procedure is not recommended unless used along with buffering techniques. Use of lot-for-lot is seen to be ineffective as it neither reduces nervousness nor improves cost performance. It is seen that buffer stock is the most effective in reducing the total number of scheduling messages. However, the additional inventory-holding cost leads to inferior cost performance. All in all, the Change cost procedure in conjunction with Wagner-Whitin algorithm seems to offer a balanced approach to nervousness and is reasonably cost effective since it reduces only the number of new unplanned orders which are most disruptive to the schedule.

29. UNCERTAINTY DAMPENING METHODS FOR REDUCING MRP SYSTEM NERVOUSNESS

Ho et al[29] introduce the different types of dampening methods used in the context of MRP systems, classifies them and identifies the operating environment in which these dampening methods can be applied effectively. Dampening methods can be viewed as a filtering method that screens out insignificant rescheduling messages. They can be classified into local and global methods. Global dampening methods can be used with any type of rescheduling problem. Production uncertainty can be resolved by either using slack or buffer like safety stock, safety lead time, safety capacity or using by the rescheduling capability of the MRP systems thereby realigning the due dates. Safety stock is the most commonly used buffer and is preferred under conditions of quantity uncertainty. Safety lead time involves in having components in stock before the expected need. Use of safety lead time is preferred under conditions of timing uncertainty. Safety capacity is another method for resolving rescheduling problems. When using safety capacity, certain percentage of the scheduled capacity is reserved to accommodate unanticipated orders and changes. MPS management is another method to reduce nervousness. The objective is to maintain a stable MPS when there are changes in customer orders. Other techniques like firm planned order, lead time compression and time fencing are also in use. Three dampening procedures commonly used are:

1. **Static Dampening Procedure** This procedure refers to a set of heuristic rules that consider due date changes involving only a few periods as trivial, i.e., the system ignores the rescheduling messages created inside a no reschedule window.
2. **Automatic Rescheduling Process** In this process, all the messages which are deemed 'feasible' are implemented and a computer automati-

cally reschedules orders. A message that reschedules an order inside its minimum lead time, which is the time required to complete an order with highest priority, is not considered feasible.

3. **Cost based dampening procedures** In this process, the concept of cost of nervousness is used. Cost of nervousness is the additional cost of disrupting previously established schedules. A rescheduling message is deemed cost effective or significant if the cost of rescheduling of a job is less than the cost of not rescheduling that job.

30. EVALUATION OF SAFETY STOCK METHODS

Zhao et al[30] evaluate methods of establishing safety stock level considering forecasting accuracy, MPS and MRP under a rolling horizon. In the first phase of simulation, demand pattern is generated for 400 periods and forecasting is done using Winters' model with focus on minimising Mean Absolute Deviation (MAD). In the second phase, based on the demand forecast for the planning horizon, MPS is developed for these periods using a lot-sizing heuristic rule. As and when more demand information is available, both demand forecast as well as MPS is revised. Planning horizon is divided into frozen and free intervals and within the frozen interval, the MPS is implemented and cannot be changed. Net requirements for free intervals are calculated using revised forecast, inventory and safety stock levels. The MRP simulation module takes the MPS as the input and develops production and ordering schedule. To calculate safety stock, it is necessary to determine safety coverage, standard deviation of forecast errors and service level. Coverage is the number of periods in which demand uncertainty is to be protected by safety stock. The three methods to calculate coverage are:

1. **T method** Here, the coverage is taken as the period from which the last order is received to the period in which the current order is to be received.
2. **LT method** In this method, the coverage equals the coverage calculated using T method and production lead time.
3. **FT method** In this method, coverage is the period between the times in which the order is first planned and the time in which the order is to be received.

It was found that the placing of safety stock at the end item level improves performance of MRP systems. It is also found that the methods used to determine coverage significantly influences the total cost in the MRP system. T method is seen to perform better when compared to the other two methods since it produces lower cost, lower instability and higher service levels. The managerial implications of this are that a manager should try to set enough safety stock to protect against uncertainty during periods that the order quantity covers.

31. INTERACTION BETWEEN FREQUENCY OF RESCHEDULING AND THE RULE OF SAFETY STOCK IN MRP SYSTEM

Most of the literature available studied the approaches for determining scheduling policy or safety stock in MRP systems, but little has been done in examining the interaction between them. Candace and Carlson,[31] study the interaction between frequency of rescheduling and the role of safety stock in terms of impact on system performance. It is assumed that lead times, yields, supply timing and quantity are certain and only the demand is uncertain. For scheduling, both fixed and flexible scheduling policies are considered and the product structure considered is a two-level structure. The study determines cost-effective safety stock levels for both finished products and to ascertain whether rescheduling is desirable. Candace and Carlson used a simulation model to study the above mentioned relationships and interactions and a range of parameters like holding cost, cycle length and demand variability were considered. Simulation results show that safety stock has no impact on an end item if the component cycle is the same as its parent and the schedule and quantity for each item is fixed during lead time. An item with the same order/production frequency as its parent will know exactly how many units are required in the next production stage.

If fixed rescheduling is used on level 1, it was found that increasing end item safety stock always increases both fill rate and cost. If flexible rescheduling is used on level 1, cost and fill rate vary for different scenarios as given below.

- Cost and fill rate increases if safety stock is used so as to reduce shortages
- Cost and fill rate decreases if emergency set-ups are prevented but availability over horizon decreases
- Cost decrease and fill rate increases if emergency set-ups are prevented but availability over horizon increases
- Cost increase and fill rate decreases if emergency set-ups are eliminated but additional safety stock offsets the savings obtained by eliminating emergency set-ups

For second level component, if fixed rescheduling is used, increasing component safety stock increases both cost and service levels except under special conditions. Simulation studies have also been done when fixed scheduling is used on level 1 and flexible on level 2, additional safety stock impacts total cost but not service levels to a great extent. Evidence also indicates that effect of safety stock in a system in which flexible rescheduling is used on both levels is highly unpredictable.

Thus, for systems operating under flexible scheduling, increasing end item safety stock may actually decrease service levels in the short run and for second component level, cost may get reduced with no significant impact on service levels. Moreover, rescheduling frequently may not be an economical option.

32. IMPACT OF SAFETY STOCK ON SCHEDUDE INSTABILITY COST AND SERVICE

Sridharan and LaForge[32] investigate the effectiveness of safety stock in reducing schedule instability when the demand is uncertain. Along with schedule instability, effect on lot-size cost and customer service is also examined. The main factors considered were demand variability, demand uncertainty, inventory-carrying cost and set-up cost, planning horizon which represents the number of periods of forecasted demand available to develop MPS schedule. The lot-sizing methods considered are Wagner-Whitin and Silver Meal Heuristics. The effects of safety stock were investigated using simulation methods under a wide range of conditions for the above mentioned experimental factors. The results indicate that safety stock may be useful only when used in limited quantities. Safety stock has a significant impact on schedule instability, total cost and service level, but both schedule instability and total cost appear to increase as the safety stock level is increased beyond a threshold. Safety stock is ineffective when demand is highly uncertain. Moreover, since both total cost and schedule instability decrease when small amounts of safety stock are used, stable production schedules can be achieved by using small quantities of safety stock if the set-up cost is low. So reducing product setup times or improving accuracy of forecasts can help reduce schedule instability.

33. IMPACT OF USING MULTIPLE-FREEZE FENCES APPROACH OF COSTS IN MRP SYSTEMS

Yeung et al[33] study the impact of environmental and cost factors on the total system cost when using multiple-freeze fences approach and comparing it with single-freeze fence. The environmental factors studied are product structure, forecast error and forecast bias and the cost factors under considerations are cost structure, holding cost, shortage cost, set-up cost and schedule change cost. Three sets of product structure with different component commonality are considered for simulation, and three types of cost structures–low, medium and high are considered. Two simulation runs are conducted–first in an environment with multiple-freeze fences and the second with a single-freeze fence. The results show that multiple-freeze fences are preferred as they can lower total inventory-holding cost in all environments. But to reduce shortage cost, single freeze fence are a better option. In general, multiple-freeze fences perform better with cost factors under conditions of high holding cost, high product structure cost and low shortage cost. It is also recommended that effort should be made by manufacturers to increase component commonality and shorter frozen intervals give MPS more flexibility,

34. SCHEDULE INSTABILITY SERVICE LEVEL AND COST IN MRP SYSTEM

Xue et al[34] aim at investigating how the four important parameters (schedule frozen interval, schedule re-planning interval, safety stock and lot-sizing rules) affect MRP system performance. The performance measurements used are schedule instability, total cost and service level. The impact of these parameters were evaluated under different levels of two operating factors–lead times of items in product structure and accuracy of demand forecast. Frozen interval is the time during which no schedule changes are allowed, whereas re-planning interval is the, time between successive revisions of MPS. The performance measure schedule instability is defined as the average weighted changes in order quantities throughout multiple planning cycles for all items at all levels, while service level is the proportion of end-item demand satisfied from stock on time. The third parameter, total cost, consists of total set-up cost, total holding cost and total cost of changing. For different combinations of parameters and operating factors, simulation was carried out. The results indicate that increasing frozen interval reduces schedule instability and total cost-but service level is worsened. Frequent re-planning improves service level and reduces cost but instability increases due to the frequent changes in the planned productions. However, contrary to popular belief, results indicate that high levels of safety stock increases instability and reduce cost. Other observations are:

- If lead time is long and forecast is less accurate, frequent re-planning can worsen system instability. So in such situations, it is advisable to choose longer re-planning interval.
- If lead time is long and forecast is more precise, increasing safety stock level may significantly worsen system instability, thus not a good option.
- If lead time is short and forecast is less accurate, system instability is insensitive to lot-sizing and cost and service level are the only parameters used in selecting lot size rule.
- If lead time is short and forecast is accurate, all three measures of performance improves, i.e., system can achieve highly stable schedule, low total cost and high service level.

REFERENCES

1. Yeung JHY, WCK Wong, and L Ma, Parameters affecting the effectiveness of MRP systems: a review, International of Production Research, 36(2), 1998, 313-331.
2. William Darrow P and Jatinder N D Gupta, Integrating Group Technology and MRP systems through Lot-sizing and Scheduling, 16(2), 1989, 287-296.
3. Enns ST, The Effect of Batch Size Selection on MRP performance, Computers and Industrial Engineering, 37, 1999, 15-19.
4. Ashutosh Agrawal, Ioannis Minis, and Rakesh Nagi, Cycle time reduction by improved MRP-based production planning, International Journal of Production Research, 38(18), 2000, 4823-4841.
5. Michael Hegedus G, Wallace J Hopp, Due Date setting with Supply constraints in systems using MRP, Computers & Industrial Engineering, 39, 2001, 293-305.
6. Peter Billington, J John ,O McClain and L Joseph Thomas, Mathematical Programming approaches to capacity-constraint MRP systems: Review, Formulation and Problem Reduction, Management Science, 29(10), 1983, 1126-1141.
7. Johannes Harl E and Larry P Ritzman, Heuristic Algorithm for Capacity Sensitive Requirements Planning, Journal of Operations Management, 5(3), 1985, 309-326.
8. Kurt Gutzmann M and Richard A Wysk, Capacity Control policies for MRP systems, International Journal of Production Research, 24(2), 1986, 359-374.
9. Pandey PC, Pisal Yenradee and Sunisa Archariyapruek, A finite capacity material requirements planning system, Production Planning & Control, 11(2), 2000, 113-121.

10. Nagendra P B and S K Das, Finite Capacity scheduling method for MRP with lot size restrictions, International Journal of Production Research, 39(8), 2001, 1603-1623.
11. Amitabh Raturi S and Arthur V Hill, An Experimental Analysis of Capacity-Sensitive Setup Parameters for MRP Lot-Sizing, Decision Sciences, 19(4), 1988, 782-800.
12. Koh SCL, S M Saad and J Padmore, Development and implementation of a generic order release scheme for modeling MRP-controlled finite-capacitated manufacturing environments, International Journal of Computer Integrated Manufacturing, 17(6), 2004, 561-576.
13. Johannes Harl E, Alternative Heuristics for Large Scale Capacitated Requirements Planning Systems, International Journal of Operations & Production Management, 4(3), 1983, 22-35.
14. Alfieri A, P Brandimarte and S D'Orazio, LP-based heuristics for the capacitated lot-sizing problem: The interaction of model formulation and solution algorithm, International Journal of Production Research, 40(2), 2002, 441-458.
15. Xiande Zhao, Kokin Lam, Lot-sizing rules and freezing the master production schedule in material requirements planning systems, International Journal of Production Economies, 53, 1997, 281-305.
16. Dellaert N and J Jeunet, Solving large unconstrained multilevel lot-sizing problems using a hybrid genetic algorithm, International Journal of Production Research, 38(5), 2000, 1083-1099.
17. Hyun-Joon Kim, Yasser A. Hosni, Manufacturing Lot-sizing under MRP-II Environment: An Improved Analytical model & Heuristic procedure, Computers and Industrial Engineering, 35(3-4), 1998, 423-426.
18. Chrwan-Jyh Ho and Shih-Jen Kathy Ho, Evaluating the effectiveness of using lot-sizing rules to cope with MRP system nervousness, Production Planning & Control, 10(2), 1999, 150-161.
19. Dellaert N, J Jeunet, N Jonard, A genetic algorithm to solve the general multi-level lot-sizing problem with time-varying cost, International Journal of Production Economics, 68, 2002, 241-257.
20. Eric Prentis L, Basheer M Khumawala, Efficient Heuristics for MRP Lot-sizing with Variable Production/Purchasing Cost, 20(3), 1989, 439-450.
21. Molinder A, Joint optimization of lot-sizes, safety stocks and safety lead times in an MRP system, International Journal of Production Research, 35(4), 1997, 983-994.
22. Earle Steinberg and H Albert Napier, Optimal multi-level lot-sizing for requirements planning systems, Management Science, 26(12), 1980, 1258-1271.
23. Huan-Neng Chiu and Tsong-Ming Lin, An Optimal model and a Heuristic technique for Multi-stage Lot-sizing Problems: Algorithms and Performance tests, Engineering Cost and Production Economics, 16, 1989, 151-160.
24. Guide V D R Jr and R Srivastava, Review of techniques for Buffering against uncertainty with MRP systems, Production Planning & Control, 11(3), 2000, 223-233.

25. Eisenhower Etienne C, Choosing Optimal Buffering Strategies for dealing with Uncertainty in MRP, Journal of Operations Management-Combined Issue, 7(1,2), 1987, 107-120.
26. Chrwan-jyh Ho, Ram Narasimhan, Steve A Melnyk, and Phillip L Carter, Research Framework for Investigating the Effectiveness of Dampening Procedures to Cope with MRP System Nervousness, International Journal of Operations & Production Management, 12(6), 1992, 30-43.
27. Chrwan-Jyh Ho, Evaluating dampening effects of alternative lot-sizing rules to reduce MRP system nervousness, International Journal of Production Research, 40(11), 2002, 2633-2652.
28. Joseph Blackburn D, Dean H Kropp and Robert A Millen, MRP System Nervousness: Causes and Cures, Engineering Cost and Production Economics, 9, 1985, 141-146.
29. C J Ho, W K Law, and R Rampal, Uncertainty dampening methods for reducing MRP system nervousness, International Journal of Production Research, 33(2), 1995, 483-496.
30. Xiande Zhao, Fujun Lai and T S Lee, Evaluation of Safety stock methods in multilevel material requirements planning (MRP) systems, Production Planning & Control, 12(8), 2001, 794-803.
31. Candace Arai Yano and Robert C Carlson, Interaction between frequency of rescheduling and the role of safety stock in material requirement planning systems, International Journal of Production Research, 25(2), 1987, 221-232.
32. Sridharan V, R Lawrence LaForge, The Impact of Safety Stock on Schedule Instability, Cost and Service, Journal of Operations Management, 8(4), 1989, 327-347.
33. Jeff Yeung H Y, Lin Ma, and Japhet S Law, The impact of using multiple freeze fences on cost in MRP systems, International Journal of Production Research, 41(10), 2003, 2201-2228.
34. Xue Bai, J Steve Davis, John J Kanet, Steve Canrell and J Wayne Patterson, Schedule instability, service level and cost in a material requirements planning system, International Journal of Production Research, 40(7), 2002, 1725-1758.

Appendix-1
Product Structures used in Research Problems

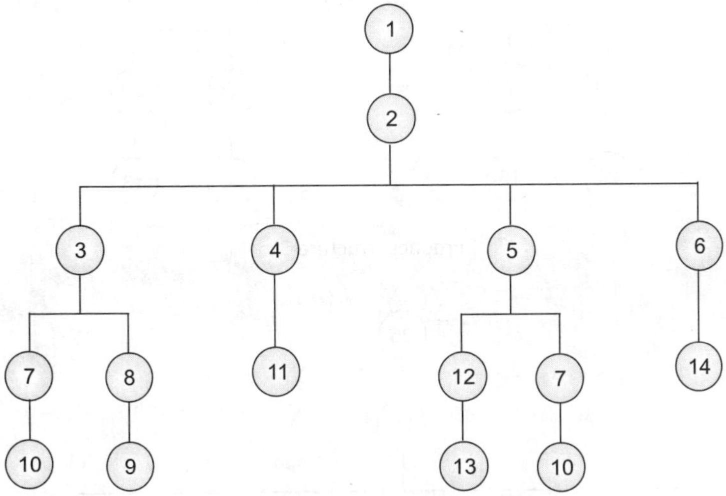

Product Structure-1

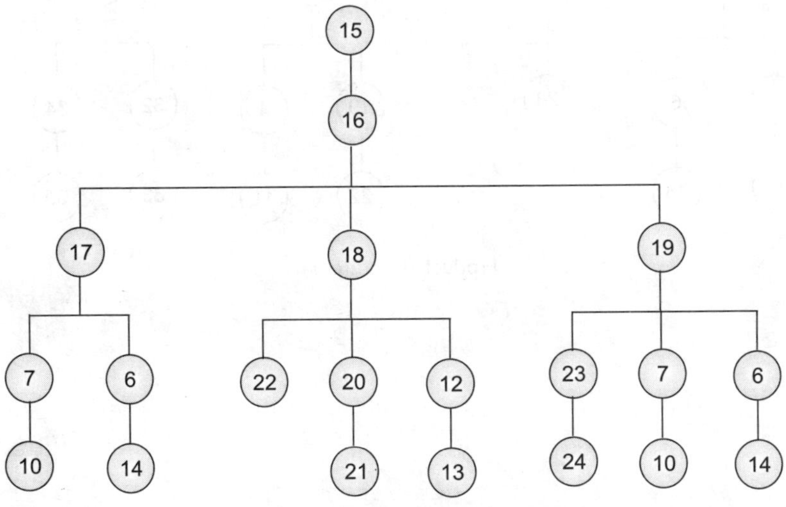

Product Structure-2

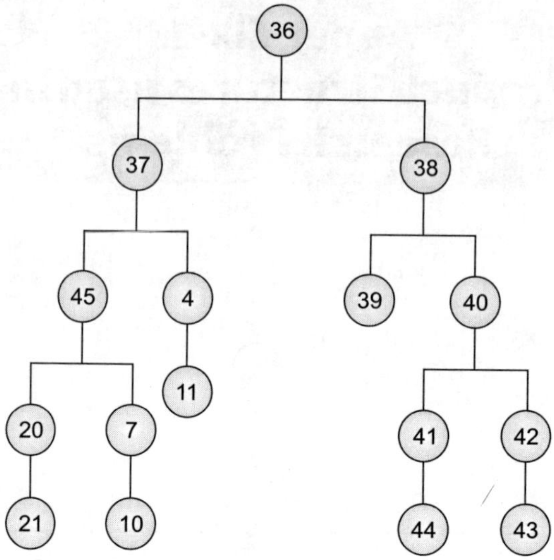

Product Structure-3

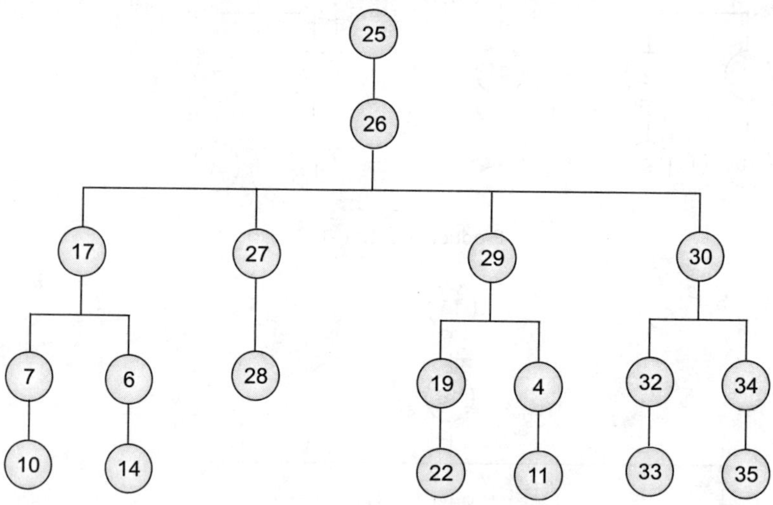

Product Structure-4

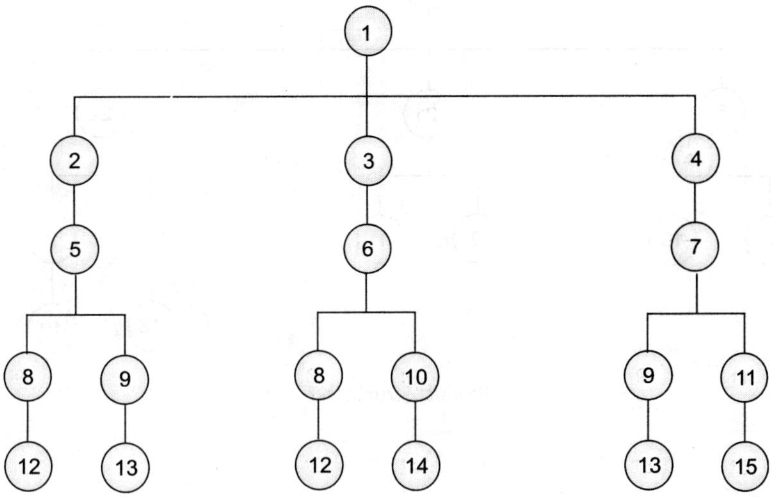

Product Structure-5

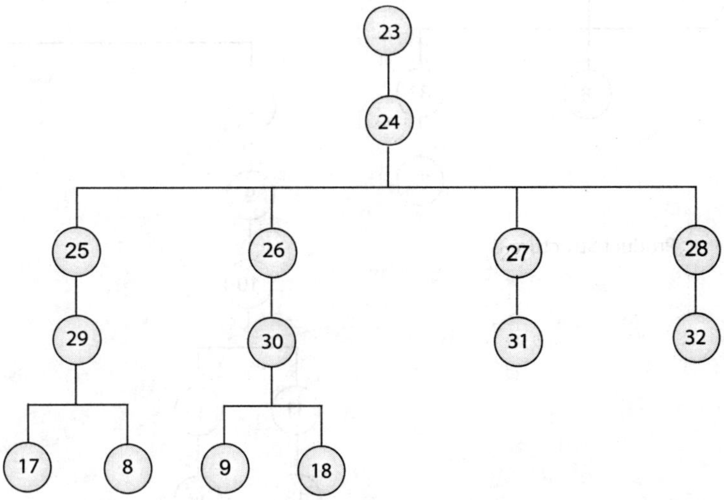

Product Structure-6

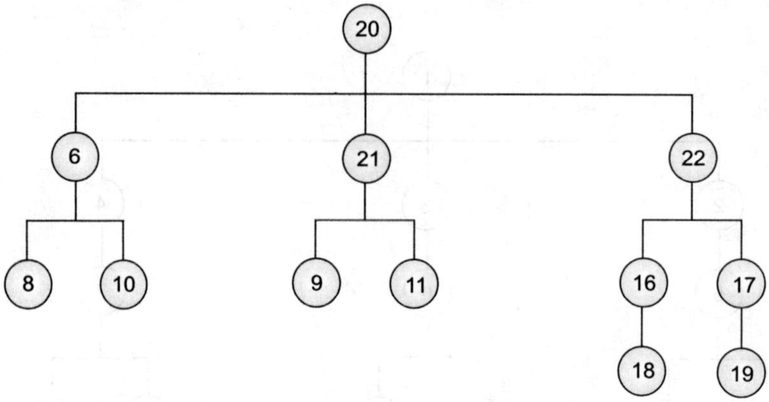

Product Structure-7

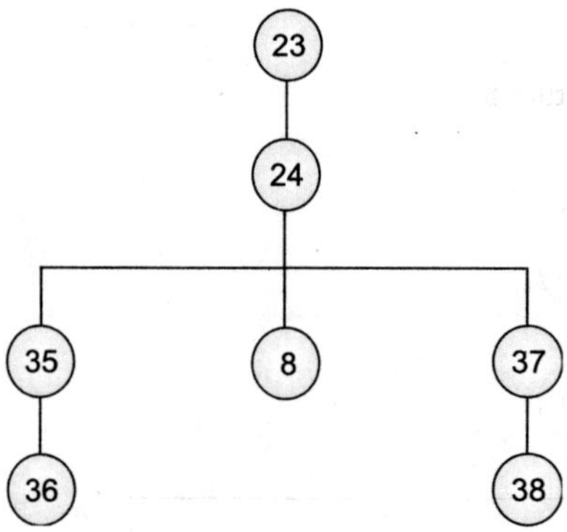

Product Structure-8

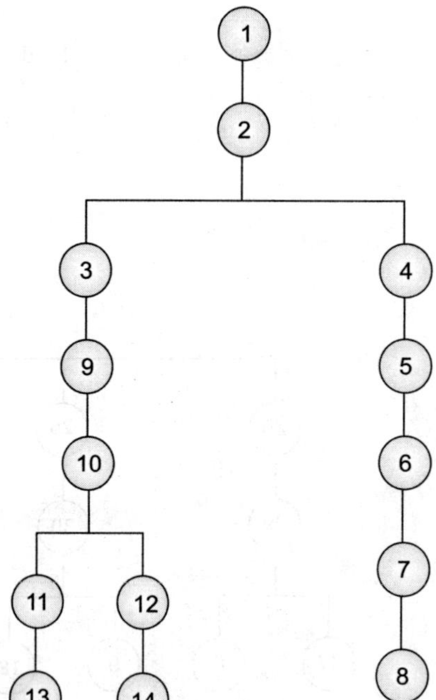

Product Structure-9

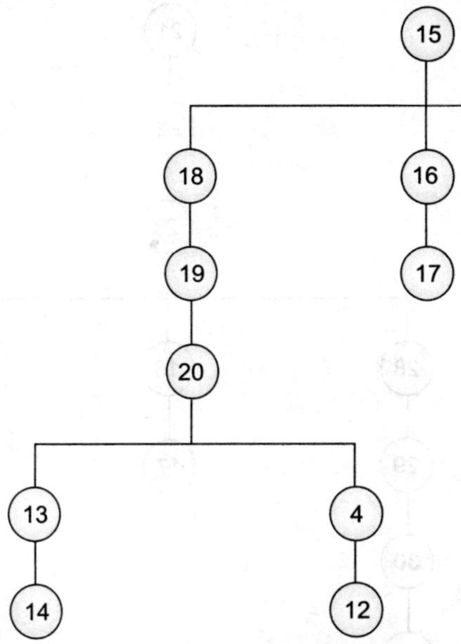

Product Structure-10

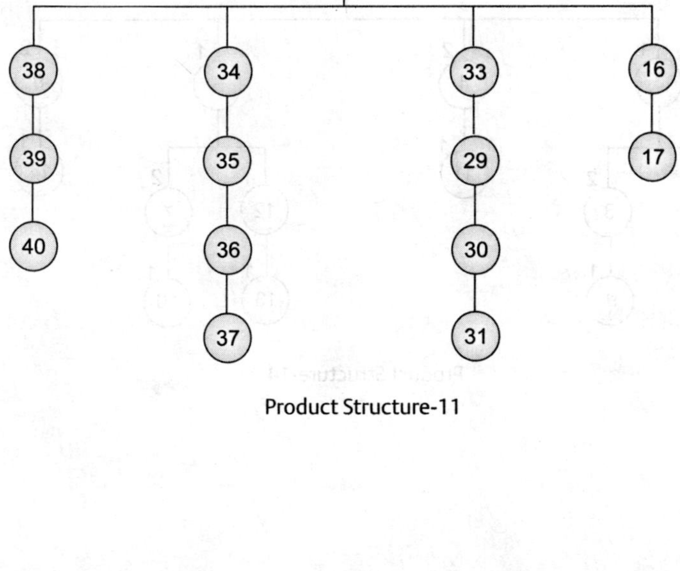

Product Structure-11

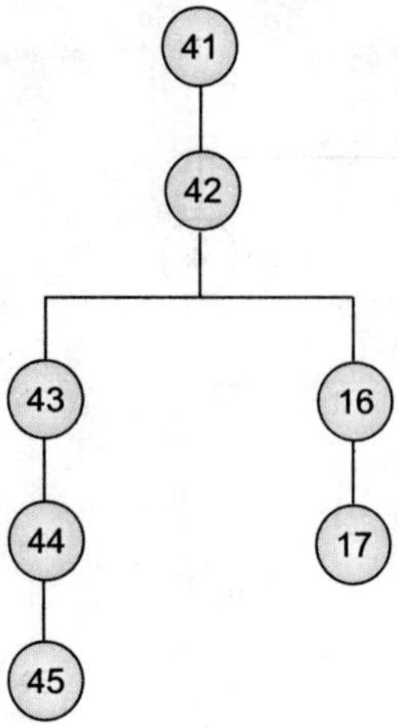

Product Structure-12

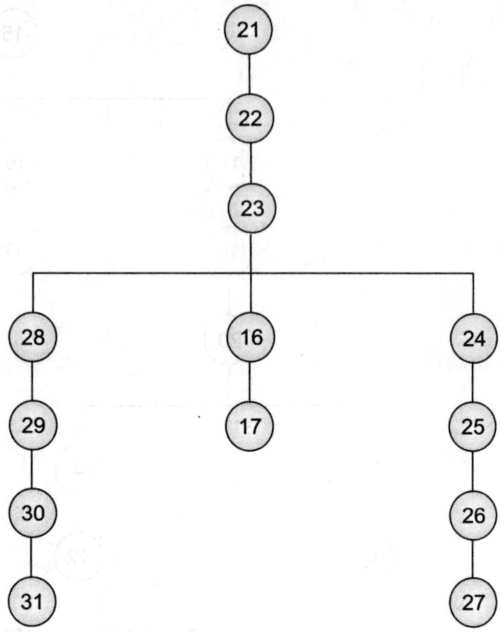

Product Structure-13

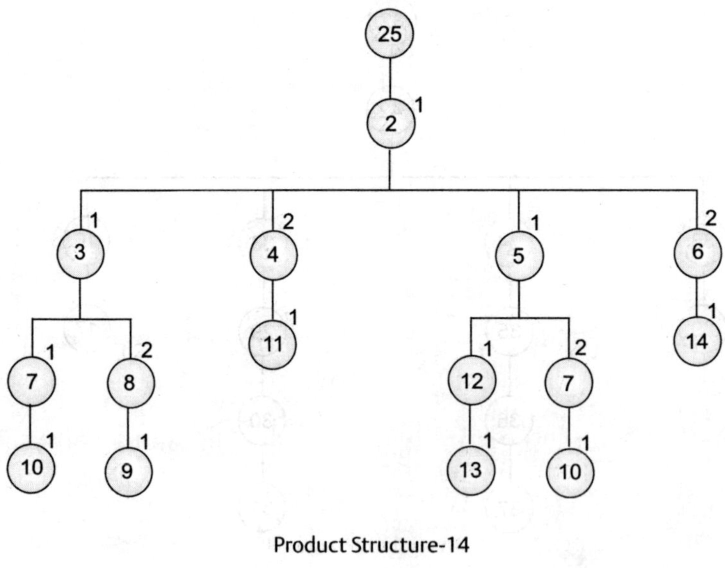

Product Structure-14

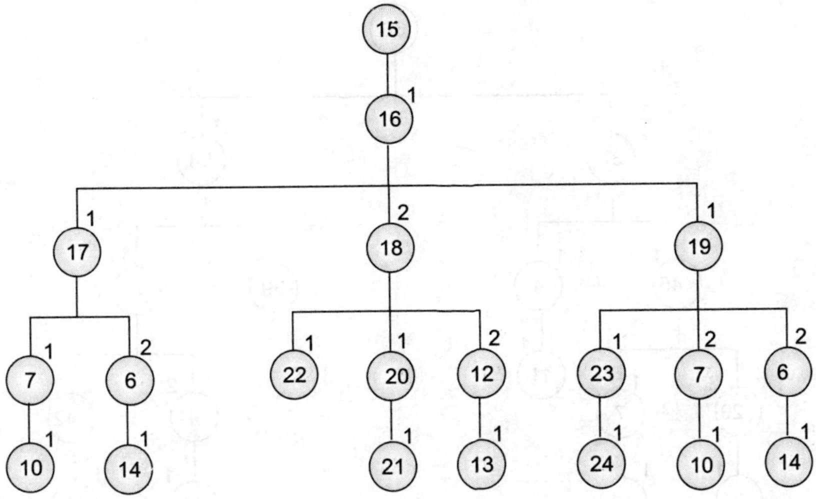

Product Structure-15

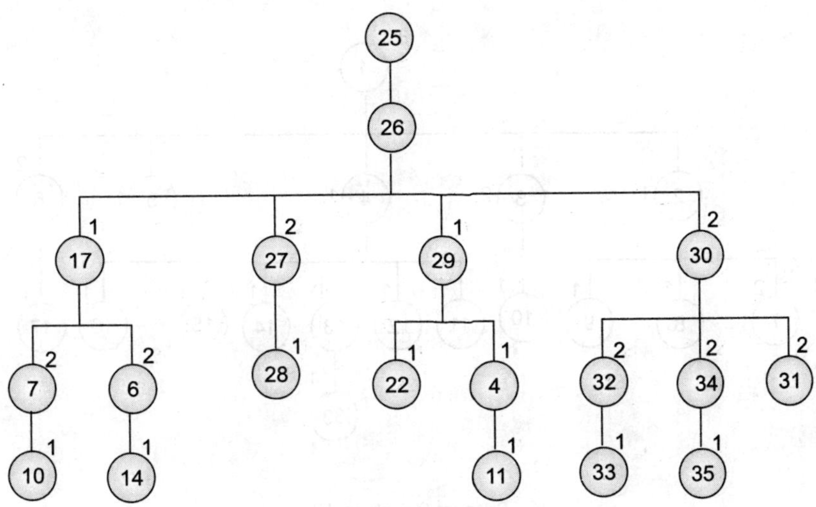

Product Structure-16

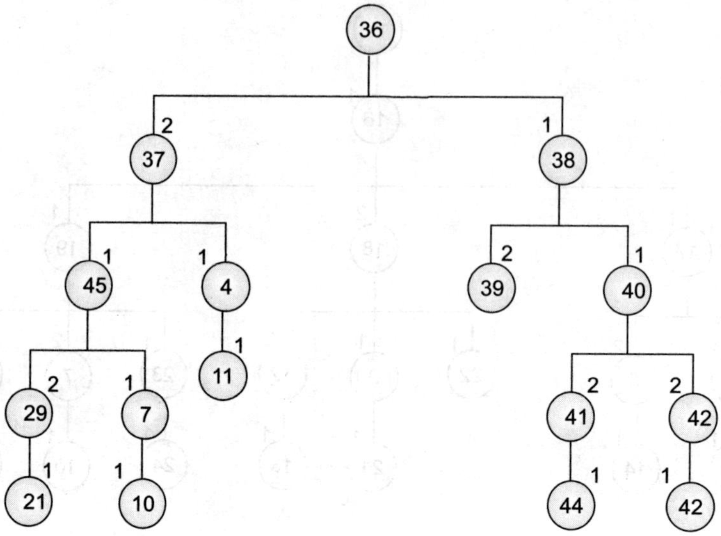

Product Structure-17

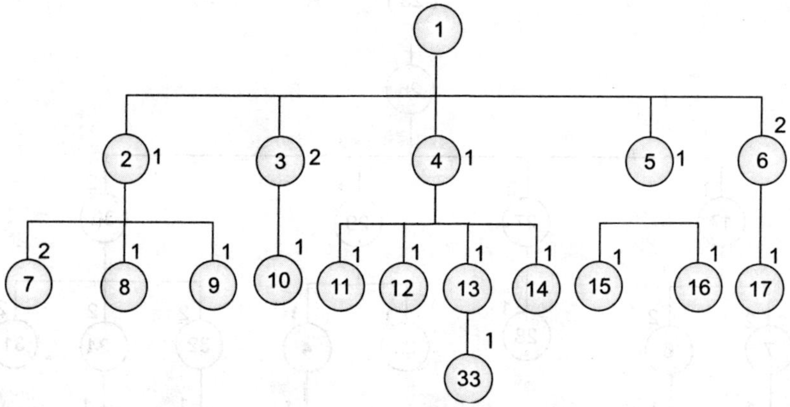

Product Structure-18

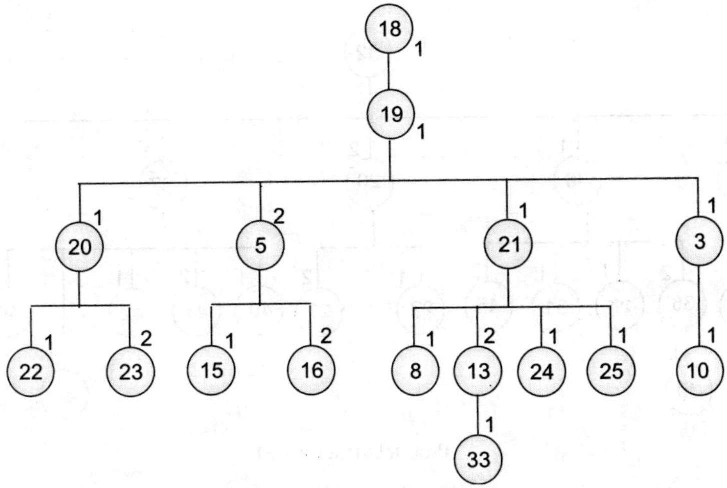

Product Structure-19

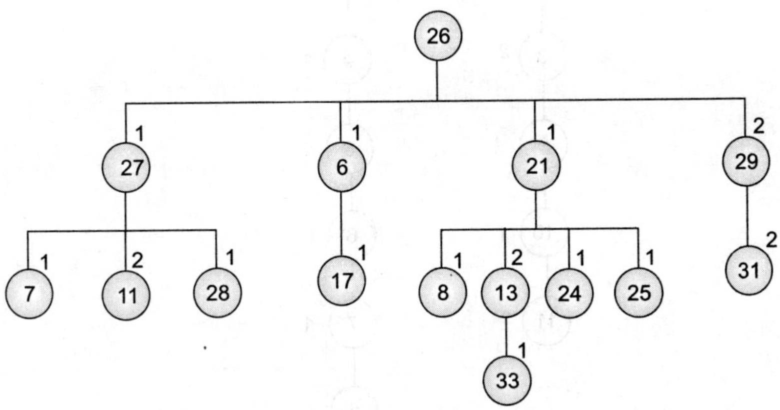

Product Structure-20

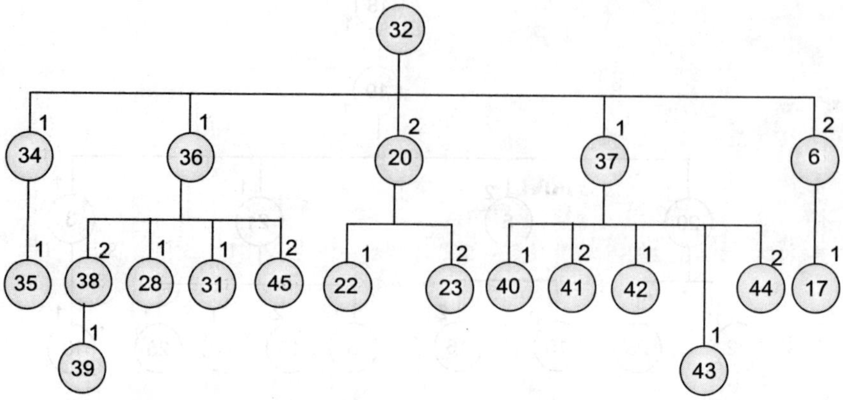

Product Structure-21

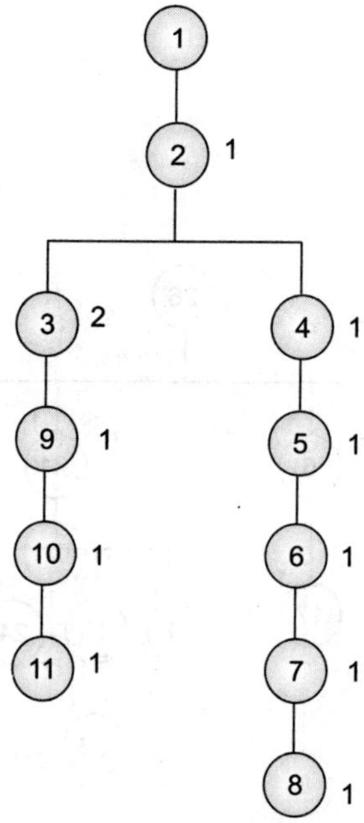

Product Structure-22

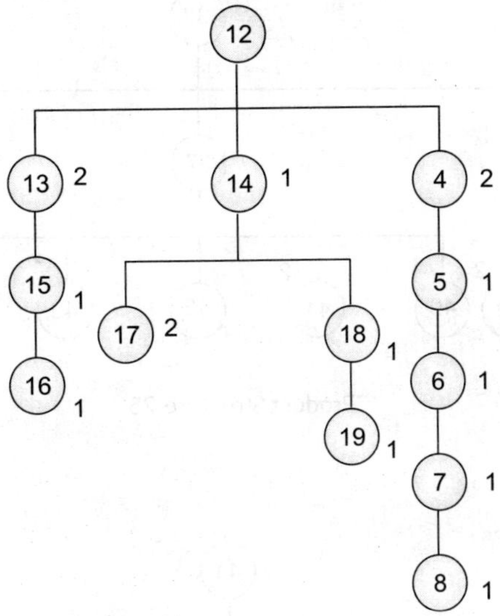

Product Structure-23

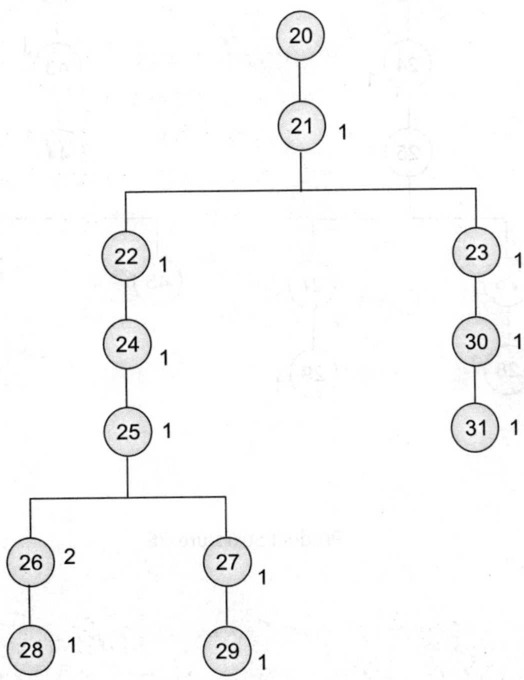

Product Structure-24

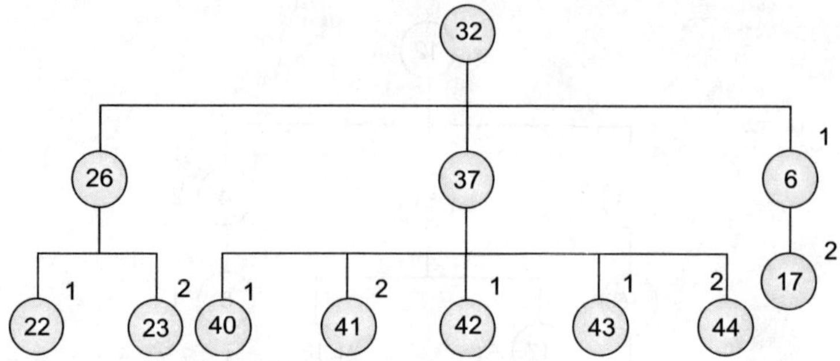

Product Structure-25

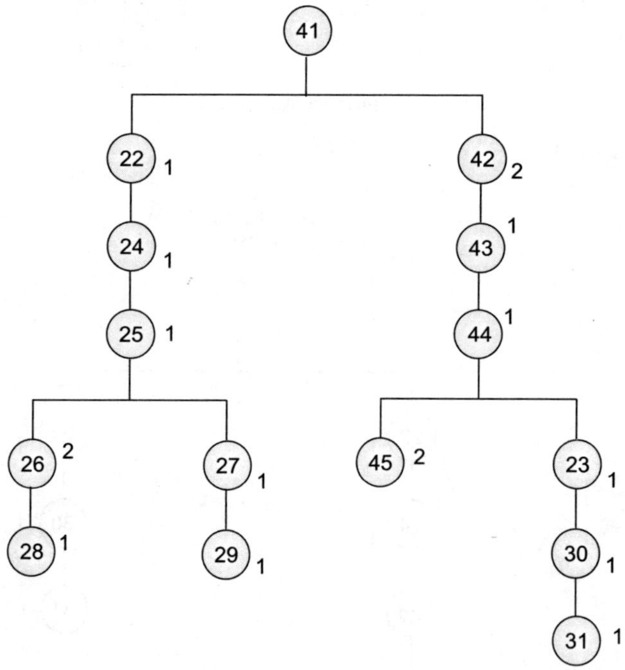

Product Structure-26

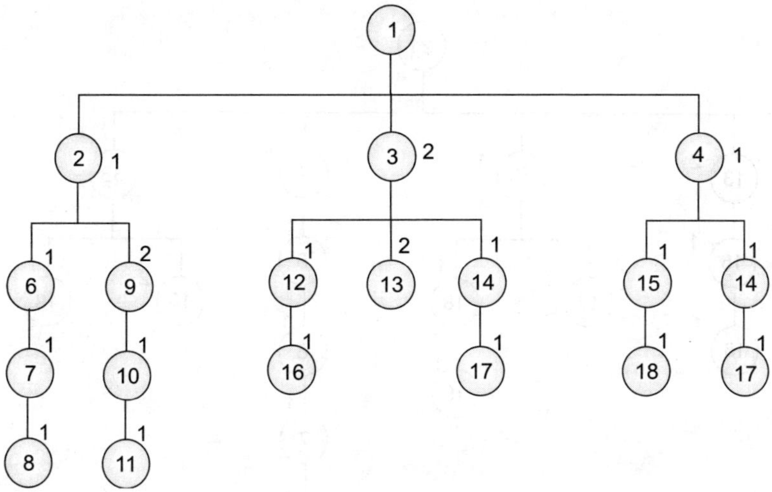

Product Structure-27

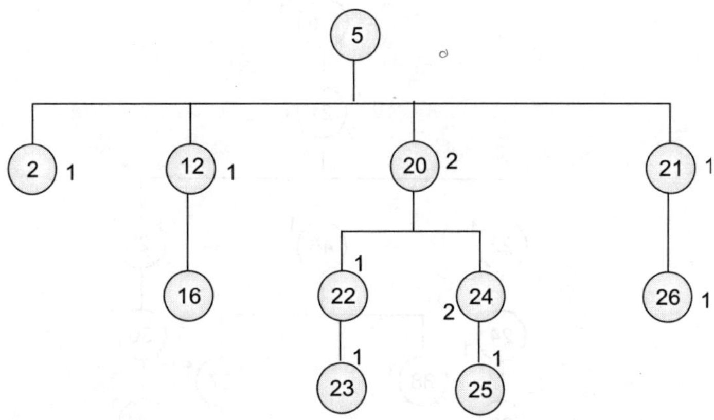

Product Structure-28

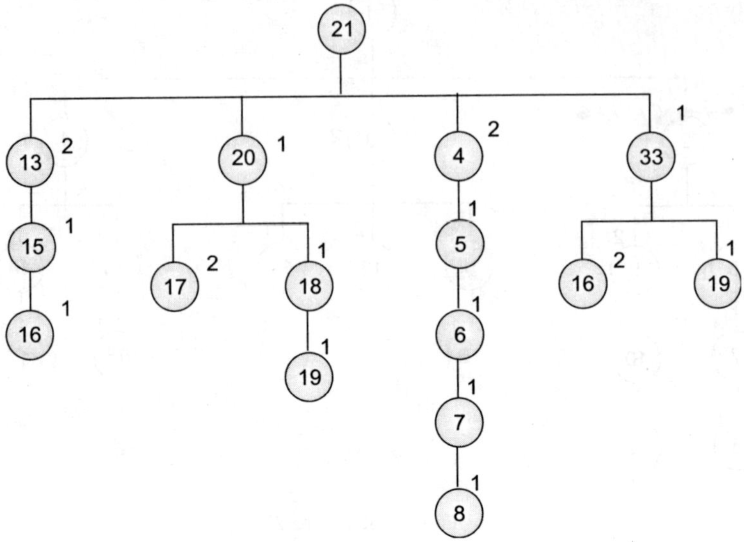

Product Structure-29

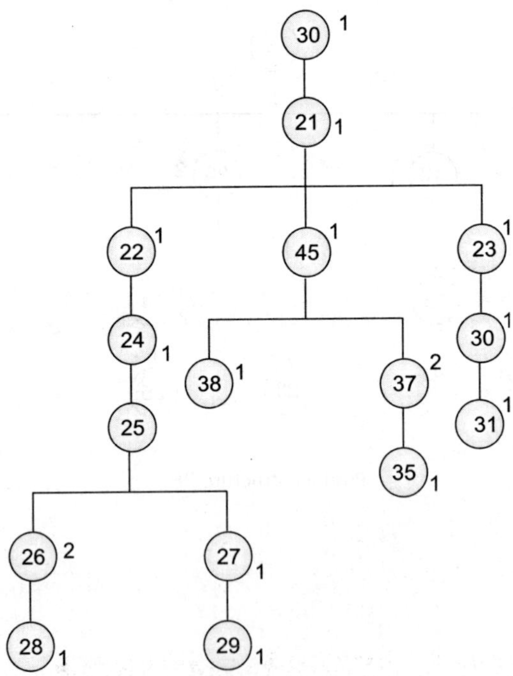

Product Structure-30

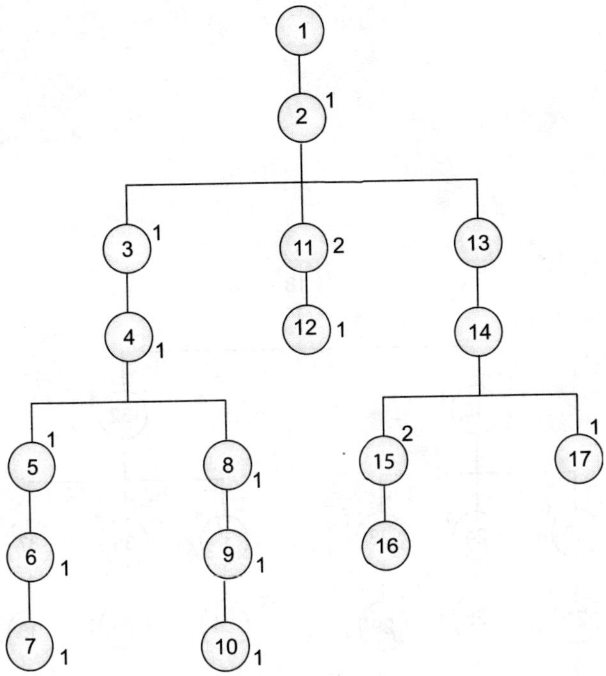

Product Structure-31

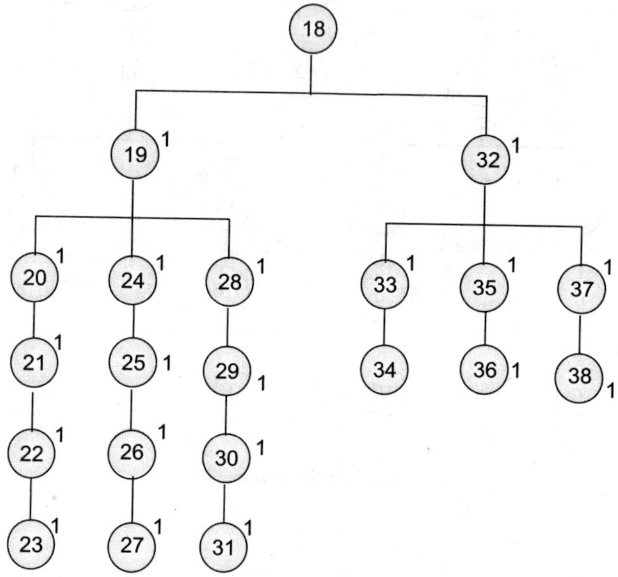

Product Structure-32

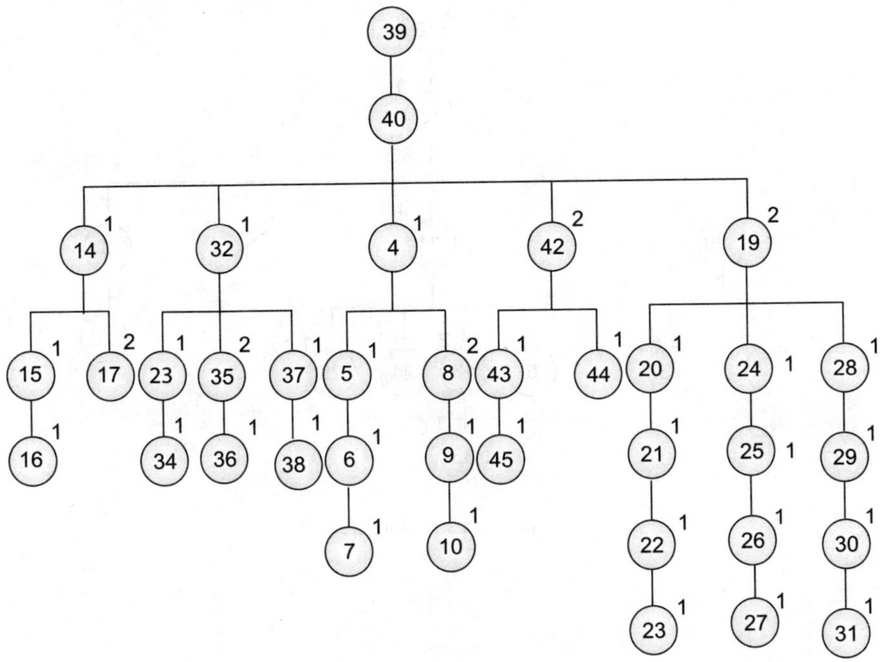

Product Structure-33

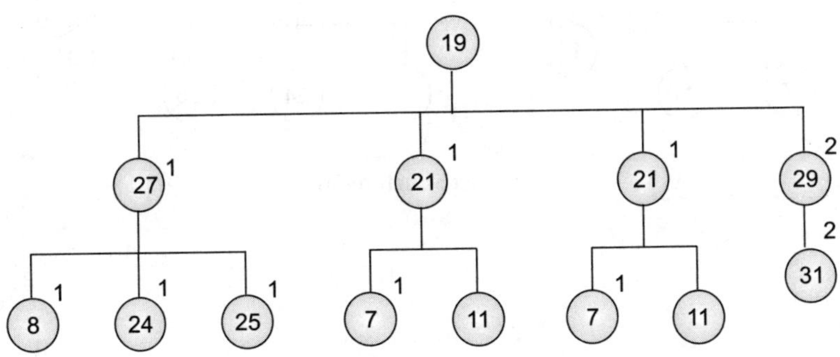

Product Structure-34

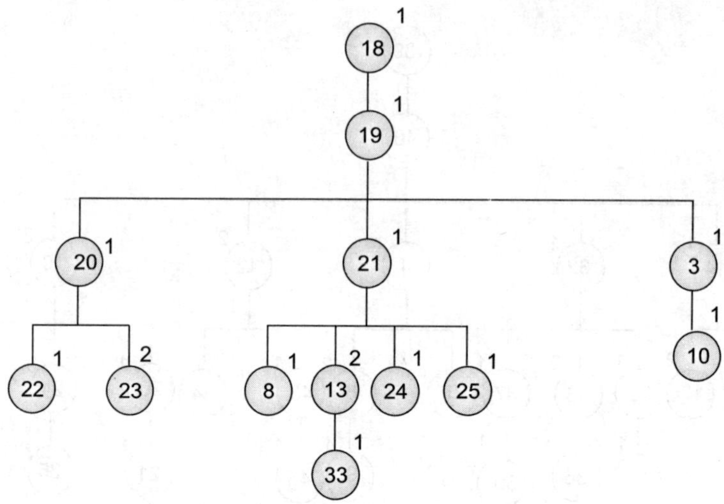

Product Structure-35

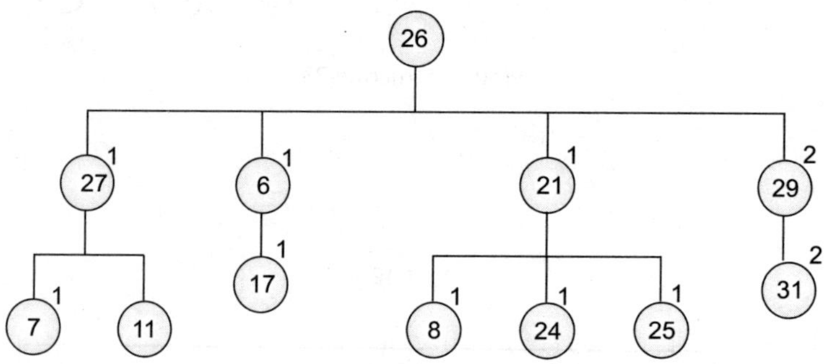

Product Structure-36

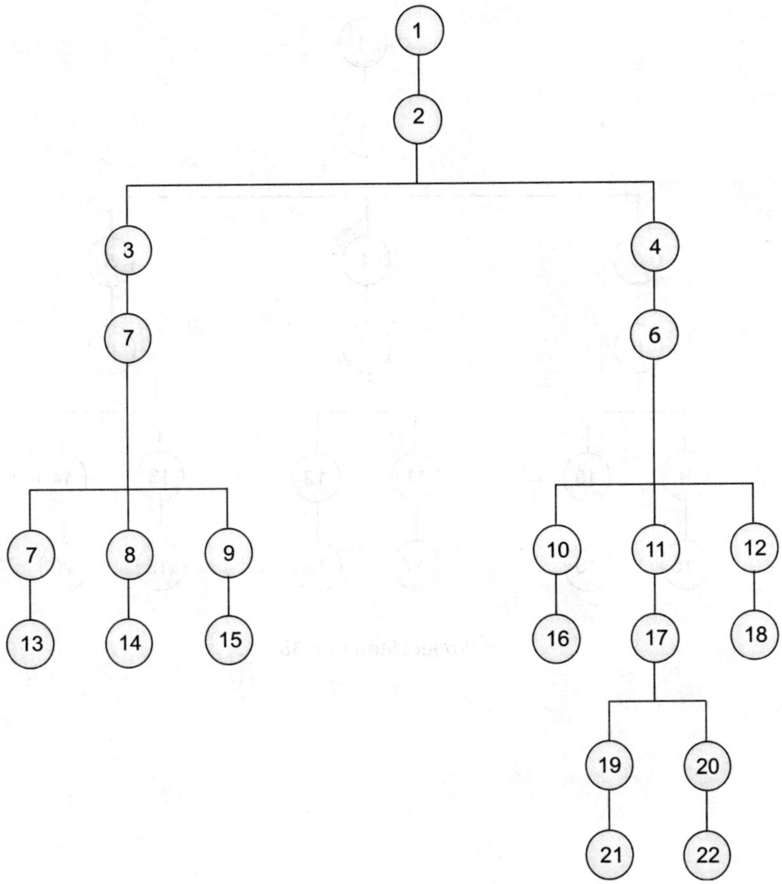

Product Structure-37

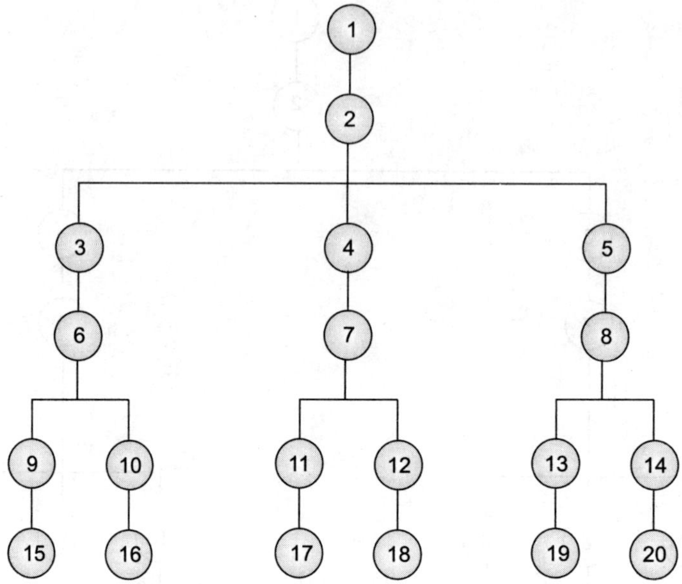

Product Structure-38

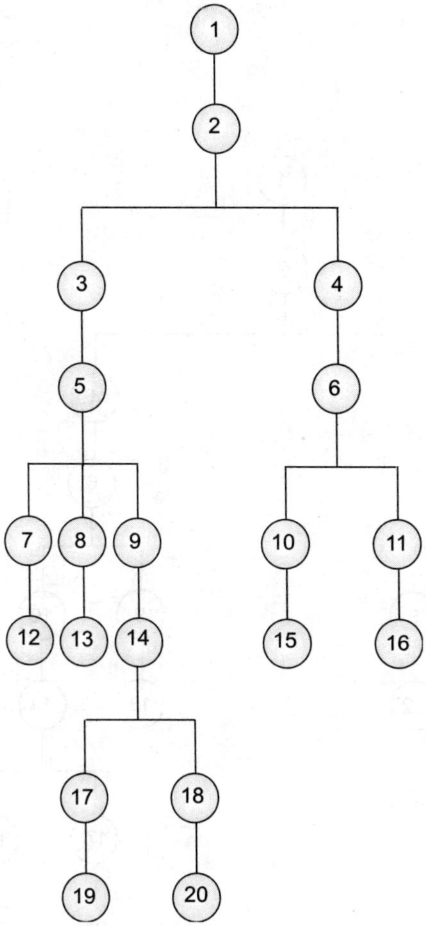

Product Structure-39

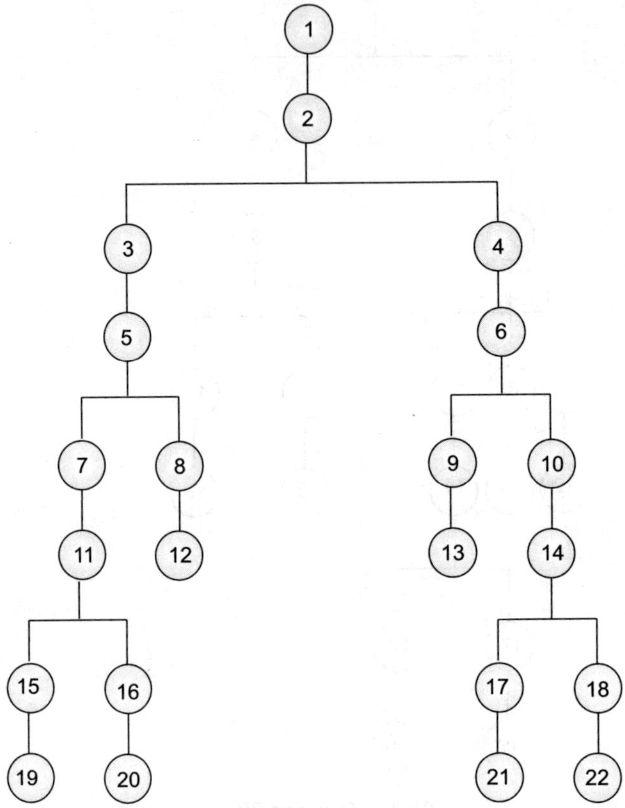

Product Structure-40

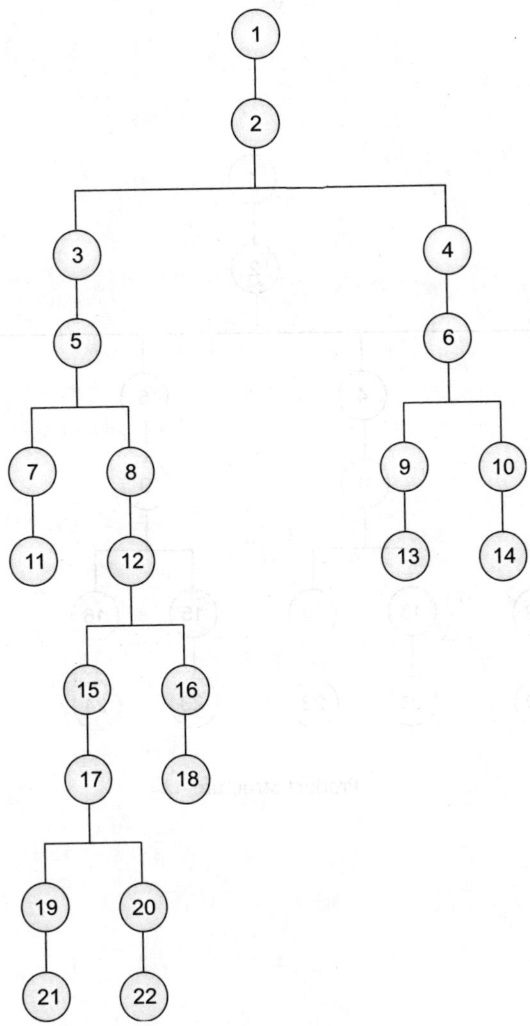

Product Structure-41

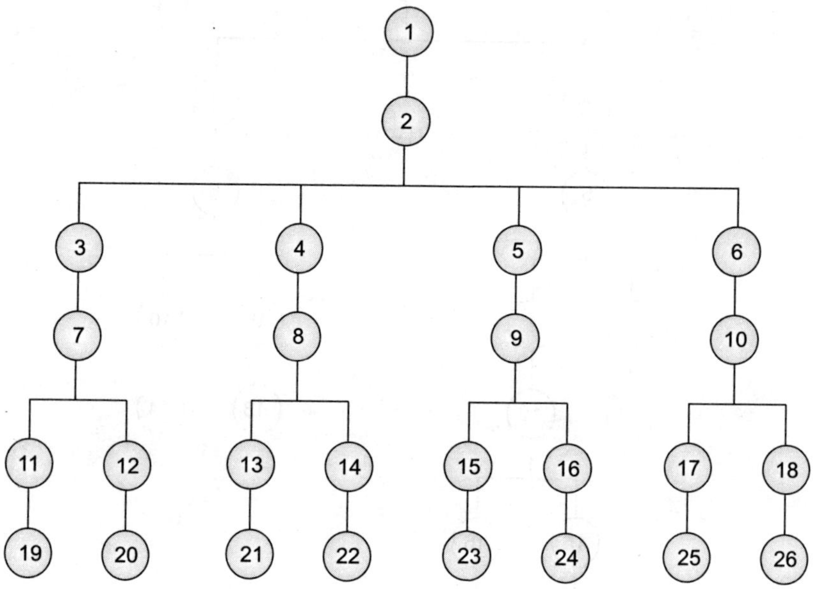

Product Structure-42

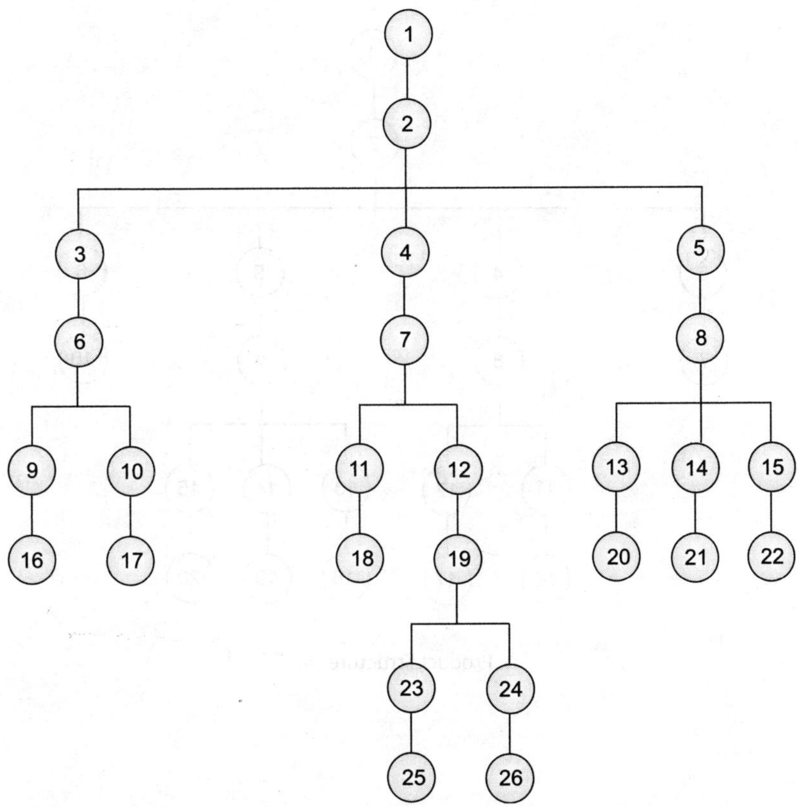

Product Structure-43

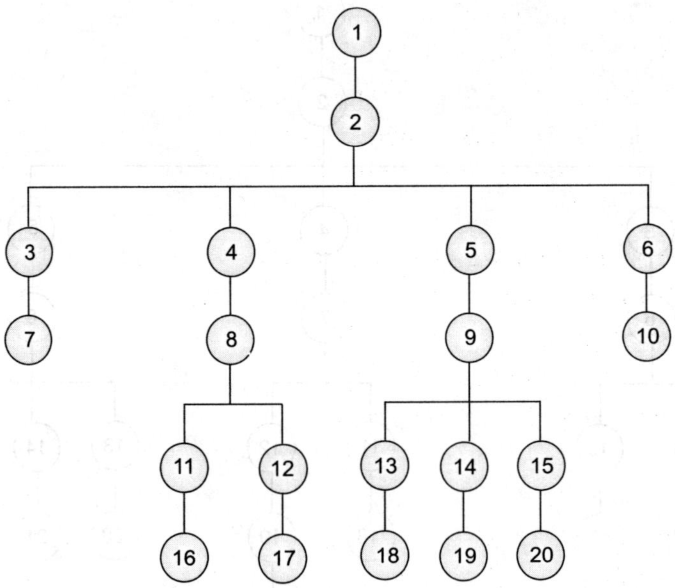

Product Structure-44

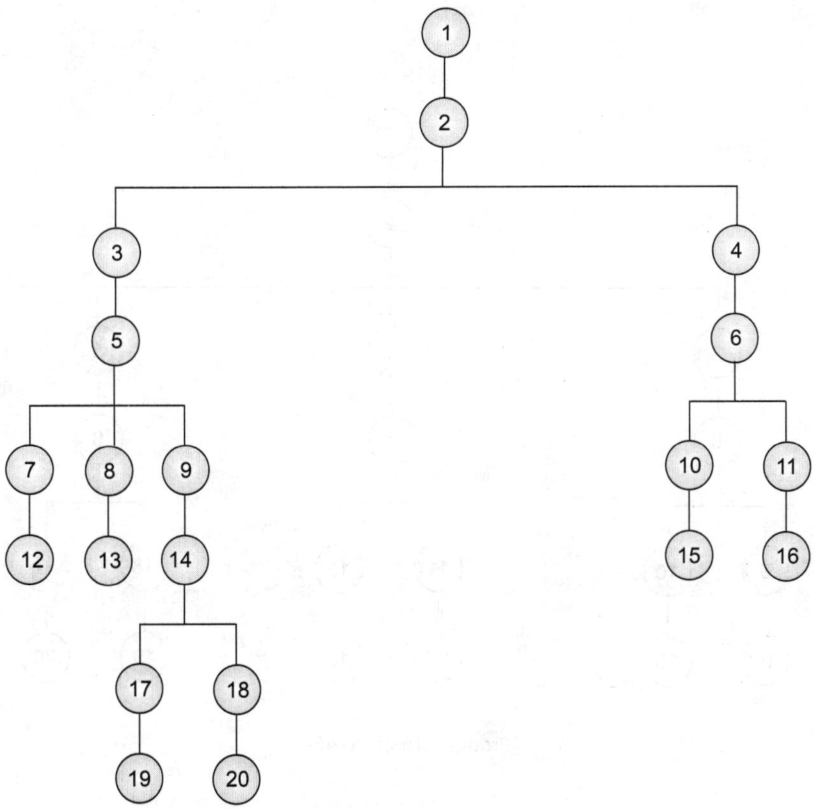

Product Structure-45

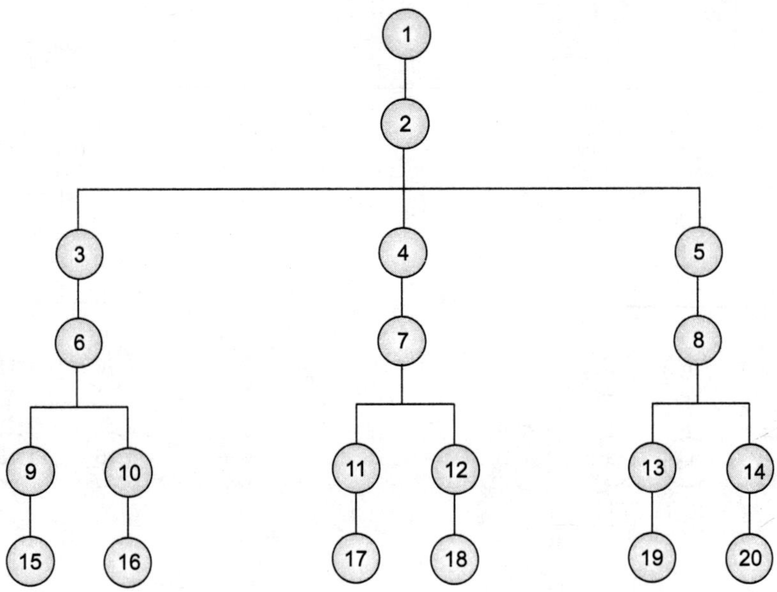

Product Structure-46

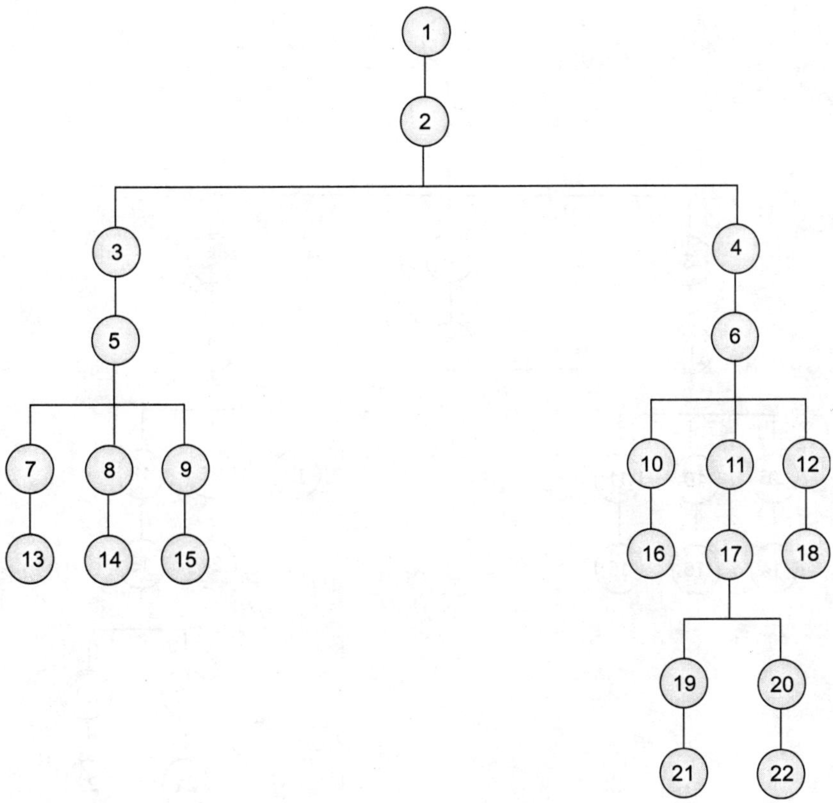

Product Structure-47

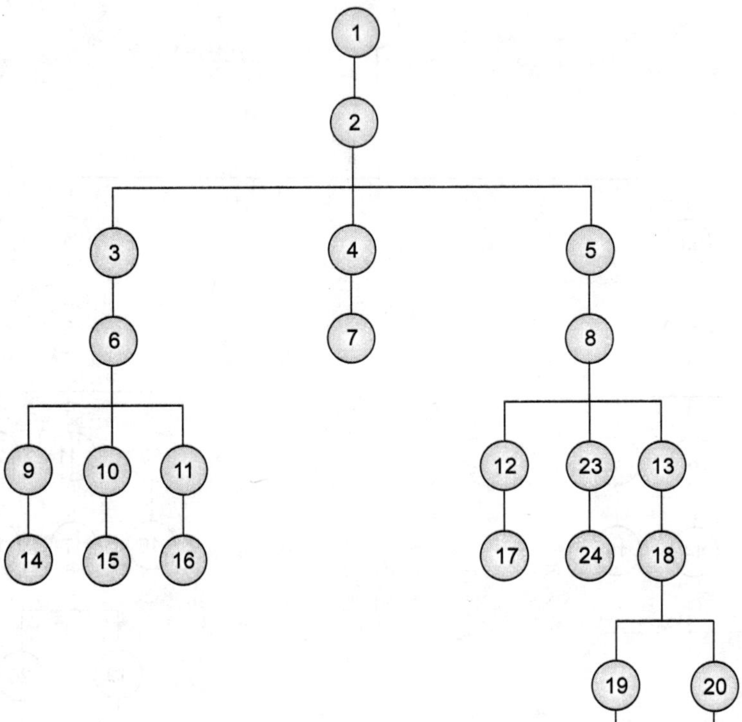

Product Structure-48

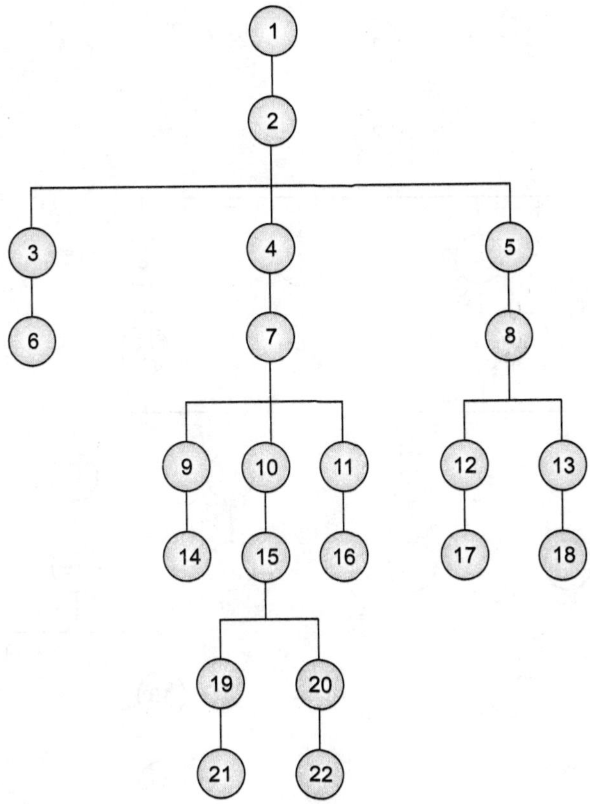

Product Structure-49

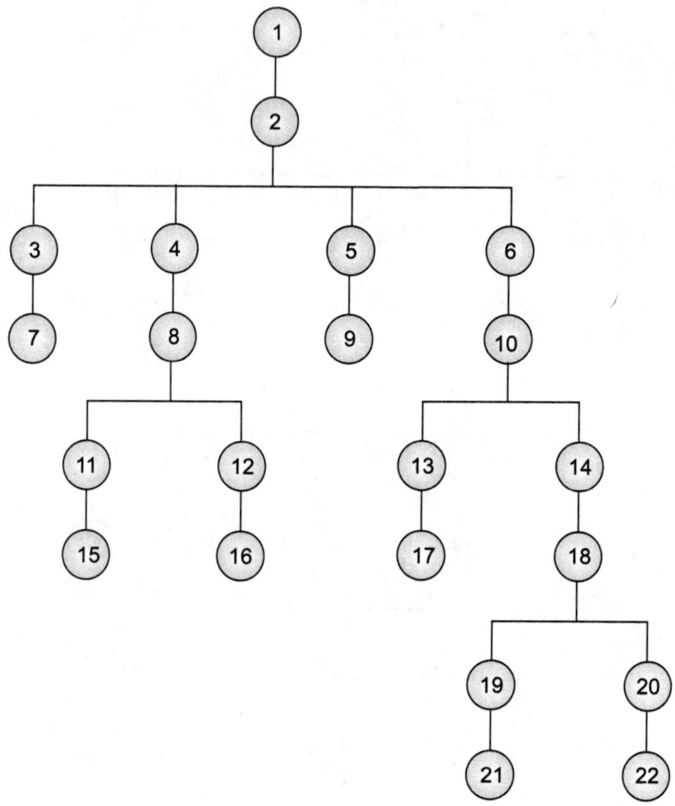

Product Structure-50

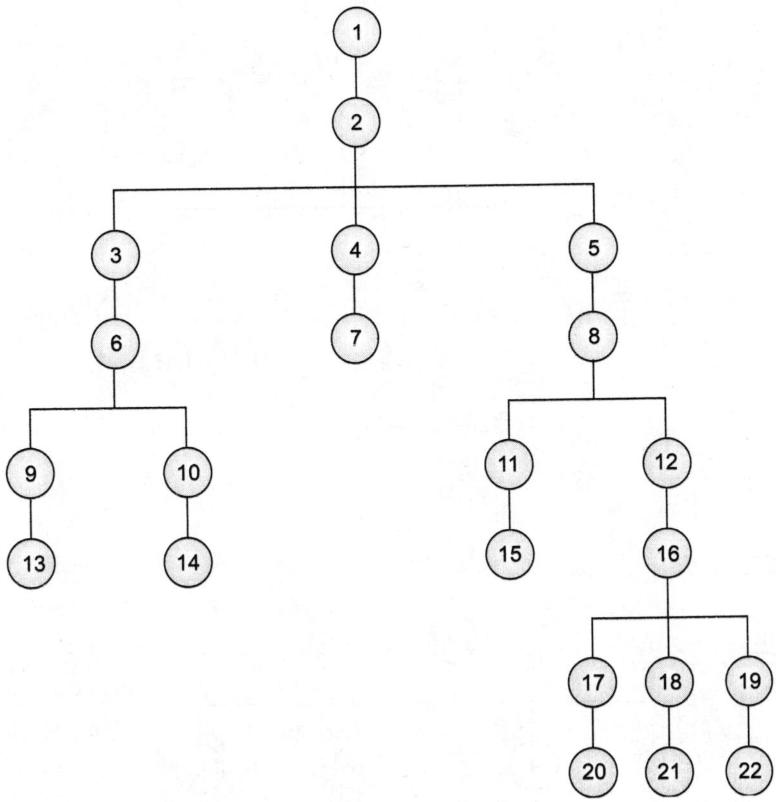

Product Structure-51

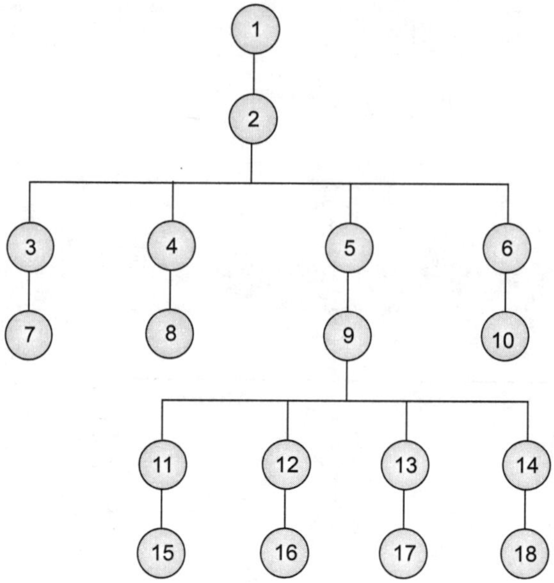

Product Structure-52

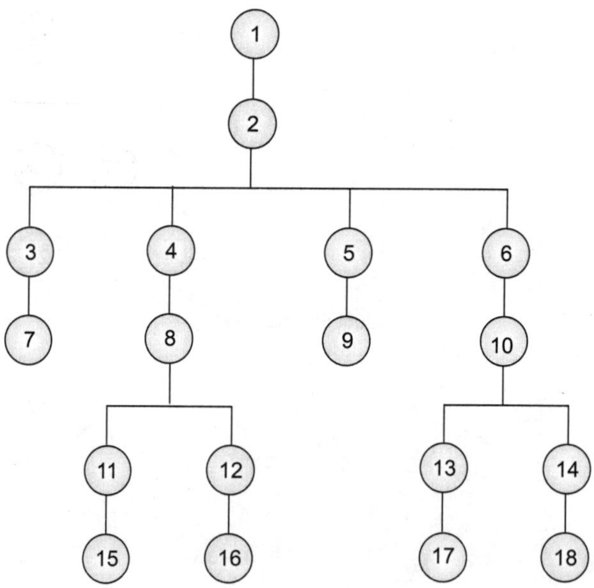

Product Structure-53

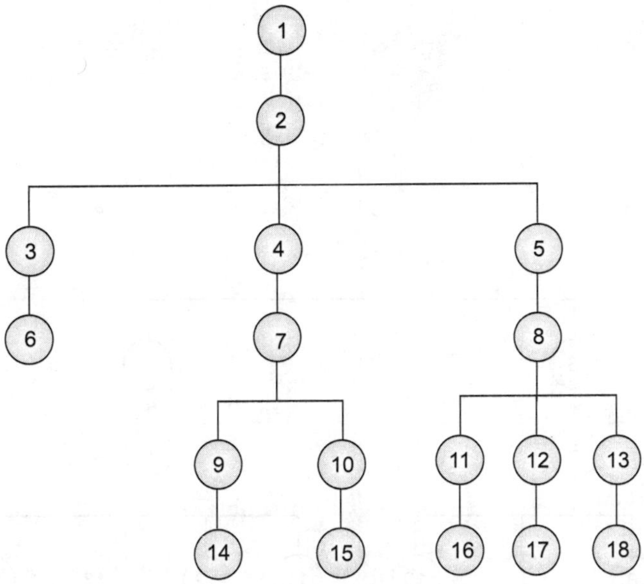

Product Structure-54

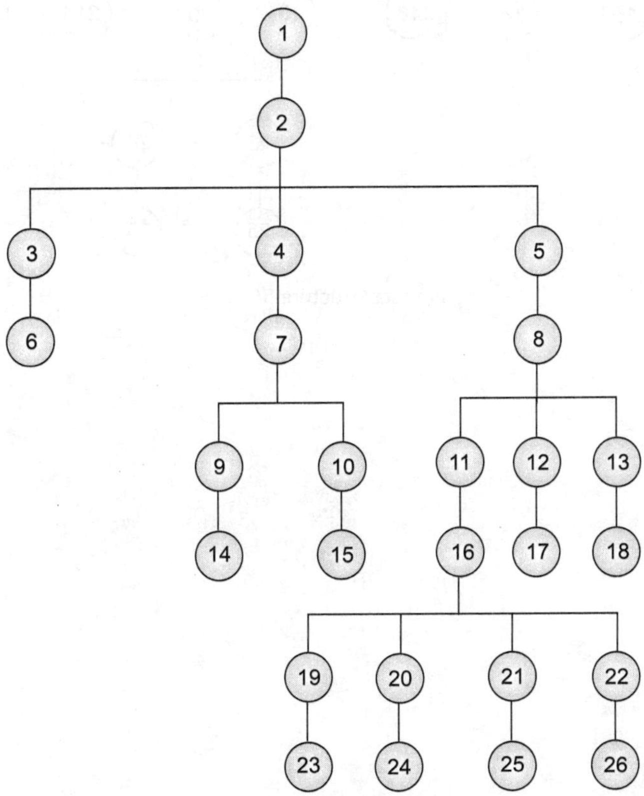

Product Structure-55

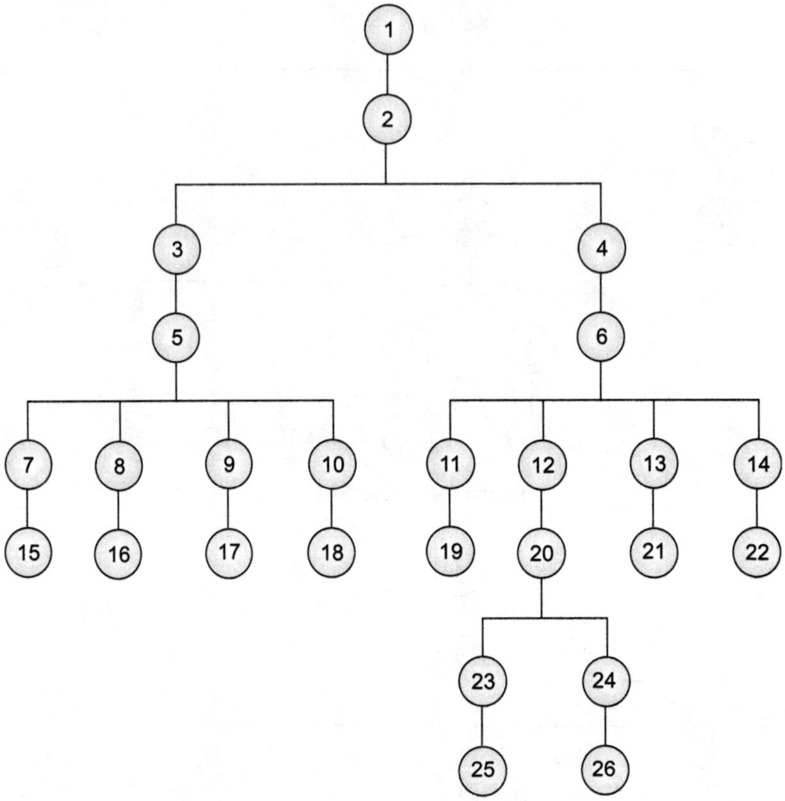

Product Structure-56

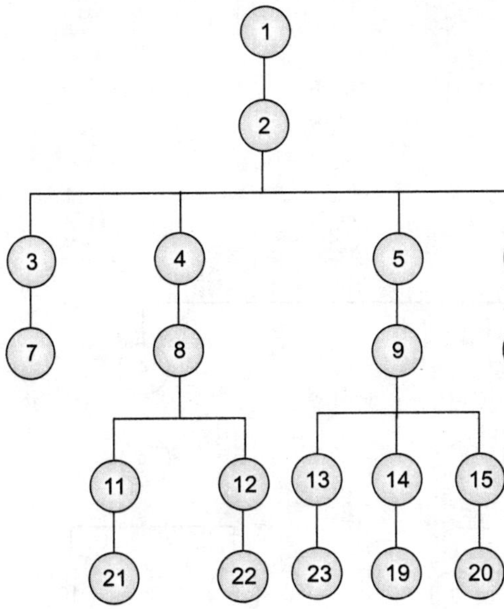

Product Structure-57

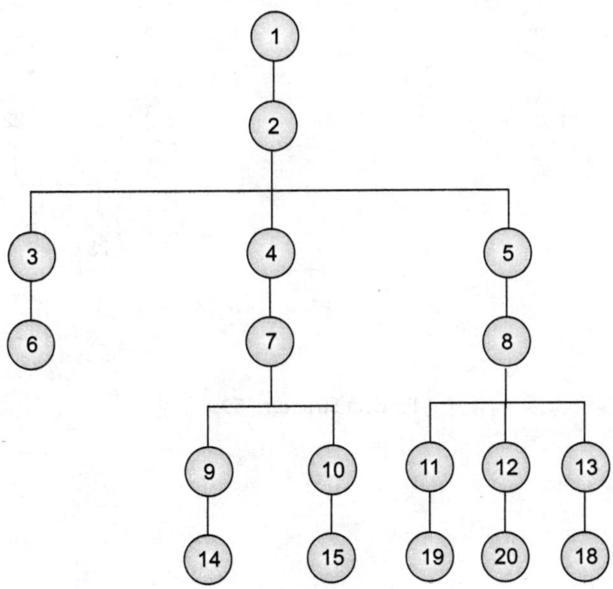

Product Structure-58

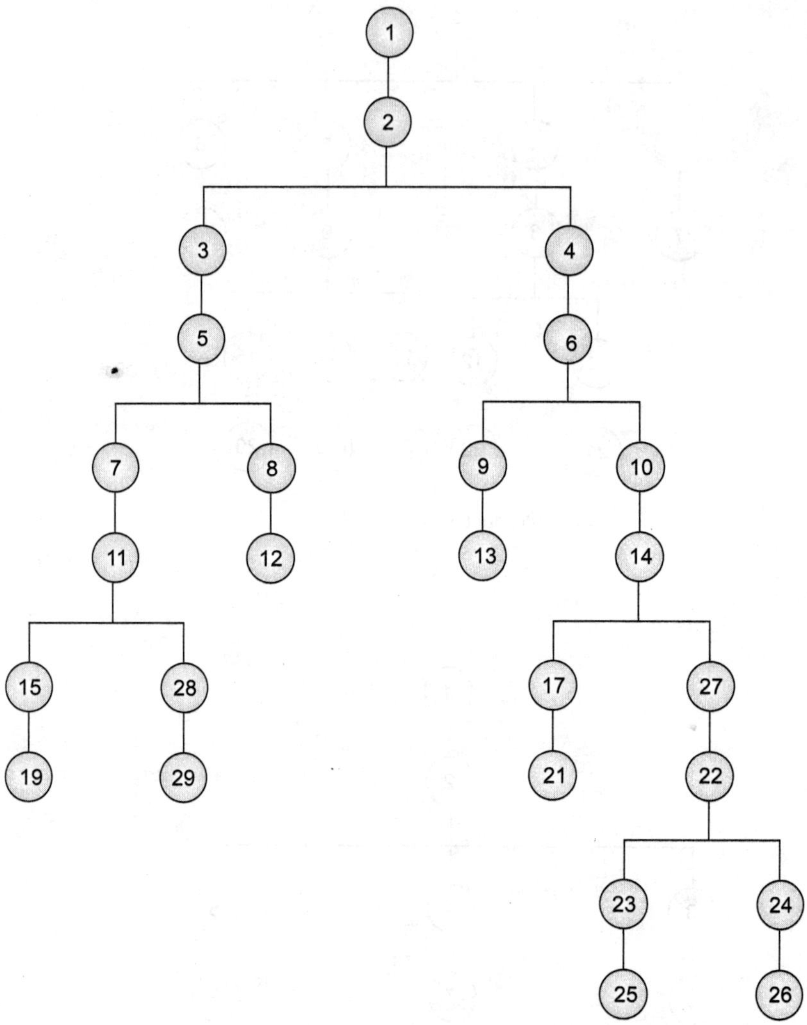

Product Structure-59

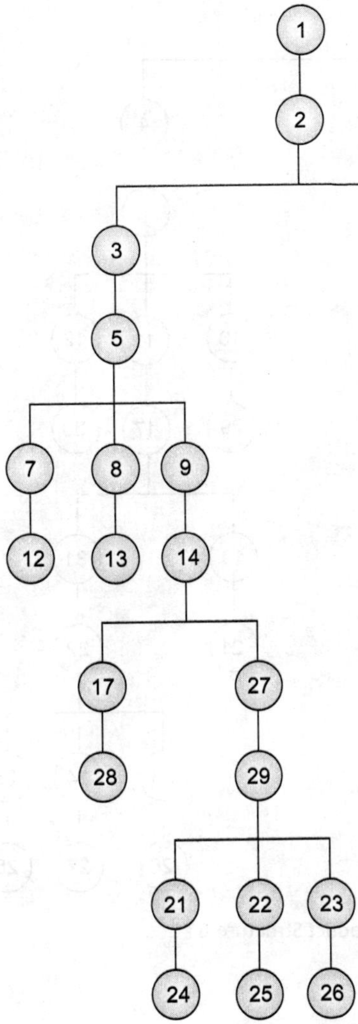

Product Structure-60

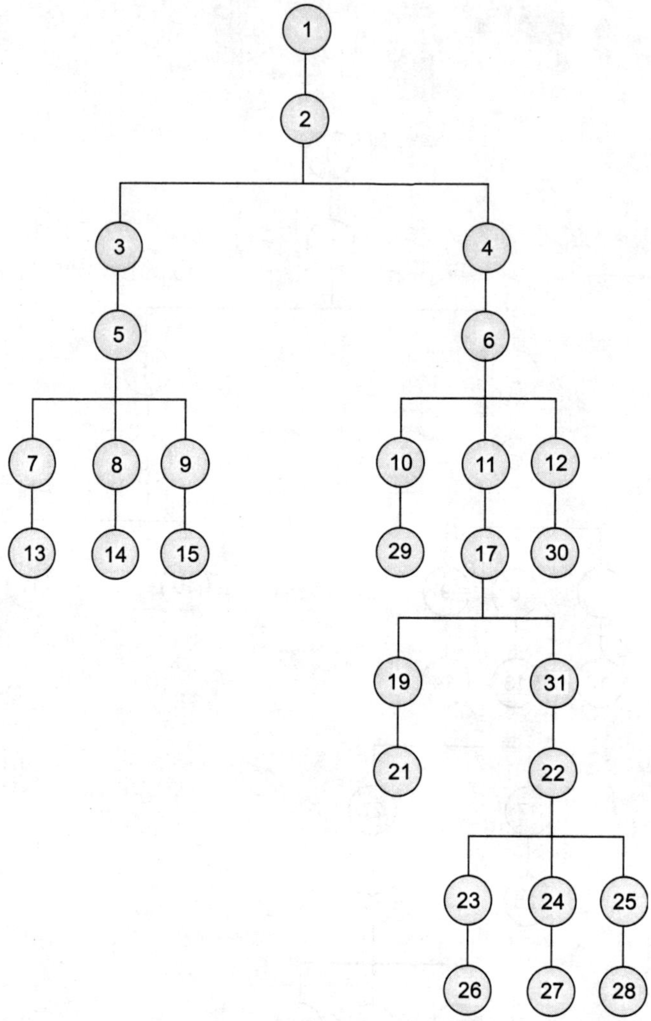

Product Structure-61

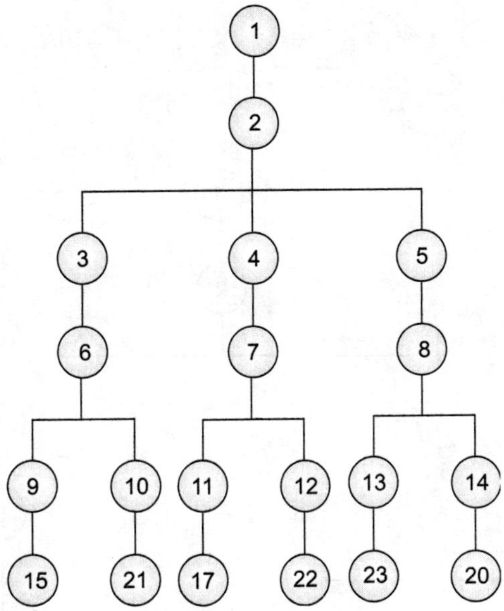

Product Sturacture-62

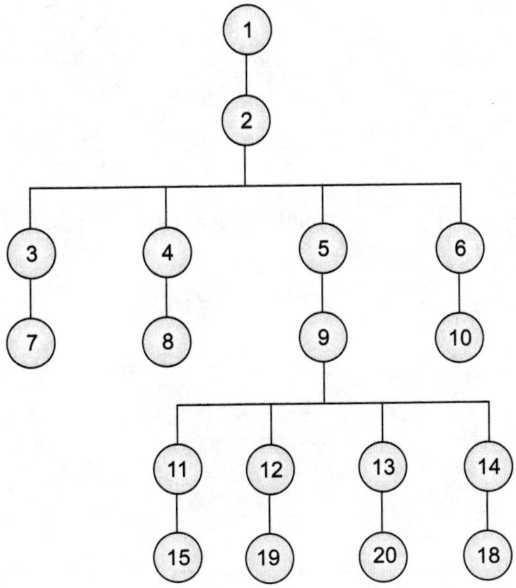

Product Structure-63

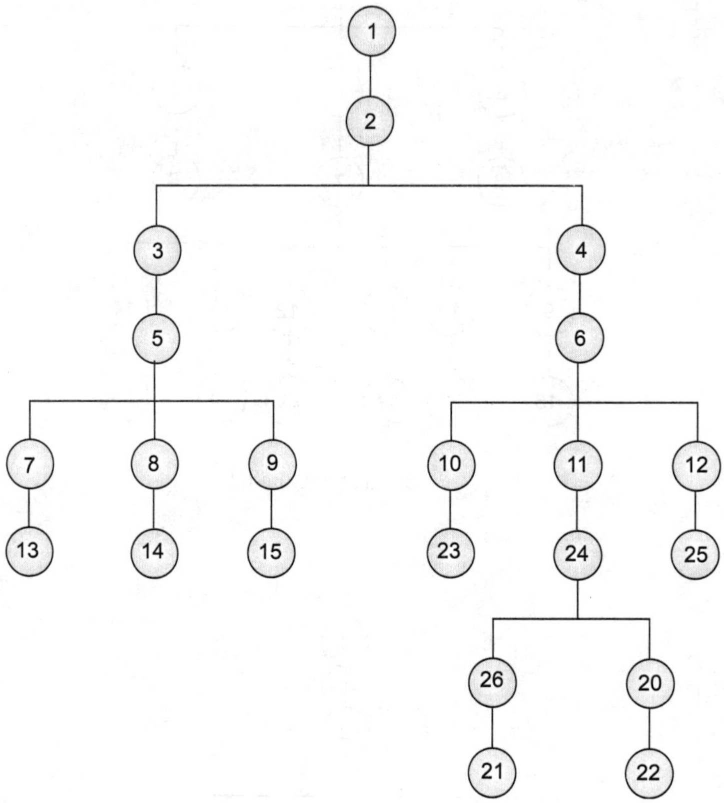

Product Structure-64

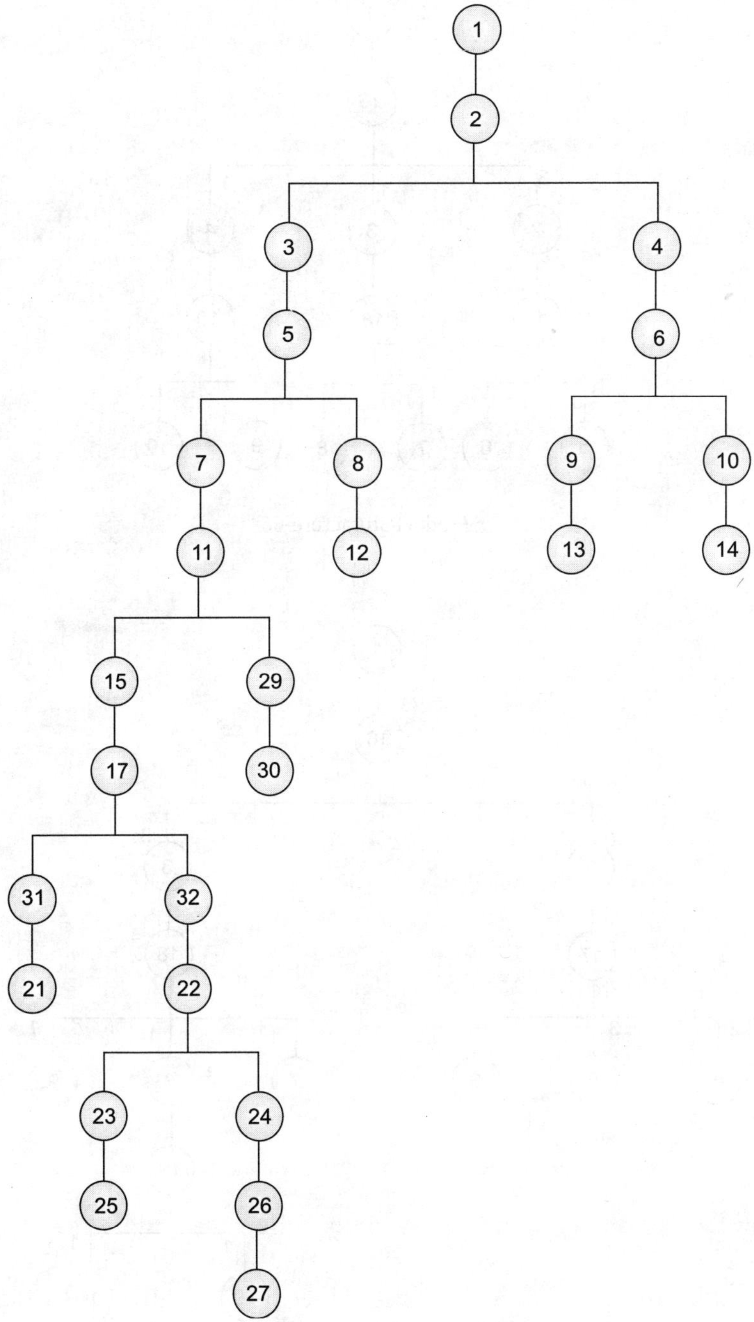

Product Structure-65

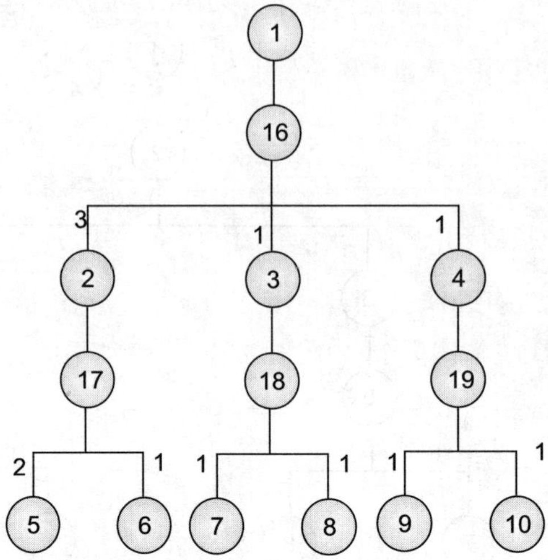

Product Sturacture-66

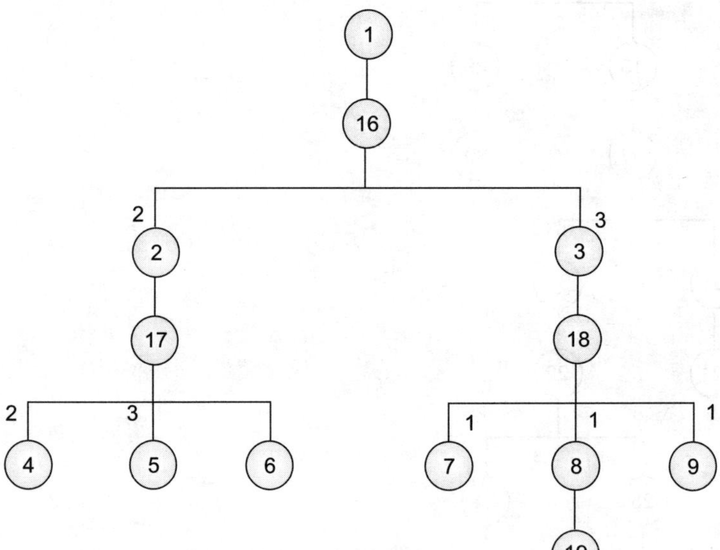

Product Structure-67

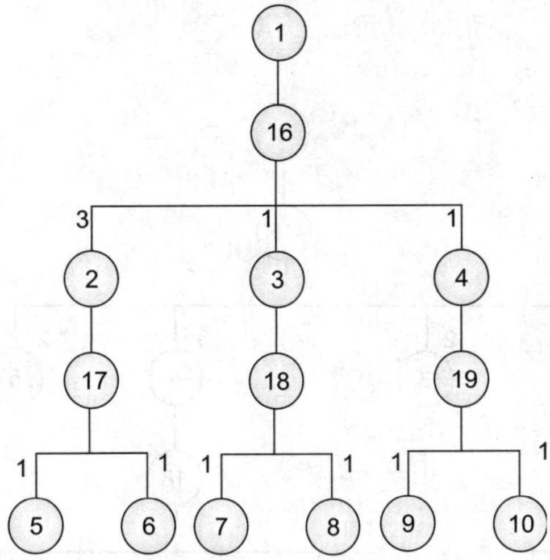

Product Structure-68

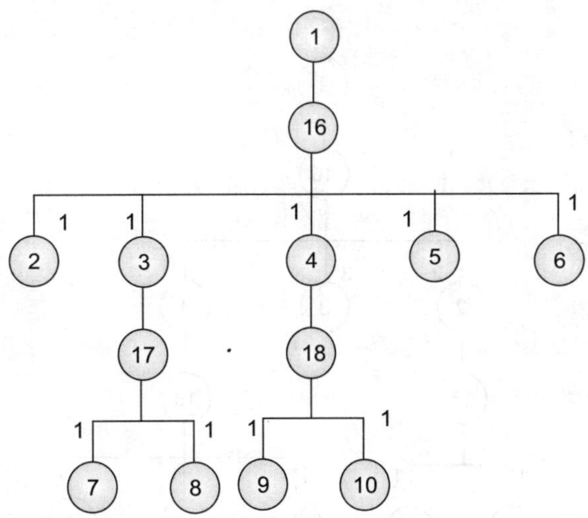

Product Structure-69

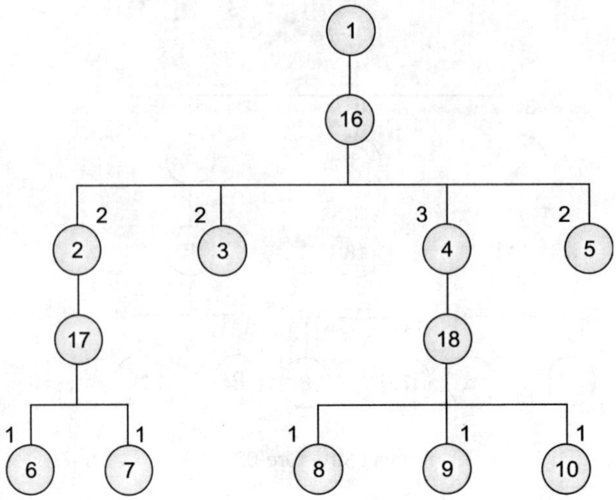

Product Structure-70

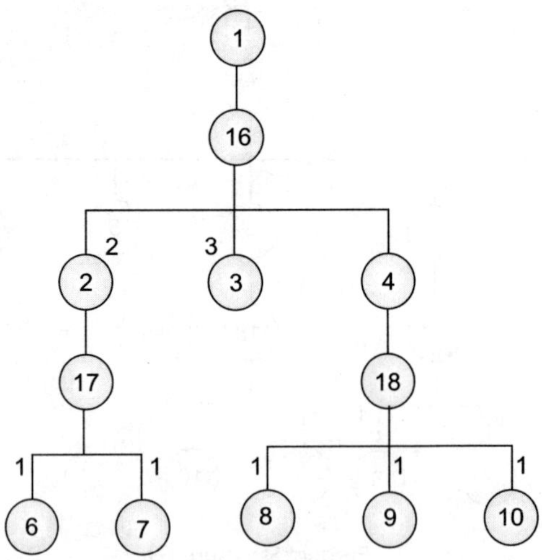

Product Structure-71

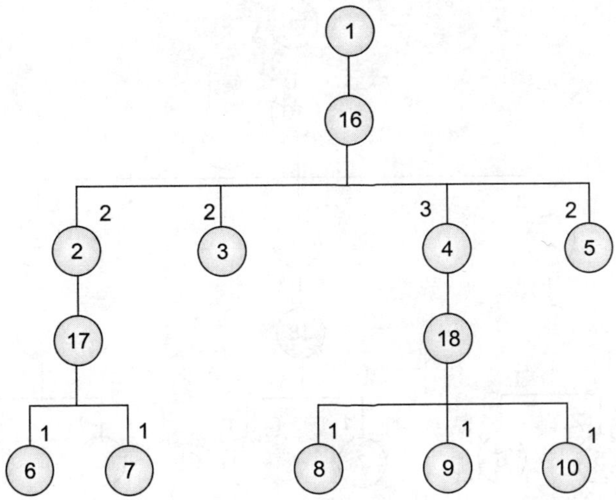

Product Structure-72

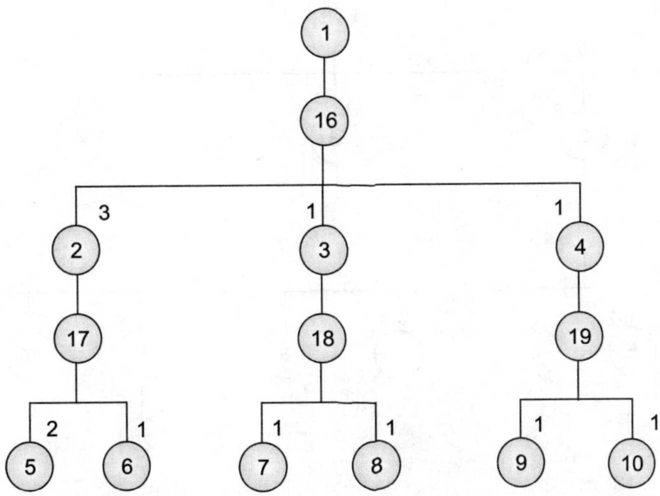

Product Structure-73

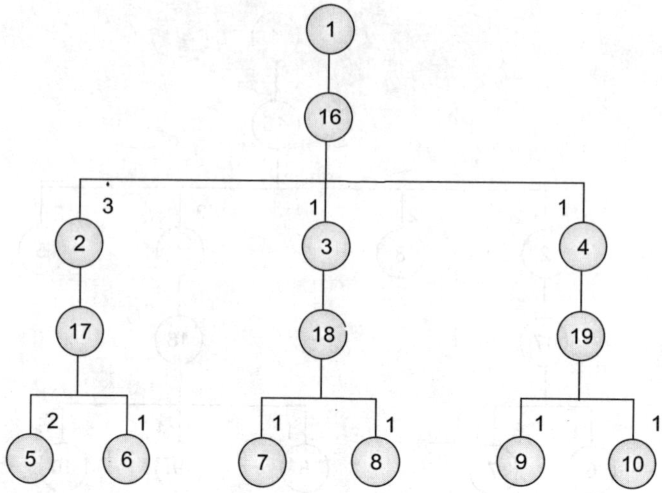

Product Structure-74

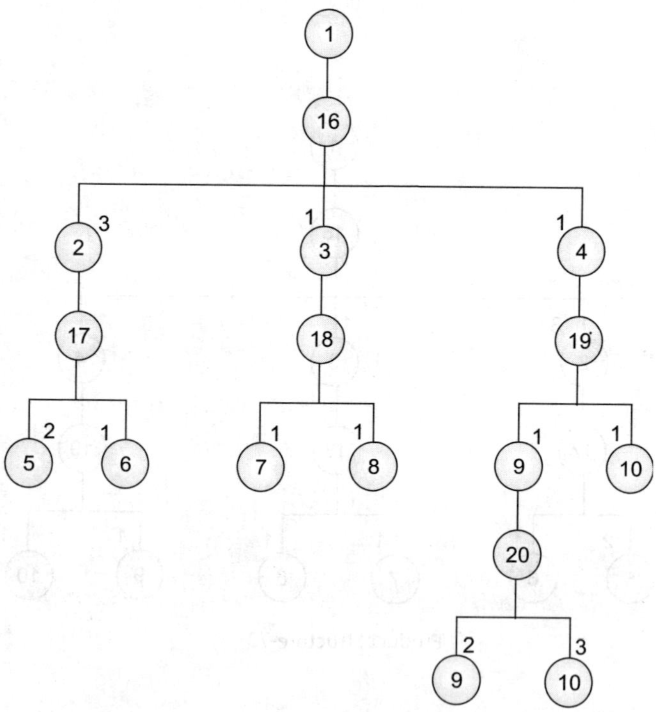

Product Structure-75

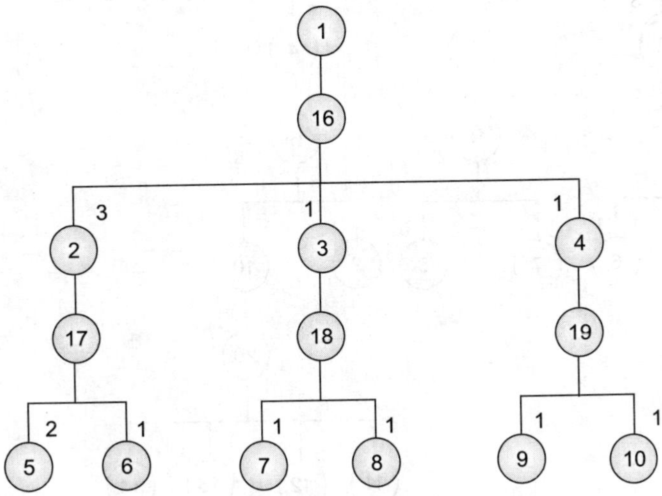

Product Structure-76

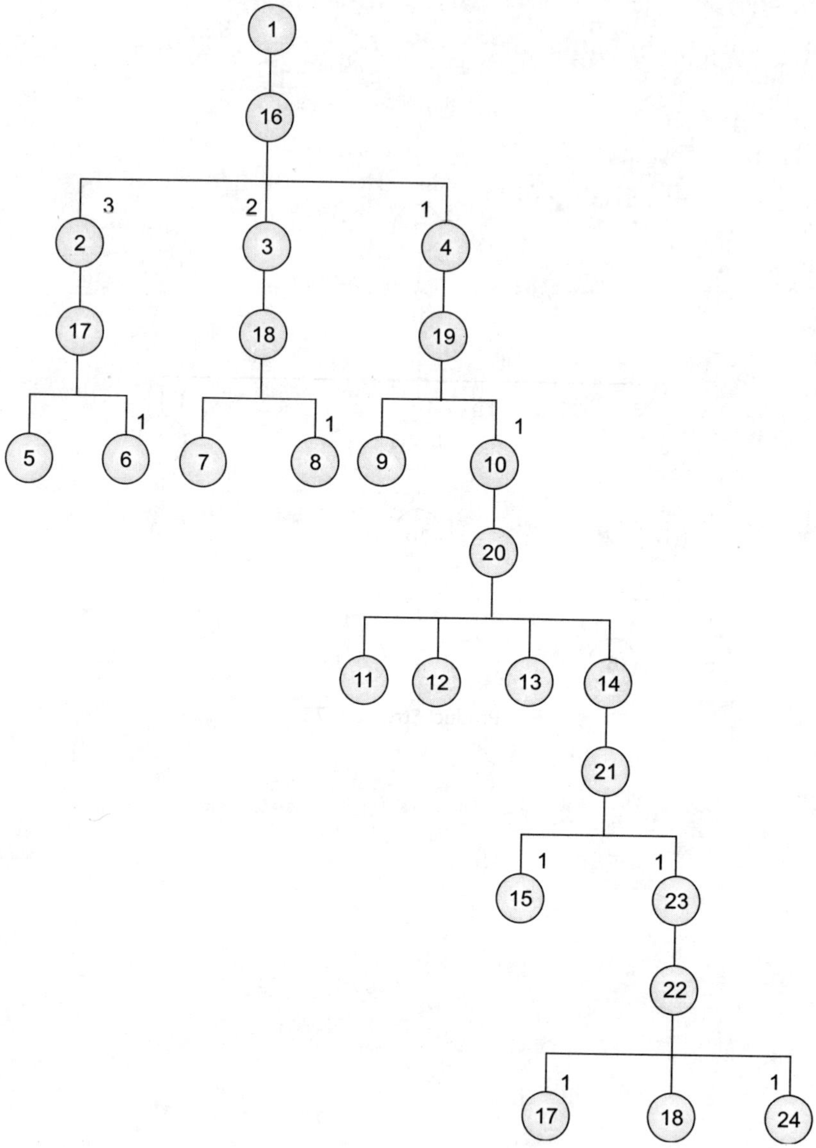

Product Structure-77

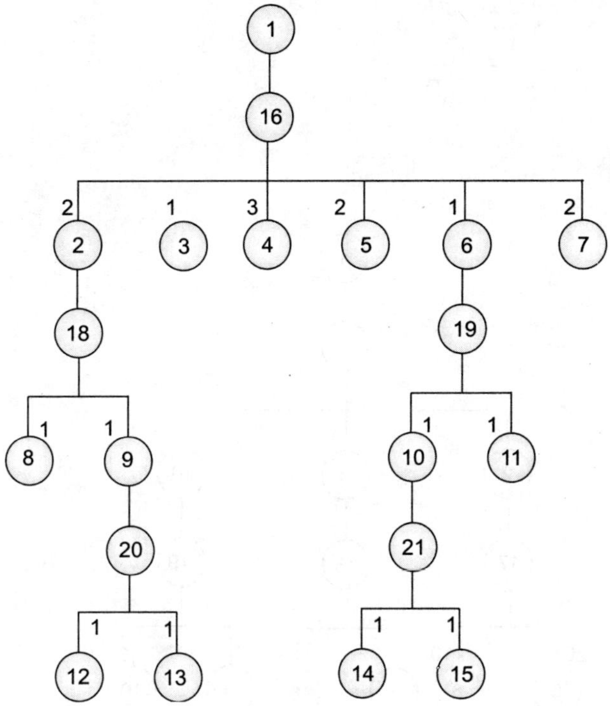

Product Structure-78

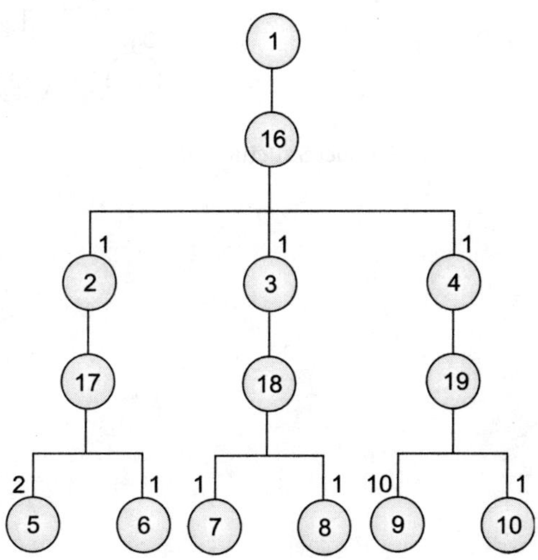

Product Structure-79

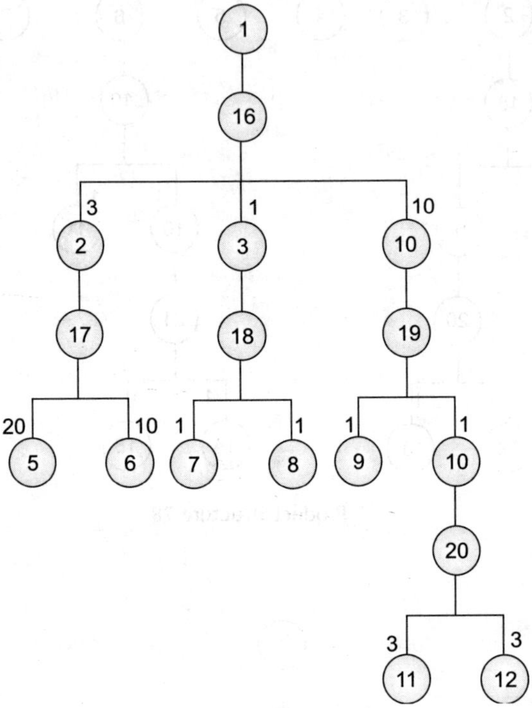

Product Structure-80

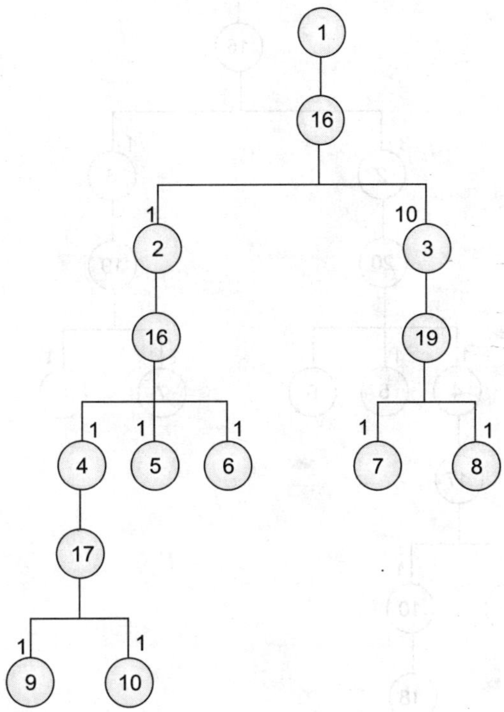

Product Structure-81

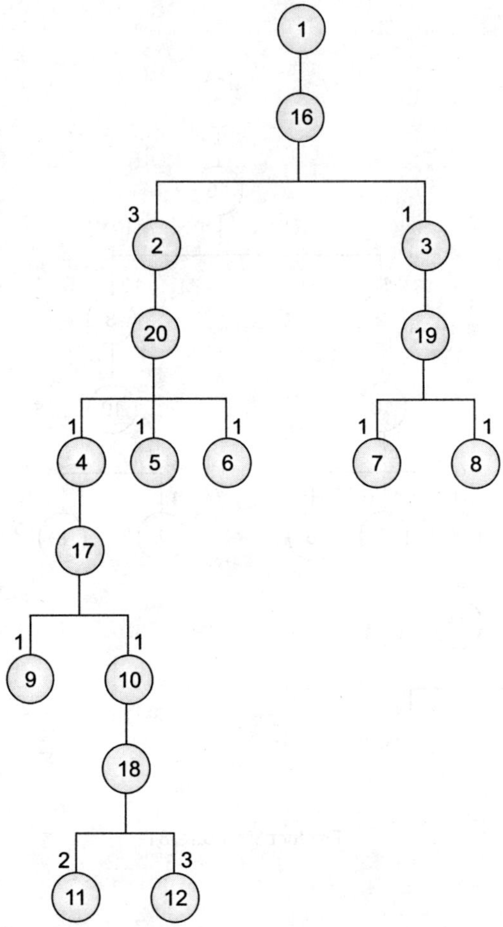

Product Structure-82

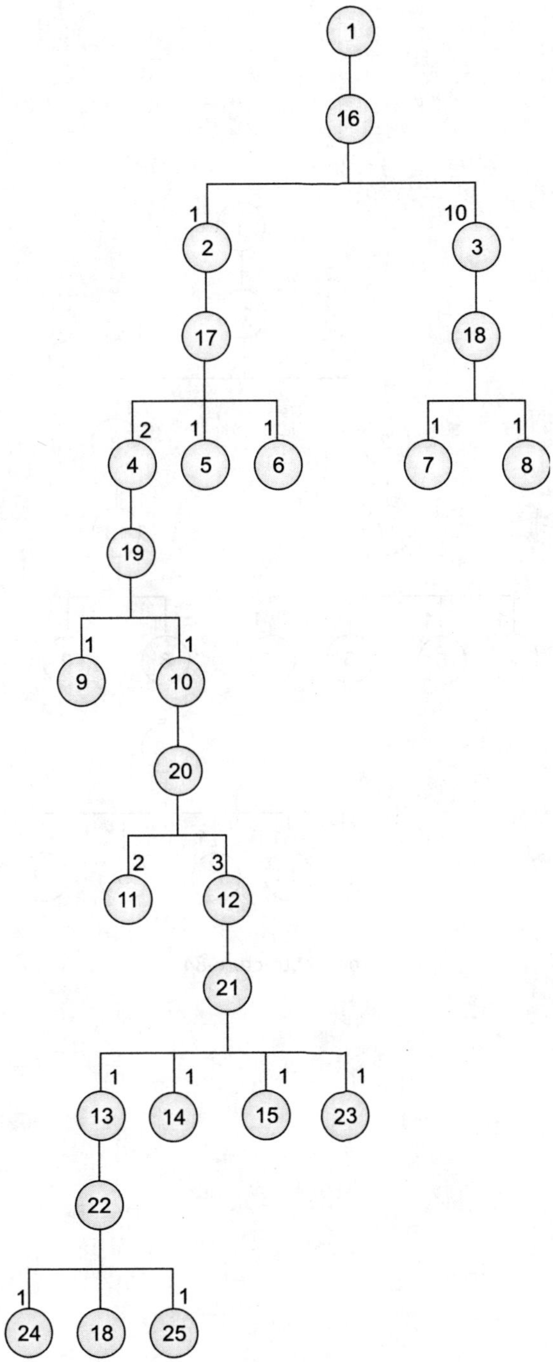

Product Structure-83

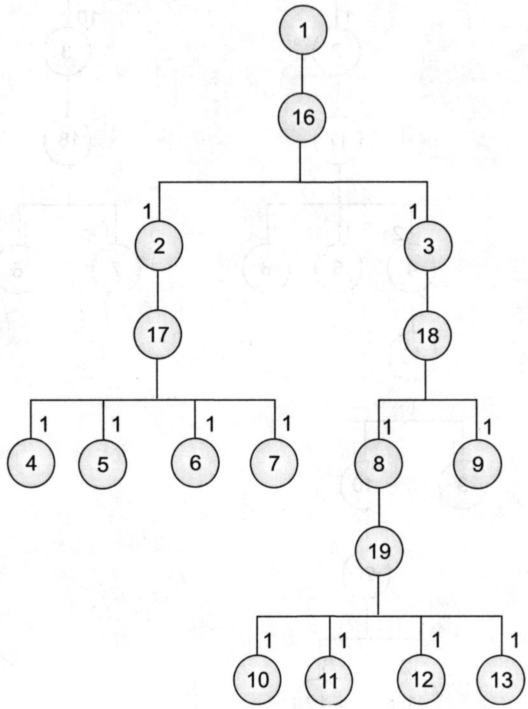

Product Structure-84

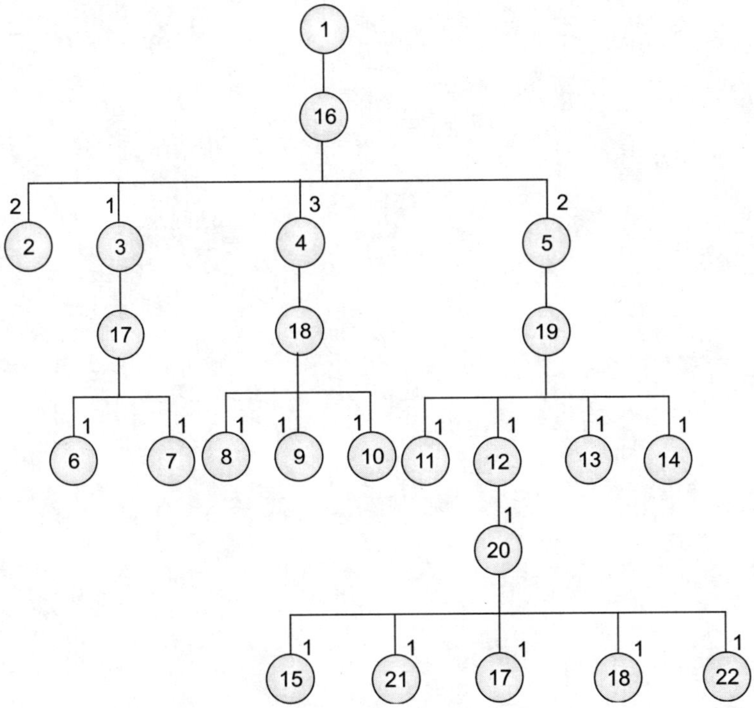

Product Structure-85

Appendix 2
Simulation Program for MRP System in PASCAL

```
program mrp(input,output);
const
      max_mc_no                                   = 15;
      max_no_of_proces_on_any_assly               = 4;
      max_assly_no                                = 20;
      Max_subassly_no_into_an_assly               = max_assly_no;
      max_period_no                               = 50;
      infinity                                    = 400000000000;
      max_statistics_pt_no                        = 4;
      computing_points_per_period_in_w_w          = 100;
      max_no_of_lots                              = max_period_no;
      max_queue_length                            = 200;
      inventory_cost_fraction                     = 0.3;
      no_of_hours_in_a_year                       = 8640;
      no_of_hours_in_a_period                     = 24;
      collect_statistics_from_time = 10.0*no_of_hours_in_a_period;
      lead_time                                   =50; simulation_time
                                                  = infinity;
      max_assly_mc_no                             = 19;
      factor                                      = 1000;
type
     range_of_assly_mcs        = 16..max_assly_mc_no;
       ptr_to_event            = ^event_record;

       event_type    = (collect_statistics_from_now_on,
         lot_enters_the_shop,
         lot_enters_the_general_mc_queue,
         lot_enters_the_assly_mc_queue,
         processing_on_general_mc_starts,
         processing_on_assly_mc_starts,
         processing_on_general_mc_gets_over,
```

```
          processing_on_assly_mc_gets_over,
          lot_enters_the_finished_product_list);

process_data = record
          mc_no : integer;
                    set-up_time,
                    processing_time_per_unit,
                    set-up_cost : real;
                 end;
   child_assly = record
          assly_no,
                    qty_to_be_contributed  : integer;
                 end;
subassly_data = record
   assly_no,
                    qty_av : integer;
               (*assly_no, qty_av :integer;*)
                 end;

lot=  record
          assly_no,
          original_size,
          qty_left,
          no_of_agm_visited,
          current_mc_no : integer;
          processing_complete : boolean;
          aggregate_lateness_of_lot,
          units_lateness_of_lot,
          actual_inventory_carrying_cost,
          priorty_value,
          percentage_completion,
              required_completion_time,
              actual_completion_time,
              cpt,
              total_wait_time_in_queues_so_far,
              tpt_completed_so_far,
              time_of_entry_into_the_shop,
              total_required_processing_time,
              time_of_joining_the_queue,
              time_when_processing_starts :real;
              end;
```

```
basic_data_about_an_assly =
        record
            assly_no,
            assly_no_after_processing, parent_no,
            no_of_child_asslys,
            no_of_children_for_assly,
            no_of_processes_needed,
            qty_for_parent,
            assly_on_mc_no : integer;

            actual_inventory_carrying_cost,
            theoretical_inventory_carrying_cost,
            total_set-up_cost,
            cost : real;
            lot_sizing_to_be_done,
            immediately_gets_into_assly,
            immediately_needs_processing : boolean;

            aps
              : array[1..max_no_of_proces_on_any_assly * 3]
                        of process_data:
            array_of_child_assly
                    : array[1..max_subassly_no_into_an_assly]
                        of child_assly;
            end;

    lot_data_about_an_assly = record
                    assly_no,
                    lot_no_which_will_enter_the_shop,
                    no_of_lots : integer;

                    dol : array[1..max_no_of_lots] of lot;
                                end;
       general_machine = record
                        tpt, total_idle_time, cu : real;
                                end;
      assly_machine = record
                        finished_assly_no : integer;
                        processing_time_per_unit,
                        tpt,
```

```
                    total_idle_time,
                    cu : real;
                       end;
      event_record = record
              event : event_type;
             array_of_relevant_nos : array[1..3] of integer;
             (* 1- assly_no 2- lot_no 3- mc_no_of_visit *)
              execution_time : real;
             next_event : ptr_to_event;
                    end;

   (* BEGIN TYPES OF EXPLOSION DETAILS*)
   explosion_details = record
              assly_no,
                 qty_to_be_exploded : integer;
               end;
   (* END TYPES FOR EXPLOSION DETAILS *)
(* BEGIN TYPES OF QUEVES *)
   lot_and_assly_no = record
             lot_no,
             assly_no : integer;
              end;

   type_for_queue_before_general_mc
               = record
             queue_length :integer;
        details_of_queue : array[1..max_queue_length]
                 of lot_and_assly_no;
                 end;

   type_for_queue_before_assly_mc
             = record
             finish_assly_no,
             no_of_subasslys_into_assly : integer;
             quantity_available :
   array[1..max_subassly_no_into_an_assly]
                of integer;
                details_of_queues :
   array[1..max_subassly_no_into_an_assly]
```

```
                    of type_for_queue_before_general_mc;
                    end;
   (* END TYPES FOR QUEUES*)

  (* BEGIN TYPE FOR WAGNER WHITIN ALGORITHM *)

  type  basic_period_data  = record
                   order_cost,
                   holding_cost :real;
                   demand : integer;
                        end;
   input_data_for_lot_sizing = array[1..max_period_no] of basic_period_
data;
     order_data = record
              period_no,
              qty_produced  : integer;
                end;
     computation_data = record
                   cost : real;
                   order_period_no  : integer;
                     end;

     output_data_of_lot_sizing =
          record
              no_of_orders_placed : integer;
     order_schedule : array[1..max_period_no] of order_data;
              total_cost,
              holding_cost,
              order_cost  :  real;
          end;

     period_wise_computations =
         record
              no_of_calculations,
              min_cost_position  : integer;
              period_wise_calculation  :
              array[1..computing_points_per_period_in_w_w] of
                  computation_data;
         end;
```

```
type_for_find_min_position = array[1..max_period_no] of real;
(* END TYPES FOR WAGNER WHITIN ALGORITHM*)
   varclock_time : real;
          demand,
          exploded_demand : array[1..max_assly_no, 1..max_pe-
riod_no] of integer;
          event_freetop,
          ptr_to_current_executable_event,
          top_of_event_list,
          new_event,
          p,q : ptr_to_event;
          abda
           : array[1..max_assly_no] of basic_data_about_an_assly;

        ala : array[1..max_assly_no] of lot_data_about_an_assly;

        agm : array[1..max_mc_no] of general_machine;

        aam : array[range_of_assly_mcs] of assly_machine;

        list_of_end_products : array[1..max_assly_no] of integer;

       (* BEGIN VARIABLES FOR EXPLOSION DETAILS *)
             no_of_asslys_on_explosion_list,
             no_of_end_products : integer;
             incremental_explosion_list :
             array[1..(50*max_assly_no)] of explosion_details;
       (* END VARIABLES FOE EXPLOSION DETAILS *)

       (* BEGIN VARIABLES FOR QUEUES *)

       queue_before_general_mc : array[1..max_mc_no] of
                      type_for_queue_before_general_mc;

       queue_before_assly_mc : array[range_of_assly_mcs] of
                      type_for_queue_before_assly_mc;

       (* END VARIBLES FOR QUEUES *)

       (* BEGIN VARIABLES FOR WAGNER WHITIN*)
```

```
input_data_for_w_w : input_data_for_lot_sizing;

output_data_of_w_w : output_data_of_lot_sizing;

omputation_table_for_w_w : array[1..max_period_no] of
                              period_wise_computations;

   array_for_output_of_w_w   : array[1..max_assly_no] of
                              output_data_of_lot_sizing;
      in_ass_dat : text;
      in_dem_dat : text;
      in_ass_mc : text;
      w_w_output : text;
      w_w_file : text;
      event_file : text;
   potty_output : text;
      s_dat : text;
      i,j : integer;
      counter : integer;
      in_out : text;
      rand : real;
      flag : boolean;
mc_busy : array[1..max_no_of_proces_on_any_assly] of boolean;

  (* END VARIABLES FOR WAGNER-WHITIN*)
  (* STARTS VARIABLES FOR POTTY'S ALGORITHM*)
  R,K,S:array[1..max_assly_no] of integer;
  theoretical_cost,actual_cost:array[1..max_assly_no] of real;
  best_sol:real;
  count,max_count: integer;
  stop,go_ahead:boolean;
  total_units_lateness:real;
  temp,max_dif:real;
  index_period:integer;
  old_orders,new_orders:integer;
  assly_after_processing:integer;
  iteration:integer;
  levels:integer;
  coordination_index,
```

```
    present_coordination_index,
    ag_coordination_index : array[1..max_assly_no] of real;
    max_time,max_index,
    present_mean_time,
    prev_mean_time : array[range_of_assly_mcs] of real;
    critical_child : array[1..max_assly_no] of integer;
    times:integer;
 arrival_time:array[1..100,1..max_assly_no,1..max_no_of_lots] of real;
    check_out:text;
    a,b,c,lots:integer;
    assly_count:array[range_of_assly_mcs] of integer;
 time_of_reaching : array[1..max_assly_no,1..max_no_of_lots] of real;
 latest_assly_time :array[1..max_assly_no,range_of_assly_mcs] of real;
    first_run : boolean;
    earliest_lot_time,
    latest_lot_time : array[range_of_assly_mcs] of real;
    prev_range : real;
    lead_times : array[1..max_assly_no] of integer;
    bottle_neck_mc : array[1..max_assly_no] of integer;
    bottle_ass : array[1..max_assly_no] of boolean;
    max_lead_time : integer;
procedure   event_addfreelist(p : ptr_to_event);
begin (*event_addfreelist*)

        p^.next_event := event_freetop;
            event_freetop := p;
end; (*event_addfreelist*)

procedure newmodified(var p : ptr_to_event);
        begin (* newmodified*)
            if (event_freetop = nil)
            then new(p)
            else begin
            p:=event_freetop;
            event_freetop:=event_freetop^.next_event;
        end;
            p^.next_event := nil;
            p^.array_of_relevant_nos[1] :=0;
            p^.array_of_relevant_nos[2] := 0;
            p^.execution_time := 0.0;
```

```
        end; (*newmodified*)

procedure   print_the_event_list ;  (* this is the changed version*)
        var
                q: ptr_to_event;
        begin (* print_the_event_list*)
            q:=ptr_to_current_executable_event;
   case q^.event of
   collect_statistics_from_now_on  :
   write(event_file,'collect_statistics_from_now_on');
   lot_enters_the_shop  :
   write(event_file,'lot_enters_the_shop');
   lot_enters_the_general_mc_queue  :
   write(event_file, ' lot_enters_the general_mc_queue');
   lot_enters_the_assly_mc_queue :
   write(event_file, ' lot_enters_the_assly_mc_queue');
   processing_on_general_mc_starts  :
   write(event_file, ' processing_on_general_mc_starts');
   processing_on_assly_mc_starts  :
   write(event_file, ' processing_on_assly_mc_starts ');
   processing_on_general_mc_gets_over :
   write(event_file, ' processing_on_general_mc_gets_over');
   processing_on_assly_mc_gets_over  :
   write(event_file,'processing_on_assly_mc_gets_over');
   lot_enters_the_finished_product_list :
   write(event_file, ' lot_enters_the_finished_product_list');
end; (*case*)

write(event_file,'assly_no:',q^.array_of_relevant_nos[1]:1,' ',
                            'lot_no:',q^.array_of_relevant_nos[2]:1,' ');
         writeln(event_file, 'exec_time',q^.execution_time:8:3);
        end;  (* print_the_event_list*)

        procedure open_print_the_event_list
        begin
            rewrite(event_file,'event_file');
        end;

        procedure close_print_the_event_list;
        begin
```

```
            close(event_file);
        end;

procedure lot_sizing_by_w_w(assly_no  :  integer);
            var period_no,
            order_can_be_placed_from_period_no:integer;
            procedure  forward_recursion_of_w_w;
            var  period_no,
            index,
            min_pos,
            scratch,
            size,
            no_of_calculations_done,
            search_index_in_previous_period,
            min_cost_pos_upto_last_period,
            order_placed_in_period : integer;
            min_cost_upto_last_period,
            cost,
            min_cost_upto_period_in_which_order_is_placed : real;
            a: type_for_find_min_position;
 procedure find_min_position(a:type_for_find_min_position;
             size:integer; var min_pos : integer);

           var index  : integer;

           min_cost : real;

          begin (* find_min_position*)
             min_cost := a[1];
             min_pos:=1;
             for index := 2 to size do
             if (a[index] < min_cost)
             then begin
             min_cost := a[index];
             min_pos:=index;
             end;
          end; (* find_min_position*)

          begin (* forward_recursion_of_w_w*)
             computation_table_for_w_w[1].no_of_calculations:=1;
```

```
            computation_table_for_w_w[1].min_cost_position:=1;
        computation_table_for_w_w[1].period_wise_calculation[1].
        cost: = input_data_for_w_w[1].order_cost;
computation_table_for_w_w[1].period_wise_calculation[1].
        order_period_no:=1;
order_can_be_placed_from_period_no :=1;
        for period_no :=2 to max_period_no do
        begin
        no_of_calculations_done:=1;
        computation_table_for_w_w[period_no].
 no_of_calculations:=period_no - order_can_be_placed_from_period_no
+ 1;
            order_placed_in_period := period_no;
            min_cost_pos_upto_last_period:=
computation_table_for_w_w[period_no-1].min_cost_position;
             min_cost_upto_last_period:=
computation_table_for_w_w[period_no -1 ].
period_wise_calculation[min_cost_pos_upto_last_period].cost;
             computation_table_for_w_w[period_no].
             period_wise_calculation[1].cost:=
             min_cost_upto_last_period +
             input_data_for_w_w[period_no].order_cost;
             computation_table_for_w_w[period_no].
            period_wise_calculation[no_of_calculations_done].

 order_period_no:=order_placed_in_period;
              search_index_in_previous_period:=1;
            order_placed_in_period:=order_placed_in_period -1;
              while (order_placed_in_period >= order_can_be_
        placed_from_period_no) do
              begin
        no_of_calculations_done := no_of_calculations_done + 1;
           min_cost_upto_period_in_which_order_is_placed :=
                  computation_table_for_w_w[period_no - 1].

 period_wise_calculation[search_index_in_previous_period].cost;
          cost:=min_cost_upto_period_in_which_order_is_placed;
   for index:= order_placed_in_period to (period_no - 1) do
   cost := cost + input_data_for_w_w[index].holding_cost *
                     input_data_for_w_w[period_no].demand;
```

```
                    computation_table_for_w_w[period_no].
        period_wise_calculation[no_of_calculations_done].cost:=cost;
                    computation_table_for_w_w[period_no].
                  period_wise_calculation[no_of_calculations_done].
                         order_period_no:=order_placed_in_period;
  search_index_in_previous_period:=search_index_in_previous_period +
1;
   order_placed_in_period:= order_placed_in_period - 1;
                  end;  (*while*)

                  size:= computation_table_for_w_w[period_no].
                      no_of_calculations;
                  for index:= 1 to size do
                  a[index]:=computation_table_for_w_w[period_no].
                    period_wise_calculation[index].cost;
                  find_min_position(a,size,min_pos);
                  computation_table_for_w_w[period_no].min_cost_
position:=min_pos;
                  order_can_be_placed_from_period_no:=
                  computation_table_for_w_w[period_no].
                  period_wise_calculation[min_pos].order_period_no;
                  end;  (*for*)

              end; (* forward_recursion_of_w_w *)

              procedure    fill_up_the_order_schedule;

                  var prodn_from_period,
                     period_no,
                        min_position,
                        no_of_orders_placed,
                        index,
                        order_qty : integer;
                        order_cost,
                        total_cost,
                        holding_cost : real;
              computations_to_continue : boolean;

  begin (* fill_up_the_order_schedule *)
```

```
min_position:= computation_table_for_w_w[max_period_no].
                          min_cost_position;
 total_cost:= computation_table_for_w_w[max_period_no].
              period_wise_calculation[min_position].cost;
              order_cost := 0.0;
              no_of_orders_placed:= 0;
              period_no := max_period_no;
              computations_to_continue:=true;
              while (computations_to_continue) do
              begin
   min_position := computation_table_for_w_w[period_no].
                          min_cost_position;
 prodn_from_period := computation_table_for_w_w[period_no].
                          period_wise_calculation[min_position].
                                    order_period_no;
 order_cost := order_cost + input_data_for_w_w[prodn_from_period].
order_cost;
          no_of_orders_placed := no_of_orders_placed + 1;
          order_qty := 0;
          for index:= prodn_from_period to period_no do
 order_qty := order_qty + input_data_for_w_w[index].demand;
 output_data_of_w_w.order_schedule[no_of_orders_placed].period_
no:=prodn_from_period;

             output_data_of_w_w.order_schedule[no_of_orders_
             placed].qty_produced:=
             order_qty;
             period_no := prodn_from_period - 1;
          if (period_no = 0) then computations_to_continue := false;
             end;
             holding_cost := total_cost - order_cost;
 output_data_of_w_w.no_of_orders_placed:=no_of_orders_placed;
             output_data_of_w_w.total_cost := total_cost;
             output_data_of_w_w.holding_cost:= holding_cost;
             output_data_of_w_w.order_cost:= order_cost;
            end; (* fill_up_the_order_schedule *)

 procedure  print_w_w_output;
            var  index,
            period_no,
```

```
            no_of_items_printed_so_far,
            no_of_items_to_be_printed,
            no_of_calculations_done  : integer;

begin (* print_w_w_output*)
        writeln(w_w_output,'assembly no. = ',assly_no:2);
        for period_no := 1 to max_period_no do
        begin
        writeln(w_w_output, ' period_no :=',period_no:2,' ' );
no_of_calculations_done:=computation_table_for_w_w[period_no].
                        no_of_calculations;
        no_of_items_to_be_printed := no_of_calculations_done;
            no_of_items_printed_so_far := 0;
            while (no_of_items_to_be_printed > 0) do
              if (no_of_items_to_be_printed <= 5)
              then
         begin
              write(w_w_output, ' ' :12);
              for index:=(no_of_items_printed_so_far + 1)
              to no_of_calculations_done do
begin
  write(w_w_output,computation_table_for_w_w[period_no].
                    period_wise_calculation[index].cost:8:3,'(');
  write(w_w_output,computation_table_for_w_w[period_no].
                         period_wise_calculation[index].
                                   order_period_no,')');
  no_of_items_to_be_printed:=no_of_items_to_be_printed - 1;
         end; (* for index *)
         writeln(w_w_output);
         no_of_items_printed_so_far := no_of_calculations_done;
             end (* then*)
             else
             begin
               write(w_w_output, ' ' :12);
               for index:=(no_of_items_printed_so_far + 1)
                             to
                        (no_of_items_printed_so_far + 5)
                                    do
          begin
  write(w_w_output, computation_table_for_w_w[period_no].
```

```
                    period_wise_calculation[index].cost:8:3,'(');
        write(w_w_output,computation_table_for_w_w[period_no].
                    period_wise_calculation[index].
                        order_period_no,')');
      end;
      writeln(w_w_output);
      no_of_items_printed_so_far := no_of_items_printed_so_far + 10;
      no_of_items_to_be_printed := no_of_items_to_be_printed - 10;
      end; (* else *)
      end; (* for period_no *)
      writeln(w_w_output);
      writeln(w_w_output);
      writeln(w_w_output);
      writeln(w_w_output,'production_scheudle is as follows');
      writeln(w_w_output,'period_no','production_quantity');
      for index:= 1 to output_data_of_w_w.no_of_orders_placed do
      writeln(w_w_output,output_data_of_w_w.order_schedule[index].
                  period_no:8,' ' :5,
                    output_data_of_w_w.order_schedule[index].
                        qty_produced);
      writeln(w_w_output,'order_cost:=',output_data_of_w_w.order_cost);
      writeln(w_w_output,'holding_cost:=',output_data_of_w_w.holding_
cost);
      writeln(w_w_output,'total_cost:=',output_data_of_w_w.total_cost);
           end;

                  begin (* lot_sizing_by_w_w *)

                  forward_recursion_of_w_w;
                    print_w_w_output;
                    fill_up_the_order_schedule;
              end; (* lot_sizing_by_w_w *)

                  procedure   read_assly_data;

                  var
                     assembly_no,
                     child_assly_no,
                     needs_process,
                     needs_assembly,
```

```
            process_no : integer;

          begin (* read_assly_data*)
             reset(in_ass_dat,'in_ass.dat');
            for assembly_no:=1 to max_assly_no do
            begin
              readln(in_ass_dat,
                 abda[assembly_no].assly_no,
                 abda[assembly_no].
           no_of_child_asslys,needs_process,needs_assembly,
                 abda[assembly_no].cost);
                 abda[assembly_no].
          immediately_needs_processing:=(needs_process = 1);
                 abda[assembly_no].
          immediately_gets_into_assly:=(needs_assembly = 1);
                 if (abda[assembly_no].
                    no_of_child_asslys >0 )

          then
                 for child_assly_no := 1 to
                    abda[assembly_no].no_of_child_asslys do
                        begin

                        readln(in_ass_dat,
                          abda[assembly_no].
  array_of_child_assly[child_assly_no].assly_no,
                 abda[assembly_no].

  array_of_child_assly[child_assly_no].qty_to_be_contributed);

  (*writeln(abda[assembly_no]. array_of_child_assly[child_assly_no].
assly_no,' ',assembly_no,'oo');*)
                    end;
           if(abda[assembly_no].immediately_needs_processing)
                 then
                  begin
                   readln(in_ass_dat,
                    abda[assembly_no].
                      no_of_children_for_assly,
                 abda[assembly_no].
```

```
                        assly_no_after_processing,
               abda[assembly_no].
                        no_of_processes_needed);
          for process_no := 1 to
               abda[assembly_no].
                        no_of_processes_needed do
         begin  (* for *)
           with abda[assembly_no].
                  aps[process_no] do
           begin (* with *)
               readln(in_ass_dat,
       mc_no, set-up_time, processing_time_per_unit,
            set-up_cost);
        end; (* with *)
                  end; (* for *)
                  end
                  else (* collect_parent_data*)
                     begin
                       abda[assembly_no].
                       no_of_processes_needed := 0;
                       readln(in_ass_dat,
                          abda[assembly_no].parent_no,
                               abda[assembly_no].
                                      qty_for_parent,
                          abda[assembly_no].
                                      assly_on_mc_no);
                  end;
                     end;  (* for *)

                  end; (* read_assly_data *)
    procedure   read_assly_demands;

    var
        assly_no,
        period_no,
        no_of_demands,
        demand_no     : integer;

    begin  (*  read_assly_demands  *)
         for assly_no := 1 to max_assly_no do
```

```
                for period_no := 1 to max_period_no do
                demand[assly_no, period_no]:=0;
                reset(in_dem_dat,'in_dem_dat');
                while not eof(in_dem_dat) do
                begin
            readln(in_dem_dat,assly_no,no_of_demands);
                 for demand_no:=1 to no_of_demands do
                begin
                 read(in_dem_dat, period_no);
            readln(in_dem_dat,demand[assly_no,period_no]);
                 end;
                end;
      end; (* read_assly_demands *)

            procedure  read_input_data;

            begin  (* read_input_data *)
              read_assly_data;
              read_assly_demands;
             end;  (* read_input_data *)
(*  procedure transfer_asslys_on_explosion_list(period_no:integer);

    var assly_no  :  integer;
             begin  * transfer_asslys_on_explosion_list *
                 no_of_asslys_on_explosion_list := 0;
                     for assly_no := 1 to max_assly_no do
                     if (demand[assly_no, period_no] >0 )
                     then
                       begin
                         no_of_asslys_on_explosion_list :=
                         no_of_asslys_on_explosion_list + 1;
     incremental_explosion_list[no_of_asslys_on_explosion_list].
                                     assly_no:=assly_no;
     incremental_explosion_list[no_of_asslys_on_explosion_list].
                                 qty_to_be_exploded :=
                           demand[assly_no,period_no];
                 end;
                    end;   * transfer_asslys_on_explosion_list *)
       procedure do_explosion;
       var  current_no,
```

```
          current_assly_no,
          current_qty_for_explosion,
          no_of_children,
          children_no,
          ending_no,
          period_no,
          assly_no,
          temp_assly,
          temp_qty,
          a,b : integer;

begin (* do explosion *)
          for a:=1 to max_assly_no do
          for b:=1 to max_period_no do
          exploded_demand[a,b]:=0;
          for period_no:=1 to max_period_no do
          exploded_demand[1,period_no]:=demand[1,period_no];
          period_no:=1;
          for period_no:=1 to max_period_no do
          begin
          for assly_no:=1 to max_assly_no do
          begin
             no_of_children:=
                abda[assly_no].no_of_child_asslys;
current_qty_for_explosion:=exploded_demand[assly_no,period_no];
              for children_no:=1 to no_of_children do
                begin
                temp_assly:=abda[assly_no].
                   array_of_child_assly[children_no].assly_no;
                temp_qty:=abda[assly_no].
      array_of_child_assly[children_no].qty_to_be_contributed*
                          current_qty_for_explosion;
           exploded_demand[temp_assly,period_no]:=
           exploded_demand[temp_assly,period_no] + temp_qty;
           end;
           end;
           end;
   end; (* do_explosion *)

   procedure  do_lot_sizing;
```

```
var  set-up_cost  : real;

    assly_no,
          assly_no_after_processing,
          period_no,
          process_no  : integer;
       begin  (* do_lot_sizing  *)
          rewrite(w_w_output,'w_w.out');
        for assly_no := 1 to max_assly_no do
        abda[assly_no].
           lot_sizing_to_be_done:=true;
         for assly_no:= 1 to max_assly_no do
         begin  (*  for *)
      if (abda[assly_no].
                     immediately_needs_processing)
            then
            begin  (* then  *)
        assly_no_after_processing:=
              abda[assly_no].
                 assly_no_after_processing;
              abda[assly_no_after_processing].
                   lot_sizing_to_be_done := false;
                      writeln('assly',assly_no);
       end;  (* then *)
 end;  (* for *)
      writeln('*');
     for assly_no := 1 to max_assly_no do
        if (abda[assly_no].
                   lot_sizing_to_be_done)
         then
         begin  (* then *)
           for period_no := 1 to max_period_no do
           input_data_for_w_w[period_no].holding_cost:=
             abda[assly_no].cost*
            inventory_cost_fraction;
            set-up_cost:=0.0;
            for process_no := 1 to
                  abda[assly_no].
                               no_of_processes_needed do
```

```
  set-up_cost:= set-up_cost + abda[assly_no].
                                        aps[process_no].set-up_cost;
  abda[assly_no].total_set-up_cost:= set-up_cost; writeln('setxp_cost',set-
up_cost);
  for period_no := 1 to max_period_no do
  input_data_for_w_w[period_no].order_cost:=
       set-up_cost;
  for period_no := 1 to max_period_no do
  begin
  input_data_for_w_w[period_no].demand:=
    exploded_demand[assly_no,period_no];
  writeln('assly_no',assly_no,' ',input_data_for_w_w[period_no].de-
mand);
        end;
        lot_sizing_by_w_w(assly_no);
        array_for_output_of_w_w[assly_no]:=output_data_of_w_w;
            if (abda[assly_no].
            immediately_needs_processing)

            then
             begin  (* then *)
               assly_no_after_processing :=
          abda[assly_no].
            assly_no_after_processing;
            array_for_output_of_w_w[assly_no_after_processing]:=
                    output_data_of_w_w;
                end; (* then *)
                end; (* then *)
                close(w_w_output);

             end; (* do_lot_sizing*)

             procedure  prepare_queue_of_lots;

             var  (* lead_time  *)

                assly_no,
                no_of_lots,
                process_no,
                    lot_no : integer;
```

```
begin (* prepare_queue_of_lots *)
   for assly_no := 1 to max_assly_no do
   begin
     ala[assly_no].assly_no:=assly_no;
ala[assly_no].no_of_lots:=
array_for_output_of_w_w[assly_no].no_of_orders_placed;
    writeln(assly_no ,ala[assly_no].no_of_lots,'lots');
    no_of_lots:=array_for_output_of_w_w[assly_no].
       no_of_orders_placed;
    for lot_no := 1 to no_of_lots do
    begin
     ala[assly_no].
       dol[lot_no].assly_no:=assly_no;
      ala[assly_no].
       dol[lot_no].original_size:=
     array_for_output_of_w_w[assly_no].
       order_schedule[lot_no].qty_produced;
(*writeln (assly_no, lot_no, array_for_output_of_w_w[assly_no].
       order_schedule[lot_no].qty_produced);*)
     ala[assly_no].
       dol[lot_no].qty_left:=
     array_for_output_of_w_w[assly_no].
order_schedule[lot_no].qty_produced;

  ala[assly_no].
         dol[lot_no].
              no_of_agm_visited:=0;
      ala[assly_no].
        dol[lot_no].
             current_mc_no:=0;
      ala[assly_no].
        dol[lot_no].
             processing_complete:=false;
      ala[assly_no].
        dol[lot_no].
      actual_inventory_carrying_cost:=0.0;
      ala[assly_no].
        dol[lot_no].
             priorty_value:=0.0;
      ala[assly_no].
```

```
     dol[lot_no].
          percentage_completion:=0.0;
   ala[assly_no].
     dol[lot_no].
       required_completion_time:=
   array_for_output_of_w_w[assly_no].
     order_schedule[lot_no].period_no*
          no_of_hours_in_a_period;
 ala[assly_no].
  dol[lot_no].
   actual_completion_time:=0.0;
 ala[assly_no].
  dol[lot_no].
   cpt:=0.0;
 ala[assly_no].
   dol[lot_no].
    total_wait_time_in_queues_so_far:=0.0;
 ala[assly_no].
   dol[lot_no].
    tpt_completed_so_far:=0.0;
 ala[assly_no].
   dol[lot_no].
    time_of_entry_into_the_shop:=
  array_for_output_of_w_w[assly_no].
 order_schedule[lot_no].period_no*1.0-  lead_times[assly_
 no]*factor;
  ala[assly_no].
    dol[lot_no].
     total_required_processing_time := 0.0;
     if not (first_run) then
     begin
       if (max_lead_time < lead_times[assly_no]) then
          max_lead_time:=lead_times[assly_no];
 end;
  for process_no:=1 to abda[assly_no].
                       no_of_processes_needed do

begin
    ala[assly_no].
      dol[lot_no].
```

```
                    total_required_processing_time:=
             ala[assly_no].
              dol[lot_no].
               total_required_processing_time +
               abda[assly_no].
                aps[process_no].
                 set-up_time +
                    abda[assly_no].
                aps[process_no].
                 processing_time_per_unit*
          array_for_output_of_w_w[assly_no].
                order_schedule[lot_no].qty_produced;
               end;
               ala[assly_no].
                dol[lot_no].
                 time_of_joining_the_queue:=0.0;
              end;
             end;

         end;  (* prepare_queue_of_lots *)

         procedure   plug_in_the_event(p : ptr_to_event);

         var  execution_time_just_greater,
            prev_to_execution_time_just_greater : ptr_to_event;

          begin  (* plug_in_the_event *)
          (*writeln('plug',p^.execution_time);*)

            counter := counter + 1;
            if (top_of_event_list = nil)
            then
             begin  (* top_of_the_event_list = nil *)
              top_of_event_list := p;
             p:=nil;
         end (* top_of_event_list := nil *)
          else
           begin  (* contains at least one event *)
            execution_time_just_greater := top_of_event_list;
      prev_to_execution_time_just_greater := top_of_event_list;
```

```
if (top_of_event_list^.execution_time < p^.execution_time)
        then
 begin  (* continue search until execution_time_just_greater *)
          execution_time_just_greater:=
           execution_time_just_greater^.next_event;
        while (execution_time_just_greater <> nil)
                and
           (execution_time_just_greater^.
                  execution_time < p^.execution_time)
                      do
          begin  (* while *)
           execution_time_just_greater:=
            execution_time_just_greater^.next_event;
           prev_to_execution_time_just_greater:=
           prev_to_execution_time_just_greater^.next_event;
          end;  (* while *)
          if (execution_time_just_greater <> nil)
          then
           begin
            p^.next_event :=
            prev_to_execution_time_just_greater^.next_event;
           prev_to_execution_time_just_greater^.next_event:=p;
            p:=nil;
           end
             else
              begin
           prev_to_execution_time_just_greater^.next_event:=p;
           p:=nil;
          end;
      end (* continue searh till execution_time_just_greater *)
      else
      begin (* execution time just greater *)
      p^.next_event:=top_of_event_list;
      top_of_event_list:=p;

      p:=nil;
 end;   (* execution time just greater *)
end;  (* contains at leat one event *)
end; (* plug in the event *)
```

```
procedure prepare_event_regarding_entry_of_the_components;

  var assly_no,
      no_of_lots,
          lot_no : integer;

begin (* prepare_event_regarding_entry_of the_components *)

for assly_no := 1 to max_assly_no do
        if (abda[assly_no].
              no_of_child_asslys = 0)

         then
         begin (* then it is a component assly *)
          no_of_lots:=ala[assly_no].no_of_lots;
          for lot_no:= 1 to no_of_lots do
          begin (* for lot_no *)
           newmodified(p);
           with p^ do
           begin
            event:=lot_enters_the_shop;
            array_of_relevant_nos[1]:=assly_no;
            array_of_relevant_nos[2]:=lot_no;
            execution_time:=ala[assly_no].
                        dol[lot_no].
                            time_of_entry_into_the_shop;
           plug_in_the_event(p);
           end;
        end; (* for lot_no *)
           end; (* then it is a component assly *)

  end; (* prepare_events_regarding_entry_of_the_components *)

          procedure prepare_collect_statistic_event;

          begin (* prepare_collect_statistic_event *)

            newmodified(p);
           with p^ do
           begin
```

```
                event:=collect_statistics_from_now_on;
                array_of_relevant_nos[1]:=0;
   array_of_relevant_nos[2]:=0;
     execution_time:=collect_statistics_from_time -lead_time*factor;
                if not (first_run) then
  execution_time:=collect_statistics_from_time - (max_lead_time - 50)*fac-
tor;

                plug_in_the_event(p);
              end;

           end; (* prepare_collect_statistic_event *)
           procedure  initialisations;

           var    mc_no,
                 assly_mc_no,
                assly_no_after_processing,
                finished_assly_no,
                assly_no,
                subassly_no,
                quelg_no : integer;
                in_ass_mc : text;

            begin  (* initialisations *)

             clock_time:=0;
             counter:=0;
             flag := false;

           (*now all mc queues and assly mc queues are intialised *)

             for mc_no := 1 to max_mc_no do
             begin
               queue_before_general_mc[mc_no].queue_length:=0;
               for quelg_no:=1 to max_queue_length do
               begin
                queue_before_general_mc[mc_no].
                details_of_queue[quelg_no].lot_no:=0;
                queue_before_general_mc[mc_no].
                details_of_queue[quelg_no].assly_no:=0;
```

```
            end;
        end;
          reset(in_ass_mc,'in_ass.mc');
          for assly_mc_no :=16 to max_assly_mc_no do
          begin
           readln(in_ass_mc,
              aam[assly_mc_no].
                     finished_assly_no,
                 aam[assly_mc_no].
                         processing_time_per_unit,
                 queue_before_assly_mc[assly_mc_no].
                          no_of_subasslys_into_assly );
                 finished_assly_no:=
                 aam[assly_mc_no].
                      finished_assly_no;
           (* queue_before_assly_mc[assly_mc_no].
                 no_of_subasslys_into_assly:=
                   abda[finished_assly_no].
                      no_of_child_asslys;    *)
     (*writeln('ffff ', finished_assly_no);*)
        for subassly_no := 1 to max_subassly_no_into_an_assly do
           begin
             queue_before_assly_mc[assly_mc_no].
details_of_queues[subassly_no].queue_length:=0;
         queue_before_assly_mc[assly_mc_no].
              quantity_available[subassly_no]:=0;  (* added *)
            for quelg_no := 1 to max_queue_length do
            begin
             queue_before_assly_mc[assly_mc_no].
                  details_of_queues[subassly_no].
                       details_of_queue[quelg_no].lot_no:=0;
             queue_before_assly_mc[assly_mc_no].
                   details_of_queues[subassly_no].
                    details_of_queue[quelg_no].assly_no:=0;
                  end;
           end;
        end;

        (* now all the queue and assly mc queues are intialised *)
```

```
(* now we do all pointer intialisations *)

 event_freetop:=nil;
 ptr_to_current_executable_event:=nil;
 top_of_event_list:=nil;
 p:=nil;

 (* pointer intialisations are compleate *)

 (* intialising general machine data *)

  for mc_no:= 1 to max_mc_no do
  with agm[mc_no] do
  begin  (* with *)
    tpt := 0.0;
    total_idle_time := 0.0;
    cu:=0.0;
    end; (* with *)

   (* end of intialisations of general machine data *)

   (* initialising assembly machine data *)

    for assly_mc_no := 16 to max_assly_mc_no  do
    with aam[assly_mc_no] do
    begin (* with *)
            tpt := 0.0;
              total_idle_time:= 0.0;
    cu:=0.0;

     end; (* with*)

     (* end of intialisations assembly machine data *)

     (* lot size needed or not is determined *)

     for assly_no :=1 to max_assly_no do
     abda[assly_no].
        lot_sizing_to_be_done:=true;
```

```
        for assly_no:=1 to max_assly_no do
        begin (* for *)
        if (abda[assly_no].
         immediately_needs_processing)
        then
        begin (* then *)
          assly_no_after_processing:=
          abda[assly_no].
             assly_no_after_processing;
          abda[assly_no_after_processing].
             lot_sizing_to_be_done:=false;
 end;  (* then *)
end;   (* for *)
for assly_no:=1 to max_assly_no do
ala[assly_no].
lot_no_which_will_enter_the_shop:=1;
for mc_no:=1 to max_no_of_proces_on_any_assly do
mc_busy[mc_no]:=false;
end; (* initializations *)
procedure   find_the_next_executable_event;
begin (* find_the_next_executable_event*)
 ptr_to_current_executable_event:=top_of_event_list;
      q:=ptr_to_current_executable_event;
 if (ptr_to_current_executable_event = nil ) then
       flag:=true
      (* no event left *)
      else
      begin
   top_of_event_list:=top_of_event_list^.next_event;
   clock_time:=ptr_to_current_executable_event^.
                 execution_time;
    end;
end; (* find_the_next_executable_event*)
    procedure   search_and_insert_for_general_mc_

queue(mc_no  : integer);

var  i,j,k,n,index,
   insert_position,
   assly_no,
```

```
            lot_no,
            current_assly_no,
            current_lot_no,
            next_assly_no,
            assly_mc_no : integer;

            priority_value_of_current_lot : real;

            insert_position_found : boolean;

begin (* search_and_insert_for_general_mc_queue *)

        current_assly_no:=ptr_to_current_executable_event^.
                          array_of_relevant_nos[1];
         current_lot_no:=ptr_to_current_executable_event^.
                          array_of_relevant_nos[2];
        if (queue_before_general_mc[mc_no].queue_length=0)
        then begin
          queue_before_general_mc[mc_no].
              details_of_queue[1].assly_no:=
         current_assly_no;
         queue_before_general_mc[mc_no].
            details_of_queue[1].lot_no:=
     current_lot_no;
  queue_before_general_mc[mc_no].queue_length:=
         queue_before_general_mc[mc_no].queue_length + 1;
        end
    else
 begin
 i:= 1; j:=queue_before_general_mc[mc_no].queue_length;
          current_assly_no:=ptr_to_current_executable_event^.
                        array_of_relevant_nos[1];
          current_lot_no:=ptr_to_current_executable_event^.
                        array_of_relevant_nos[2];
  next_assly_no:=abda[current_assly_no].assly_no_after_processing;
writeln('current',current_assly_no,' ',current_lot_no,' ',next_assly_no,' '
,mc_no);
        assly_mc_no:=abda[next_assly_no].assly_on_mc_no;
        (*coordination_index[current_assly_no]:=
          1 + (latest_assly_time[current_assly_no,assly_mc_no] -
```

```
            prev_mean_time[assly_mc_no])*0.1;writeln(first_run);*)
               priority_value_of_current_lot:=
ala[current_assly_no].
  dol[current_lot_no].priorty_value*1;
insert_position_found:=false;

repeat
  k:=(i+j)div 2;
  assly_no:=
  queue_before_general_mc[mc_no].details_of_queue[k].assly_no;
  lot_no:=
  queue_before_general_mc[mc_no].details_of_queue[k].lot_no;
          if (priority_value_of_current_lot >
              ala[assly_no].
               dol[lot_no].priorty_value)
         then begin  (* then *)
          if (k=1)
          then begin
     insert_position_found:=true;
             insert_position:=1;
             end
           else
           begin
             assly_no:=
             queue_before_general_mc[mc_no].
                   details_of_queue[k-1].assly_no;
                    lot_no:=

             queue_before_general_mc[mc_no].

                   details_of_queue[k-1].lot_no;
           if (priority_value_of_current_lot <=
                  ala[assly_no].
                        dol[lot_no].priorty_value)

       then begin
             insert_position_found:=true;
             insert_position:=k;
            end
           else  j:=k-1;
```

```
            end;
                       end  (* then *)
                  else begin (* else  *)
       if (k=queue_before_general_mc[mc_no].queue_length)
                            then begin
                              insert_position_found:=true;
                              insert_position:=
                                 queue_before_general_mc[mc_no].
                                      queue_length + 1;
         end
   else
   begin
    assly_no:=
    queue_before_general_mc[mc_no].
          details_of_queue[K+1].assly_no;
     lot_no:=
     queue_before_general_mc[mc_no].
            details_of_queue[k+1].lot_no;
             if (priority_value_of_current_lot >=
                   ala[assly_no].
                        dol[lot_no].priorty_value)
         then begin
         insert_position_found:=true;
         insert_position:=k+1;
         end
         else i:=k+1;
         end;
         end;  (* else *)

         until (insert_position_found);

  for index:=queue_before_general_mc[mc_no].queue_length
                                downto
                             insert_position
                                      do
            queue_before_general_mc[mc_no].
                  details_of_queue[index+1]:=
            queue_before_general_mc[mc_no].
                  details_of_queue[index];
            queue_before_general_mc[mc_no].
```

```
                details_of_queue[insert_position].assly_no:=
          current_assly_no;
          queue_before_general_mc[mc_no].
                details_of_queue[insert_position].lot_no:=
           current_lot_no;
          queue_before_general_mc[mc_no].queue_length:=
          queue_before_general_mc[mc_no].queue_length + 1;
         end;

        end; (* search_and_insert_for_general_mc_queue *)

   procedure search_and_insert_for_assembly_mc_queue(mc_no  :  integer
);

            var finish_assly_no,
            current_assly_no,
            current_lot_no,
            que_len,
            upper_search_lim,
            search_no : integer;
            position_found : boolean;

          begin  (* search_and_insert_for_assembly_mc_queue  *)

            current_assly_no:=ptr_to_current_executable_event^.
                                      array_of_relevant_nos[1];
            current_lot_no:=ptr_to_current_executable_event^.
                                      array_of_relevant_nos[2];
            finish_assly_no:=aam[mc_no].finished_assly_no;
            writeln('finish_assly_no',finish_assly_no,' ',current_assly_no,'
',mc_no);
            if (mc_no=16) then
            finish_assly_no:=2;
            upper_search_lim:=abda[finish_assly_no].no_of_child_asslys;
            (*upper_search_lim:=abda[finish_assly_no].
                              no_of_children_for_assly;*)
            search_no := 1;  position_found:=false;
            writeln(upper_search_lim,'lim');

   while  (search_no <= upper_search_lim)  and not (position_found) do
```

```
begin
if (abda[finish_assly_no].
        array_of_child_assly[search_no].assly_no =
            current_assly_no)
then position_found:= true
else search_no := search_no + 1;
writeln(abda[finish_assly_no].
        array_of_child_assly[search_no].assly_no,'qq');
end;

  if not(position_found)
  then begin
       writeln('assly_no not found in insert queue for assly mc');
          halt;
          end
          else  (* position has beeb found*)
          begin (* else *)
      queue_before_assly_mc[mc_no].details_of_queues[search_no].
            queue_length:=
      queue_before_assly_mc[mc_no].details_of_queues[search_no].
             queue_length + 1;
que_len:=
      queue_before_assly_mc[mc_no].details_of_queues[search_no].
            queue_length;
queue_before_assly_mc[mc_no].details_of_queues[search_no].
      details_of_queue[que_len].assly_no:=current_assly_no;
queue_before_assly_mc[mc_no].details_of_queues[search_no].
      details_of_queue[que_len].lot_no:=current_lot_no;
             queue_before_assly_mc[mc_no].
                   quantity_available[search_no]:=
             queue_before_assly_mc[mc_no].
                   quantity_available[search_no]+
                      ala[current_assly_no].
                        dol[current_lot_no].
                            original_size;
          end;  (* else  *)
          end;   (* search_and_insert_for_assly_mc_queue *)

          procedure   execute_collect_statistics_from_now_on;
```

```
var  machine_no,
     queue_no,
     no_of_queues,
     queue_length,
     queue_length_index,
     assly_no,
     lot_no : integer;

     (* collect_statistics_from_time*)

     begin  (* execute_collect_statistics_from_now_on*)
     for machine_no := 1 to max_mc_no do
     begin  (* for general machine_no *)
        agm[machine_no].tpt:=0.0;
     end;  (* for general machine_no *)
     for machine_no:= 16 to max_assly_mc_no do
     begin  (* for machine_no*)
        aam[machine_no].tpt:=0.0;
     end; (* for machine_no*)
     for machine_no:= 1 to max_mc_no do
     begin  (* for general_machine_no *)
queue_length:=queue_before_general_mc[machine_no].queue_length;
    for queue_length_index:=1 to queue_length do
    begin  (* for queue_no  *)
    assly_no := queue_before_general_mc[machine_no].
         details_of_queue[queue_length_index].assly_no;
    lot_no := queue_before_general_mc[machine_no].
    details_of_queue[queue_length_index].lot_no;
    ala[assly_no].
          dol[lot_no].total_wait_time_in_queues_so_far:=0.0;
           ala[assly_no].
           dol[lot_no].time_of_entry_into_the_shop:=
           collect_statistics_from_time;
        end;  (* for queue no*)
     end;  (* for general machine no *)
     for machine_no:= 16 to max_assly_mc_no  do
     begin  (* for assly machine_no *)
      no_of_queues:= queue_before_assly_mc[machine_no].
                 no_of_subasslys_into_assly;
 for queue_no:= 1 to no_of_queues do
```

```
            begin (* for queue_no *)
            queue_length:=queue_before_assly_mc[machine_no].
                  details_of_queues[queue_no].queue_length;
            for queue_length_index:= 1 to queue_length do
            begin (* for queue_length_index *)
             assly_no :=
             queue_before_assly_mc[machine_no].
               details_of_queues[queue_no].
             details_of_queue[queue_length_index].assly_no;
             lot_no:=
             queue_before_assly_mc[machine_no].
              details_of_queues[queue_no].
               details_of_queue[queue_length_index].lot_no;
             ala[assly_no].
              dol[lot_no].total_wait_time_in_queues_so_far:=0.0;
             ala[assly_no].
              dol[lot_no].time_of_entry_into_the_shop:=
             collect_statistics_from_time;
        end; (* for queue_length_index *)
     end; (* for queue_no *)
   end; (* for assly_machine_no *)
 end; (* execute_collect_statistics_from_now_on *)

            procedure  execute_lot_enters_the_shop;

            var assly_no,
            mc_no,
            lot_no   : integer;

        begin (* execute_lot_enters_the_shop *)

          newmodified(new_event);
            new_event^.array_of_relevant_nos[1]:=
  ptr_to_current_executable_event^.array_of_relevant_nos[1];
             new_event^.array_of_relevant_nos[2]:=
ptr_to_current_executable_event^.array_of_relevant_nos[2];
             new_event^.execution_time:=
             ptr_to_current_executable_event^.execution_time
  assly_no:=ptr_to_current_executable_event^.array_of_relevant_nos[1];
  lot_no:=ptr_to_current_executable_event^.array_of_relevant_nos[2];
```

```
                if(abda[assly_no].
                        immediately_gets_into_assly)
                then begin
            new_event^.event:=lot_enters_the_assly_mc_queue;
                mc_no:=abda[assly_no].
                        assly_on_mc_no;
            new_event^.array_of_relevant_nos[3]:=mc_no;
                end
                else if (abda[assly_no].
                        immediately_needs_processing)
                 then begin
        new_event^.event:=lot_enters_the_general_mc_queue;
                        mc_no:=abda[assly_no].
                              aps[1].mc_no;
                 new_event^.array_of_relevant_nos[3]:=mc_no;
                        end
else new_event^.event:=lot_enters_the_finished_product_list;
                ala[assly_no].
                   dol[lot_no].time_of_entry_into_the_shop
                :=ptr_to_current_executable_event^.execution_time;
                      plug_in_the_event(new_event);
            end; (* execute_lot_enters_the_shop *)

    procedure  execute_lot_enters_the_general_mc_queue;

            var  assly_no,
                  lot_no,
                 queue_lg,
                 mc_no_to_visit,
                 process_no :integer;

   begin (* execute_lot_enters_the_general_mc_queu *)
assly_no:=ptr_to_current_executable_event^.array_of_relevant_nos[1];
lot_no:=ptr_to_current_executable_event^.array_of_relevant_nos[2];
     mc_no_to_visit:=ptr_to_current_executable_event^.
             array_of_relevant_nos[3];
 process_no:=ala[assly_no].dol[lot_no].no_of_agm_visited + 1;
 ala[assly_no].
  dol[lot_no].current_mc_no:=mc_no_to_visit;
        ala[assly_no].
```

```
dol[lot_no].time_of_joining_the_queue:=
        ptr_to_current_executable_event^.execution_time;
  ala[assly_no].
  dol[lot_no].cpt:=
            ala[assly_no].
              dol[lot_no].original_size *
            abda[assly_no].
             aps[process_no].
              processing_time_per_unit
             +
                abda[assly_no].
                  aps[process_no].
                   set-up_time;writeln('098');
      search_and_insert_for_general_mc_queue(mc_no_to_visit);

queue_lg:=queue_before_general_mc[mc_n_to_visit].queue_length;
       if (queue_lg = 1) and (mc_busy[mc_no_to_visit]=false) then
        begin
         newmodified(new_event);
         new_event^.event:=processing_on_general_mc_starts;
            new_event^.array_of_relevant_nos[1]:=assly_no;
            new_event^.array_of_relevant_nos[2]:=lot_no;
         new_event^.array_of_relevant_nos[3]:=mc_no_to_visit;
            new_event^.execution_time:=
            ptr_to_current_executable_event^.execution_time;
            plug_in_the_event(new_event);
           end;
         end; (* execute_lot_enters_the_general_mc_queue*)
         function  processing_can_start_on_assly_mc
                  ( mc_no_to_visit  : integer ) : boolean;

       var processing_can_start : boolean;

          pos_of_lot_no,
             lot_size,
             no_of_children,
             children_index,
             quantity_to_be_contributed,
             finish_assly_no : integer;
```

```
begin (* processing_vcan_start_on_assly_mc *)
        finish_assly_no:= aam[mc_no_to_visit].
                    finished_assly_no;
 {queue_before_assly_mc[mc_no_to_visit].finish_assly_no;}
        pos_of_lot_no:=
        ala[finish_assly_no].
          lot_no_which_will_enter_the_shop;
        lot_size:=
        ala[finish_assly_no].
         dol[pos_of_lot_no].original_size;
         no_of_children:=abda[finish_assly_no].
         no_of_children_for_assly;(*writeln('lot_size',lot_size);*)
          processing_can_start:=true;
          children_index:=1;
          while (processing_can_start)
                and
         (children_index <= no_of_children)
                do
    begin (* while *)
        quantity_to_be_contributed:=
        abda[finish_assly_no].
  array_of_child_assly[children_index].qty_to_be_contributed*
                  lot_size;

 writeln('quantity_to_be_contributed',quantity_to_be contributed,'lot_
size',lot_size);
 writeln('finish_assly_no',finish_assly_no,'children_index',children_in-
dex);
 writeln('assly_no',abda[finish_assly_no].array_of_child_ ssly[children_in-
dex].assly_no);
 writeln('quantity_available',queue_before_assly_mc[mc_no_to_visit].
quantity_available[children_index]);
       if (quantity_to_be_contributed >
         queue_before_assly_mc[mc_no_to_visit].
          quantity_available[children_index])
 then processing_can_start:=false
 else children_index:=children_index + 1;
 end; (* while *) (*writeln(children_index , processing_can_start, fin-
ish_assly_no,' finish');*)
 processing_can_start_on_assly_mc:=processing_can_start;
```

```
end; (* processing_can_start_on_assly_mc*)
procedure     execute_lot_enters_the_assly_mc_queue;

var   assly_no,

      finished_assly_no,
      pos_of_lot_no,
      lot_no,
      queue_lg,
      mc_no_to_visit : integer;
  begin    (* execute_lot_enters_the_assly_mc_queue *)
assly_no:=ptr_to_current_executable_event^.array_of_relevant_nos[1];
lot_no:=ptr_to_current_executable_event^.array_of_relevant_nos[2];
      mc_no_to_visit:=ptr_to_current_executable_event^.
                 array_of_relevant_nos[3];
            if(mc_no_to_visit>15) then
        begin
              assly_count[mc_no_to_visit]:=
              assly_count[mc_no_to_visit] + 1;
              ala[assly_no].
                dol[lot_no].time_of_joining_the_queue:=
                  ptr_to_current_executable_event^.execution_time;
                time_of_reaching[assly_no,lot_no]:=
                     ptr_to_current_executable_event^.execution_time;
               present_mean_time[mc_no_to_visit]:=
((assly_count[mc_no_to_visit]-1)*present_mean_time[mc_no_to_visit]+

time_of_reaching[assly_no,lot_no])/assly_count[mc_no_to_visit];

if (time_of_reaching[assly_no,lot_no]>
                   present_mean_time[mc_no_to_visit])
                   then
               latest_assly_time[assly_no,mc_no_to_visit]:=
                        time_of_reaching[assly_no,lot_no];
              arrival_time[times+1,assly_no,lot_no]:=
                time_of_reaching[assly_no,lot_no];
 search_and_insert_for_assembly_mc_queue(mc_no_to_visit);
                  writeln(assly_no,    lot_no,'  lott');
              if (processing_can_start_on_assly_mc(mc_no_to_visit))
 then
```

```
begin (* then fire the event processing_starts_on_assly_mc *)
        (*writeln(assly_no,lot_no,'mc_no_to_visit');*)
  if (ptr_to_current_executable_event^.execution_time<
                earliest_lot_time[mc_no_to_visit]) then
      earliest_lot_time[mc_no_to_visit]:=
 ptr_to_current_executable_event^.execution_time
      else if
       (ptr_to_current_executable_event^.execution_time>
                     latest_lot_time[mc_no_to_visit]) then
          latest_lot_time[mc_no_to_visit]:=
       ptr_to_current_executable_event^.execution_time;
       finished_assly_no:=
          abda[assly_no].parent_no;
          newmodified(new_event);
          new_event^.event:=processing_on_assly_mc_starts;
      new_event^.array_of_relevant_nos[1]:=finished_assly_no;
          pos_of_lot_no:=
          ala[finished_assly_no].
                 lot_no_which_will_enter_the_shop;
      (*writeln('pos_of_lot_no',pos_of_lot_no);*)
      new_event^.array_of_relevant_nos[2]:=pos_of_lot_no;
      new_event^.array_of_relevant_nos[3]:=mc_no_to_visit;
      new_event^.execution_time:=
      ptr_to_current_executable_event^.execution_time;
      plug_in_the_event(new_event);
     ala[finished_assly_no].lot_no_which_will_enter_the_shop:=
    ala[finished_assly_no].lot_no_which_will_enter_the_shop +1;
end; (* then fire the event processing_starts_on_assly_mc *)
          end;writeln('---')
          end; (* execute_lot_enters_the_assly_mc_starts *)
         procedure execute_processing_on_general_mc_starts;
         var assly_no,
            lot_no,
            queue_lg,
            queue_lg_no,
            size,
            mc_no_to_visit : integer;
            process_finish_time : real;
          begin (* execute_processing_on_general_mc_starts
assly_no:=ptr_to_current_executable_event^.array_of_relevant_nos[1];
```

```
lot_no:=ptr_to_current_executable_event^.array_of_relevant_nos[2];
     mc_no_to_visit:=ptr_to_current_executable_event^.
            array_of_relevant_nos[3];
     mc_busy[mc_no_to_visit]:=true;
     size:=ala[assly_no].
     dol[lot_no].
                    original_size;
            process_finish_time:=
            ptr_to_current_executable_event^.execution_time +
            ala[assly_no].
              dol[lot_no].cpt;
(* now insert an event called processing gets over on the same machine
*)
  newmodified(new_event);
  new_event^.event:=processing_on_general_mc_gets_over;
  new_event^.array_of_relevant_nos[1]:=assly_no;
  new_event^.array_of_relevant_nos[2]:=lot_no;
  new_event^.array_of_relevant_nos[3]:=mc_no_to_visit;
  new_event^.execution_time:=process_finish_time;
  plug_in_the_event(new_event);

(* the event has been inserted *)

queue_lg:=queue_before_general_mc[mc_no_to_visit].queue_length;
for queue_lg_no:=2 to queue_lg do
queue_before_general_mc[mc_no_to_visit].
details_of_queue[queue_lg_no -1] :=
queue_before_general_mc[mc_no_to_visit].
details_of_queue[queue_lg_no];
queue_before_general_mc[mc_no_to_visit].queue_length:=
queue_before_general_mc[mc_no_to_visit].queue_length - 1;
(* now we modify the assly-no and lot - no data  *)
ala[assly_no].dol[lot_no].time_when_processing_starts:=
ptr_to_current_executable_event^.execution_time;
with ala[assly_no].
dol[lot_no] do
            begin  (* with *)

            current_mc_no:=mc_no_to_visit;
            total_wait_time_in_queues_so_far:=
```

```
        total_wait_time_in_queues_so_far +
       { ptr_to_current_executable_event^.execution_time - }
        time_when_processing_starts -
        time_of_joining_the_queue;
      end;  (* with *)

    end;  (* execute processing_on_general_mc_starts *)

     procedure  execute_processing_on_assly_mc_starts;

      var  assly_no,
         lot_no,
         queue_lg,
         size,
         lot_size,
         last_quantity_available,
         quantity_available,
         quantity_to_be_contributed,
         children_index,
         no_of_children,
         lowlim,
         lowlim_index,
         lot_no_of_child,
         assly_no_of_child,
         qty_picked_up,
         mc_no_to_visit  : integer;
         process_finish_time  : real;
    begin  (* execute_processing_on_assly_mc_starts *)
 assly_no:=ptr_to_current_executable_event^.array_of_relevant_nos[1];
lot_no:=ptr_to_current_executable_event^.array_of_relevant_nos[2];
   mc_no_to_visit:=ptr_to_current_executable_event^.
        array_of_relevant_nos[3];
   lot_size:=
      ala[assly_no].
       dol[lot_no].original_size;
        no_of_children:=abda[assly_no].
              no_of_children_for_assly;
        for children_index:=1 to no_of_children do
        begin  (* for children_index *)
         quantity_to_be_contributed:= abda[assly_no].
```

```
array_of_child_assly[children_index].qty_to_be_contributed
            * lot_size;
            lowlim:=1;
            lot_no_of_child:=
            queue_before_assly_mc[mc_no_to_visit].
            details_of_queues[children_index].
               details_of_queue[lowlim].
             lot_no;
           assly_no_of_child:=
           queue_before_assly_mc[mc_no_to_visit].
              details_of_queues[children_index].
                details_of_queue[lowlim].
                  assly_no;
           last_quantity_available:=0;
           (*quantity_available:=
           ala[assly_no_of_child].
            dol[lot_no_of_child].qty_left;*)
  quantity_available:=queue_before_assly_mc[mc_no_to_visit].
            quantity_available[children_index];
 (*writeln('qty_available = ',quantity_available,'assly_no',assly_no_of_
child);
            writeln('lot_no_of_child',lot_no_of_child);*)
  while ( quantity_available < quantity_to_be_contributed ) do
            begin (* while *)
  qty_picked_up:=quantity_available - last_quantity_available;
            ala[assly_no_of_child].
              dol[lot_no_of_child].
                total_wait_time_in_queues_so_far:=
             ala[assly_no_of_child].
               dol[lot_no_of_child].
                 total_wait_time_in_queues_so_far +
            ((ptr_to_current_executable_event^.execution_time -
             ala[assly_no_of_child].
                 dol[lot_no_of_child].
             time_of_entry_into_the_shop)*qty_picked_up/
             ala[assly_no_of_child].
               dol[lot_no_of_child].original_size);
              lowlim := lowlim + 1;
             lot_no_of_child:=
             queue_before_assly_mc[mc_no_to_visit].
```

```
                    details_of_queues[children_index].
                      details_of_queue[lowlim].
                            lot_no;
                assly_no_of_child:=
                 queue_before_assly_mc[mc_no_to_visit].
                   details_of_queues[children_index].
                     details_of_queue[lowlim].
                       assly_no;
last_quantity_available:=quantity_available;
quantity_available:=
quantity_available +
ala[assly_no_of_child].
dol[lot_no_of_child].qty_left;
end; (* while *)
if (quantity_available = quantity_to_be_contributed)
then
else (*
quantity_available > quantity_to_be_contributed*)

      begin
         qty_picked_up:=quantity_available - last_quantity_available;
                    ala[assly_no_of_child].
                      dol[lot_no_of_child].qty_left:=
                      quantity_available - quantity_to_be_contributed;
                  ala[assly_no_of_child].
                    dol[lot_no_of_child].
                      total_wait_time_in_queues_so_far:=
                    ala[assly_no_of_child].
                      dol[lot_no_of_child].
                        total_wait_time_in_queues_so_far +
                 ((ptr_to_current_executable_event^.execution_time -
                    ala[assly_no_of_child].
                       dol[lot_no_of_child].
                           time_of_entry_into_the_shop)*qty_picked_up/
                  ala[assly_no_of_child].
                     dol[lot_no_of_child].original_size);
                   lowlim := lowlim - 1;
                  end;

                queue_lg:=
```

```
            queue_before_assly_mc[mc_no_to_visit].
             details_of_queues[children_index].
              queue_length;
            for lowlim_index:=(lowlim+1) to queue_lg do
            queue_before_assly_mc[mc_no_to_visit].
             details_of_queues[children_index].
               details_of_queue[lowlim_index - lowlim]:=
            queue_before_assly_mc[mc_no_to_visit].
             details_of_queues[children_index].
               details_of_queue[lowlim_index];
               if (queue_lg >= lowlim ) then
            queue_before_assly_mc[mc_no_to_visit].
             details_of_queues[children_index].
              queue_length:=queue_lg - lowlim
             else
            queue_before_assly_mc[mc_no_to_visit].
             details_of_queues[children_index].
              queue_length:=0;
            queue_before_assly_mc[mc_no_to_visit].
             quantity_available[children_index]:=
              quantity_available - quantity_to_be_contributed;
    (* writeln(queue_before_assly_mc[mc_no_to_visit].
quantity_available[children_index],'assly_no',assly_no_of child,'aa');*)
            end; (* for children_index*)
           process_finish_time:=
           ptr_to_current_executable_event^.execution_time +
           lot_size *
           aam[mc_no_to_visit].processing_time_per_unit;
           newmodified(new_event);
   new_event^.event:=processing_on_assly_mc_gets_over;
   new_event^.array_of_relevant_nos[1]:=assly_no;
   new_event^.array_of_relevant_nos[2]:=lot_no;
   new_event^.array_of_relevant_nos[3]:=mc_no_to_visit;
  new_event^.execution_time:=process_finish_time;

   plug_in_the_event(new_event);
   end; (* execute_processing_on_general_mc_gets_over*)

   procedure   execute_processing_on_general_mc_gets_over;
```

```
        var assly_no,
                lot_no,
                queue_lg,
                queue_lg_no,
                size,
                next_process_no,
                mc_no_to_visit   : integer;
            begin (* execute_processing_on_general_mc_gets_over *)
assly_no:=ptr_to_current_executable_event^.array_of_relevant_nos[1];
lot_no:=ptr_to_current_executable_event^.array_of_relevant_nos[2];
      mc_no_to_visit:=ptr_to_current_executable_event^.
            array_of_relevant_nos[3];
      mc_busy[mc_no_to_visit]:=false;
if(queue_before_general_mc[mc_no_to_visit].queue_length > 0 ) then
                begin
                  newmodified(new_event);
              new_event^.event:=processing_on_general_mc_starts;
              new_event^.array_of_relevant_nos[1]:=
                  queue_before_general_mc[mc_no_to_visit].
                      details_of_queue[1].assly_no;
              new_event^.array_of_relevant_nos[2]:=
                  queue_before_general_mc[mc_no_to_visit].
                      details_of_queue[1].lot_no;
            new_event^.array_of_relevant_nos[3]:=mc_no_to_visit;
                        new_event^.execution_time:=
                ptr_to_current_executable_event^.execution_time;
                        plug_in_the_event(new_event);
                        end;
              (* begining of intializations ans updations *)
               ala[assly_no].
                 dol[lot_no].no_of_agm_visited
                   :=
                 ala[assly_no].
                 dol[lot_no].no_of_agm_visited + 1;
               ala[assly_no].
                 dol[lot_no].tpt_completed_so_far:=
                 ala[assly_no].
                 dol[lot_no].tpt_completed_so_far +
                 ala[assly_no].
                  dol[lot_no].cpt;
```

```
agm[mc_no_to_visit].tpt:=
agm[mc_no_to_visit].tpt + ala[assly_no].
    dol[lot_no].cpt;
ala[assly_no].
 dol[lot_no].priorty_value:=
 (ala[assly_no].
 dol[lot_no].total_required_processing_time -
 ala[assly_no].
 dol[lot_no].tpt_completed_so_far -
 (clock_time -
  ala[assly_no].
  dol[lot_no].required_completion_time) )/
  ala[assly_no].
    dol[lot_no].total_required_processing_time;
(* end of intialisations and updations *)
if (ala[assly_no].
  dol[lot_no].
   no_of_agm_visited) =
 (abda[assly_no].
     no_of_processes_needed)
  then (* all the processes are done *)
  begin (* then *)
 ala[assly_no].
  dol[lot_no].
     processing_complete:=true;
 ala[assly_no].
   dol[lot_no].actual_completion_time:=
 ptr_to_current_executable_event^.execution_time;
 assly_no:=
 abda[assly_no].
  assly_no_after_processing;
 ala[assly_no].
  dol[lot_no].time_of_entry_into_the_shop:=
 ptr_to_current_executable_event^.execution_time;
 if (abda[assly_no].parent_no = 0)
 then
 begin
 newmodified(new_event);
new_event^.event:=lot_enters_the_finished_product_list;
    new_event^.array_of_relevant_nos[1]:=assly_no;
```

```
                new_event^.array_of_relevant_nos[2]:=lot_no;
                new_event^.array_of_relevant_nos[3]:=0;
                new_event^.execution_time:=
                ptr_to_current_executable_event^.execution_time;
                plug_in_the_event(new_event);
                end
                else (* joins the assly machine queue *)
                begin
                mc_no_to_visit:=
                abda[assly_no].assly_on_mc_no;
         newmodified(new_event);
    new_event^.event:=lot_enters_the_assly_mc_queue;
                new_event^.array_of_relevant_nos[1]:=assly_no;
                new_event^.array_of_relevant_nos[2]:=lot_no;
              new_event^.array_of_relevant_nos[3]:=mc_no_to_visit;
                new_event^.execution_time:=
                ptr_to_current_executable_event^.execution_time;
                plug_in_the_event(new_event);
                end;
               end (* then *)
               else (* joins the next machine *)
             if (ala[assly_no].
              dol[lot_no].
               no_of_agm_visited) <
             (abda[assly_no].
                   no_of_processes_needed)
             then
             begin (* else *)
              next_process_no:=
              ala[assly_no].
                dol[lot_no].
                 no_of_agm_visited + 1;
                   mc_no_to_visit:=
                  abda[assly_no].
               aps[next_process_no].mc_no;
             newmodified(new_event);
           new_event^.event:=lot_enters_the_general_mc_queue;
                new_event^.array_of_relevant_nos[1]:=assly_no;
                new_event^.array_of_relevant_nos[2]:=lot_no;
          new_event^.array_of_relevant_nos[3]:=mc_no_to_visit;
```

```
                new_event^.execution_time:=
                ptr_to_current_executable_event^.execution_time;
                plug_in_the_event(new_event);
                end; (* else *)
        end;  (* execute_processing_on_general_mc_gets-over *)
  procedure  execute_processing_on_assly_mc_gets_over;
  var   assly_no,
      finished_assly_no,
          lot_no,
          next_process_no,
          mc_no_to_visit           : integer;
        begin (* execute_processing_on_assly_mc_gets_over *)
assly_no:=ptr_to_current_executable_event^.array_of_relevant_nos[1];
lot_no:=ptr_to_current_executable_event^.array_of_relevant_nos[2];
    mc_no_to_visit:=ptr_to_current_executable_event^.
          array_of_relevant_nos[3];
         (*ala[assly_no].
               lot_no_which_will_enter_the_shop:=
         ala[assly_no].
               lot_no_which_will_enter_the_shop + 1;*)
          ala[assly_no].
              dol[lot_no].time_of_entry_into_the_shop:=
        ptr_to_current_executable_event^.execution_time;
        ala[assly_no].dol[lot_no].actual_completion_time:=
        ptr_to_current_executable_event^.execution_time;
        if (abda[assly_no].
              immediately_gets_into_assly)
   then
          begin  (* gets into assly *)
          finished_assly_no:=
          abda[assly_no].parent_no;
          mc_no_to_visit:=
          abda[finished_assly_no].assly_on_mc_no;
        newmodified(new_event);
 new_event^.event:=lot_enters_the_assly_mc_queue;
                new_event^.array_of_relevant_nos[1]:=assly_no;
                new_event^.array_of_relevant_nos[2]:=lot_no;
           new_event^.array_of_relevant_nos[3]:=mc_no_to_visit;
                new_event^.execution_time:=
                ptr_to_current_executable_event^.execution_time;
```

```
                    plug_in_the_event(new_event);
                    end (* gets into assly *)
                    else if (abda[assly_no].
                            immediately_needs_processing)
                            then
                            begin (* processing of the assembly starts *)
                           mc_no_to_visit:=
                           abda[assly_no].
                             aps[1].mc_no;
                             newmodified(new_event);
new_event^.event:=lot_enters_the_general_mc_queue;
                    new_event^.array_of_relevant_nos[1]:=assly_no;
                    new_event^.array_of_relevant_nos[2]:=lot_no;
                 new_event^.array_of_relevant_nos[3]:=mc_no_to_visit;
                    new_event^.execution_time:=
                    ptr_to_current_executable_event^.execution_time;
                    plug_in_the_event(new_event);
                    end (* gets into assly *)
                   else
                    begin (* gets into the finished product list *)
                (*    newmodified(new_event);
new_event^.event:=lot_enters_the_general_mc_queue;

                    new_event^.array_of_relevant_nos[1]:=assly_no;
                    new_event^.array_of_relevant_nos[2]:=lot_no;
                 new_event^.array_of_relevant_nos[3]:=mc_no_to_visit;
                          new_event^.execution_time:=
                    ptr_to_current_executable_event^.execution_time;
                    plug_in_the_event(new_event);
                    end  gets into assly
                    else
                     begin gets into the finished product list *)
                    newmodified(new_event);
              new_event^.event:=lot_enters_the_finished_product_list;
                    new_event^.array_of_relevant_nos[1]:=assly_no;
                    new_event^.array_of_relevant_nos[2]:=lot_no;
                    new_event^.array_of_relevant_nos[3]:=0;
                    new_event^.execution_time:=
                    ptr_to_current_executable_event^.execution_time;
                    plug_in_the_event(new_event);
```

```
                end (* gets into assly *)
              end;  (* execute processing on assly mc get over *)
        procedure execute_lot_enters_the_finished_product_list;
              var
                     assly_no,
                          lot_no    : integer;
           begin
assly_no:=ptr_to_current_executable_event^.array_of_relevant_nos[1];
lot_no:=ptr_to_current_executable_event^.array_of_relevant_nos[2];

ala[assly_no].dol[lot_no].actual_completion_time:=clock_time;
         end;
              procedure   execute_the_event;
              begin  (* execute_the_event *)
                case ptr_to_current_executable_event^.event of
                  collect_statistics_from_now_on  :
                       execute_collect_statistics_from_now_on;
                     lot_enters_the_shop       :
                       execute_lot_enters_the_shop;
                     lot_enters_the_general_mc_queue :
                       execute_lot_enters_the_general_mc_queue;
                     lot_enters_the_assly_mc_queue   :
                       execute_lot_enters_the_assly_mc_queue;
                     processing_on_general_mc_starts :
            execute_processing_on_general_mc_starts;
                     processing_on_assly_mc_starts   :
                       execute_processing_on_assly_mc_starts;
processing_on_general_mc_gets_over   :
execute_processing_on_general_mc_gets_over;
processing_on_assly_mc_gets_over  :
                       execute_processing_on_assly_mc_gets_over;
                     lot_enters_the_finished_product_list:
                     execute_lot_enters_the_finished_product_list;
                           end; (* case *)
          event_addfreelist(ptr_to_current_executable_event);
             end;  (* execute_the_event *)
             procedure   collect_and_print_statistics;
             var   assly_no,
                  lot_no,
                     no_of_orders_placed,
```

```
                    order_no,
                    current_demand_qty,
                    current_demand_period,
                    current_supply_qty,
                    current_supply_period,
                    machine_no,
                    queue_length,
                    queue_length_index,
                    no_of_queues,
                    queue_no,
                    no_of_lots,
                    general_mc,
                    qty, period,
                    mc_no    : integer;
                    set-up_cost,
                    total_set-up_cost,
                    set-up_cost_reductions,
                    total_aggregate_lateness,
                    inventory_carrying_cost,
                    total_theoretical_inventory_carrying_cost,
                    theoretical_inventory_carrying_cost,
                    total_inventory_carrying_cost  :  real;
                    sum_util,
                    av_util,
                    sum_range,
                    coordination_range  : real;
                    range:array[range_of_assly_mcs]  of real;

        begin  (* collect_and_print_statistics  *)

        (* calculating theoritical inventory carrying cost  *)

theoretical_inventory_carrying_cost:=0.0;
for assly_no:=1 to max_assly_no do
begin (* for assly_no *)
(* theoretical_inventory_carrying_cost:=
heoretical_inventory_carrying_cost +
array_for_out_put_of_w_w[assly_no].holding_cost;
theoretical_cost[assly_no]:=
array_for_output_of_w_w[assly_no].holding_cost;  *)
```

```
qty:=0;
period:=1;
for order_no:=1 to array_for_output_of_w_w[assly_no].
                no_of_orders_placed do
begin

   qty:= qty + array_for_output_of_w_w[assly_no].
                order_schedule[order_no].qty_produced;
          while (qty-demand[assly_no,period]>0) and
                              (period<max_period_no) do
          begin
             theoretical_cost[assly_no]:=
                    (qty-demand[assly_no,period]) *
                    abda[assly_no].cost*inventory_cost_fraction
                              + theoretical_cost[assly_no];
            theoretical_inventory_carrying_cost:=
            theoretical_inventory_carrying_cost +
                    (qty-demand[assly_no,period]) *
                    abda[assly_no].cost*inventory_cost_fraction;
          period:=period + 1;
          qty:=qty - demand[assly_no,period];
          end; (* while qty *)
      end; (* for order_no *)
         no_of_lots:=ala[assly_no].no_of_lots;
         for lot_no:=1 to no_of_lots do
         begin (* for lot_no *)
          actual_cost[assly_no]:=actual_cost[assly_no] +
          ala[assly_no].
             dol[lot_no].total_wait_time_in_queues_so_far *
             abda[assly_no].cost * inventory_cost_fraction;
           end; (* for lot no *)
          end; (* for assly_no *)

           (* end of calculating inventory carrying cost *)

           (* adding waiting times foe asslys in queues also *)

              for machine_no:=1 to max_mc_no do
              begin (* for general_mc_no *)
 queue_length:=queue_before_general_mc[machine_no].queue_length;
```

```
for queue_length_index:=1 to queue_length do
begin (* for queue_no *)
assly_no:=queue_before_general_mc[machine_no].
        details_of_queue[queue_length_index].assly_no;
   lot_no:=queue_before_general_mc[machine_no].
          details_of_queue[queue_length_index].lot_no;
   ala[assly_no].
    dol[lot_no].total_wait_time_in_queues_so_far:=
   ala[assly_no].
    dol[lot_no].total_wait_time_in_queues_so_far +
    simulation_time -
    ala[assly_no].
     dol[lot_no].time_of_joining_the_queue;
    end; (* for queue_no *)
   end; (* for general_machine_no *)
  for machine_no:=16 to max_assly_mc_no do
  begin (* for assly_mc_no *)
   no_of_queues:=queue_before_assly_mc[machine_no].
              no_of_subasslys_into_assly;
    for queue_no := 1 to no_of_queues do
    begin (* for queue_no *)
   queue_length:=queue_before_assly_mc[machine_no].
       details_of_queues[queue_no].queue_length;
  for queue_length_index:=1 to queue_length do
  begin (* for queue_length_index *)
  assly_no:=
  queue_before_assly_mc[machine_no].
    details_of_queues[queue_no].
     details_of_queue[queue_length_index].assly_no;
   lot_no:=
   queue_before_assly_mc[machine_no].
     details_of_queues[queue_no].
       details_of_queue[queue_length_index].lot_no;
   ala[assly_no].
    dol[lot_no].total_wait_time_in_queues_so_far:=
   ala[assly_no].
    dol[lot_no].total_wait_time_in_queues_so_far +
    simulation_time -
    ala[assly_no].
    dol[lot_no].time_of_joining_the_queue;
```

```
      end;  (* for queue_length_index *)
     end;  (* for assly_machine_no *)
     end;

 (* end of adding waiting times for asslys in queues also *)

     (* calculating actual inventory carrying cost *)

     total_inventory_carrying_cost:=0.0;
     for assly_no:=1 to max_assly_no do
     begin (* for assly no *)
      no_of_lots:=ala[assly_no].no_of_lots;
      for lot_no := 1 to no_of_lots do
      begin (* for lot_no *)
       inventory_carrying_cost:=
      ala[assly_no].
        dol[lot_no].total_wait_time_in_queues_so_far*
        abda[assly_no].cost * inventory_cost_fraction/
                        no_of_hours_in_a_period;
     { inventory_carrying_cost/no_of_hours_in_a_year}
     ala[assly_no].
       dol[lot_no].actual_inventory_carrying_cost:=
      inventory_carrying_cost;
      total_inventory_carrying_cost:=
   total_inventory_carrying_cost + inventory-carrying cost;
      abda[assly_no].
        actual_inventory_carrying_cost:=
        abda[assly_no].
        actual_inventory_carrying_cost+
       inventory_carrying_cost;
      end;  (* for lot_no *)
     end; (* foe assly_no *)

     (* end of calculating actual inventory-carrying cost *)

     (* calculating set-up cost *)

      total_set-up_cost:=0.0;
      set-up_cost_reductions:=0.0;
      for assly_no:=1 to max_assly_no do
```

```
                begin (* for *)
set-up_cost:=array_for_output_of_w_w[assly_no].order_cost;
                total_set-up_cost:=total_set-up_cost + set-up_cost;
                no_of_orders_placed:=
array_for_output_of_w_w[assly_no].no_of_orders_placed;
              for order_no:= 1 to no_of_orders_placed do
              begin  (* for order_no *)
               if  (array_for_output_of_w_w[assly_no].
                   order_schedule[order_no].period_no *
                      no_of_hours_in_a_period <
                 collect_statistics_from_time)
                     then set-up_cost_reductions:=
                     set-up_cost_reductions +
                     abda[assly_no].total_set-up_cost
                    else if (array_for_output_of_w_w[assly_no].
                        order_schedule[order_no].period_no  *
                           no_of_hours_in_a_period >
                          simulation_time)
                then set-up_cost_reductions:=
                  set-up_cost_reductions +
                     abda[assly_no].
                         total_set-up_cost;
                   end;  (* for order_no*)
                 end; (* for *)
 total_set-up_cost:=total_set-up_cost - set-up_cost_reductions;

                 (* end of calculating set-up costs *)

                 (* calculating the aggregate lateness *)

                 total_aggregate_lateness:=0.0;
                 for assly_no:=1 to max_assly_no do
                 begin (* for assly_no *)
                  no_of_lots:=ala[assly_no].no_of_lots;
                  for lot_no:= 1 to no_of_lots do
                  begin  (* for lot_no *)
                  if (assly_no = 1) then
             ala[1].dol[lot_no].actual_completion_time:=clock_time;
                  ala[assly_no].
                   dol[lot_no].aggregate_lateness_of_lot:=
                       (ala[assly_no].
```

```
   dol[lot_no].actual_completion_time -
 ala[assly_no].
   dol[lot_no].required_completion_time)*
   ala[assly_no].
   dol[lot_no].original_size;
   total_aggregate_lateness:=
   total_aggregate_lateness +
   ala[assly_no].
     dol[lot_no].aggregate_lateness_of_lot;
   end; (* for lot*no *)
 end; (* for assly_no*)
 total_units_lateness:=0.0;
 for assly_no:=1 to max_assly_no do
 begin  (* for assly_no*)
 no_of_lots:=ala[assly_no].no_of_lots;
 current_demand_qty:=0;
 current_demand_period:=0;
 for lot_no:= 1 to no_of_lots do
 begin  (* for lot_no *)
   current_supply_qty:=
   ala[assly_no].
     dol[lot_no].original_size;
   current_supply_period:=
   trunc(ala[assly_no].
           dol[lot_no].actual_completion_time/
                 no_of_hours_in_a_period) + 1;
 while (current_supply_qty > 0 )
            and
   ( current_demand_period < max_period_no )
            do
 begin  (* while_current_supply_qty > 0*)
   current_demand_period:=current_demand_period + 1;
current_demand_qty:=demand[assly_no,current_demand_period];
     if (current_supply_period > current_demand_period)
        then
        begin (* then *)
          ala[assly_no].
            dol[lot_no].units_lateness_of_lot:=
      (current_supply_period - current_demand_period) *
        current_demand_qty;
```

```
                    total_units_lateness:=
                    total_units_lateness +
            (current_supply_period - current_demand_period) *
                    current_demand_qty;
            end; (* then *)
  current_supply_qty:=current_supply_qty - current_demand_qty;
            end; (* while current_supply_qty > 0 *)
            end; (* for lot*no *)
            end; (* for assly_no *)

            (* end of calculating units_lateness *)

            (* calculating mc utilisation statistics *)
             for machine_no:=1 to max_mc_no do
             begin (* for machine_no *)
             agm[machine_no].cu:=
             agm[machine_no].tpt/
             (clock_time - collect_statistics_from_time);
             end; (* for machine_no *)
             for machine_no:=16 to max_assly_mc_no do
             begin (* for machine_no *)
             aam[machine_no].cu:=
             aam[machine_no].tpt/
             (clock_time - collect_statistics_from_time);
             end; (* for machine_no *)
             if (total_units_lateness < best_sol) then
             begin
                rewrite(potty_output,'s.res');
writeln(potty_output,'total_units_lateness=',total_units_lateness);
writeln(potty_output,'total_aggregate_lateness=',
                    total_aggregate_lateness);
writeln(potty_output,'total_set-up_cost=',total_set-up_cost );
writeln(potty_output,'total_inventory_carrying_cost=',
                    total_inventory_carrying_cost);
writeln(potty_output,'theoretical_inventory_carrying_cost = ',
             theoretical_inventory_carrying_cost);
sum_util:=0.0;
for general_mc:=1 to max_no_of_proces_on_any_assly do
sum_util:=sum_util + agm[general_mc].cu;
av_util:=sum_util/max_no_of_proces_on_any_assly;
```

```
for general_mc:=1 to max_no_of_proces_on_any_assly do
writeln(potty_output,
  'utilisation for general machine',general_mc,' =',
                                      agm[general_mc].cu:5);

writeln(potty_output,'average_utilisaton is',' ',av_util:5);
sum_range:=0;
for mc_no:= 16 to max_assly_mc_no do
begin
range[mc_no]:=latest_lot_time[mc_no]-
        earliest_lot_time[mc_no];
writeln(potty_output,'coordination_range for assly centre',mc_no:2,
                'is',range[mc_no]);
           sum_range:=sum_range+range[mc_no];
           end;
  coordination_range:=sum_range/(max_assly_mc_no-15);
           if first_run then
           prev_range:=coordination_range;
  writeln(potty_output,'previous_coordination_range is',' =',
                                   prev_range  : 5);
  writeln(potty_output,'improved_coordination_range is',' =',
                  coordination_range  : 5);
      close(potty_output);
         rewrite(s_dat,'s.dat');
         writeln(s_dat,total_aggregate_lateness);
         writeln(s_dat,total_set-up_cost);
         writeln(s_dat,total_units_lateness);
         writeln(s_dat,total_inventory_carrying_cost);
         writeln(s_dat,theoretical_inventory_carrying_cost);
         writeln(s_dat,av_util);
         writeln(s_dat,coordination_range);close(s_dat);
         for general_mc:=1 to max_no_of_proces_on_any_assly do
         writeln('utilisation for general machine',general_mc:2,' =',
                                   agm[general_mc].cu:5);
         writeln('average utilisation is',' =',av_util:5);
      end;
         end; (* collect_and_print_statistics*)
         procedure set_parameters;
         var
             assly,
```

```
          assly_no,
          lot_no,
          no_of_lots,
          mc_no      : integer;

      begin
          for assly_no := 1 to max_assly_no do
          if abda[assly_no].immediately_needs_processing then
          begin
              assly:=abda[assly_no].assly_no_after_processing;
            critical_child[assly]:=assly_no;
            no_of_lots:=array_for_output_of_w_w[assly_no].
                            no_of_orders_placed;
            for lot_no:= 1 to no_of_lots do
            begin
              time_of_reaching[assly_no,lot_no]:=0;
             end;
               coordination_index[assly_no]:=1;
            for mc_no:= 16 to max_assly_mc_no do
            latest_assly_time[assly_no,mc_no]:=0;
            end;
            for mc_no:=16 to max_assly_mc_no do
            begin
               latest_lot_time[mc_no]:=0;
               earliest_lot_time[mc_no]:=0;
               max_time[mc_no]:=0;
               assly_count[mc_no]:=0;
               present_mean_time[mc_no]:=0;
            end;
            end;

            procedure next_set_parameters;
            var
               assly,
               assly_no,
               lot_no,
               no_of_lots,
               mc_no         :integer;
            begin
              for assly_no:=1 to max_assly_no do
```

```
    if abda[assly_no].immediately_needs_processing then
    begin
        no_of_lots:=array_for_output_of_w_w[assly_no].
                            no_of_orders_placed;
      for lot_no:=1 to no_of_lots do
      begin
        time_of_reaching[assly_no,lot_no]:=0;
      end;
     for mc_no:= 16 to max_assly_mc_no do
     latest_assly_time[assly_no,mc_no]:=0;
     end;
     for mc_no:=16 to max_assly_mc_no do
     begin
        latest_lot_time[mc_no]:=0;
        earliest_lot_time[mc_no]:=0;
        max_time[mc_no]:=0;
prev_mean_time[mc_no]:=present_mean_time[mc_no];
        present_mean_time[mc_no]:=0;
      end;
     end;

procedure run;
     var
       a,b:integer;
begin
      read_input_data;
      do_explosion;
      do_lot_sizing;
      initialisations;
      best_sol:=infinity;
      set_parameters;
      prepare_queue_of_lots;
 prepare_event_regarding_entry_of_the_components;
      prepare_collect_statistic_event;

 (* decide_times_of_entry_into_the_shop; *)
       open_print_the_event_list;
 while (clock_time < simulation_time) and (flag = false)  do
       begin (*writeln(flag);*)
       find_the_next_executable_event;
```

```
        if (flag=false)
        then
        begin
        print_the_event_list;
        execute_the_event;
        end;
        end;
        close_print_the_event_list;
        collect_and_print_statistics;
        end;
      procedure next_run;
      var
      a,b:integer;
      begin
        do_lot_sizing;
        initialisations;
        next_set_parameters;
       prepare_queue_of_lots;
       prepare_event_regarding_entry_of_the_components;
        prepare_collect_statistic_event;
       open_print_the_event_list;
while (clock_time < simulation_time) and (flag = false) do
       begin
        find_the_next_executable_event;
        if (flag=false) then
        begin
          print_the_event_list;
          execute_the_event;
        end;
       end;
       close_print_the_event_list;
       collect_and_print_statistics;
      end;

      var

max_util : real;
      i,j,current_no,k1: integer;
      search : boolean;
      parent_assly : array[1..max_assly_no] of integer;
```

```
begin (* main*)
times:=0;
for i:=1 to max_assly_no do
begin
lead_times[i]:=lead_time;
parent_assly[i]:=0;
end;
first_run:=true;
run;
first_run:=false;

for i:= 1 to max_mc_no do
  begin
  if (max_util <= agm[i].cu) then
   begin
   max_util := agm[i].cu;
   bottle_neck_mc[1] := i;
   end;
  end;
j:=2;
  for i:=1 to max_mc_no do
  begin
 if (agm[i].cu >= 0.85*agm[bottle_neck_mc[1]].cu) and not
(i=bottle_neck_mc[1]) then
    begin
     bottle_neck_mc[j]:=i;
     writeln('bottle_neck_mc[j]=',bottle_neck_mc[j]);
     j:=j+1;
     end;
   end;
writeln('bottle_neck_mc',bottle_neck_mc[1]);

  k1:=1;
  while (bottle_neck_mc[k1]<>0) do
  begin
   for i:=1 to max_assly_no do
  bottle_ass[i]:=false;
  for i:=1 to max_assly_no do
   begin
    if(abda[i].immediately_needs_processing) then
```

```
            begin
             for j:=1 to abda[i].no_of_processes_needed do
              begin
             if (abda[i].aps[j].mc_no = bottle_neck_mc[k1]) then
                   bottle_ass[i]:=true;
              end;
              if (bottle_ass[i] = true) then
              begin
              lead_times[i]:=lead_times[i] + 100;
              writeln('bottle_ass',i);
              end;
            end;
           end;


   for i:=max_assly_no downto 1 do
        begin
          if(abda[i].immediately_needs_processing) then
           parent_assly[i]:=abda[i].assly_no_after_processing
          else
           parent_assly[i]:=abda[i].parent_no;
        writeln('parent_assly of',i,'is',parent_assly[i]);
        end;

        for i:=max_assly_no downto 2 do
        begin
          current_no:=i;
          search:=false;
          while(search = false) do
           begin
             if (parent_assly[current_no] > 1) then
             begin
               current_no:=parent_assly[current_no];
                   writeln('current_no',current_no);
                   if (bottle_ass[current_no] = true) then
                    lead_times[i]:=lead_times[i] + 100;
             end;
                 if (parent_assly[current_no] = 1 ) then
                 search:=true;
```

```
      end;
      writeln('lead_time of',i,'is',lead_times[i]);
    end;
  k1:=k1+1;
  end;

(* while (total_units_lateness < = best_sol) and (time<10) do*)
  while (times<5) do
  begin
    times:= times + 1;
    writeln(times,'iteration');
    if (total_units_lateness<best_sol) then
    begin
      writeln('improved',total_units_lateness);
      best_sol:=total_units_lateness;
    end;
   next_run;
  end;
  end.
```